It's Always Uphill from the Dock

THE STORY OF THE PUGET SOUND ISLANDS

ANN B. IRISH

NORTH
WEST
CORNER
BOOKS

Kenmore, WA

NORTH WEST CORNER BOOKS

6524 NE 181st St., Suite 2, Kenmore, WA 98028

Epicenter Press is a regional press publishing nonfiction
books about the arts, history, environment, and diverse cultures
and lifestyles of Alaska and the Pacific Northwest.
For more information, visit www.EpicenterPress.com

Library of Congress Control Number: 2022938118

ISBN: 978-1-941890-41-7 (Hardcover)
ISBN: 978-1-684920-73-0 (Trade Paperback)
ISBN: 978-1-684920-74-7 (Ebook)

Cover and interior design by Scott Book & Melisssa Vail Coffman

To my sister Mary Bahnsen Mullen
with love and thanks

Contents

III THE PRESENT AND THE FUTURE

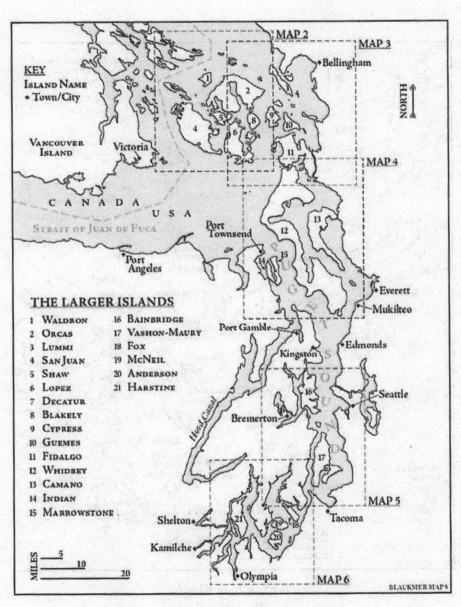

KEY
ISLAND NAME
◆ Town/City

VANCOUVER
ISLAND

THE LARGER ISLANDS

1 WALDRON
2 ORCAS
3 LUMMI
4 SAN JUAN
5 SHAW
6 LOPEZ
7 DECATUR
8 BLAKELY
9 CYPRESS
10 GUEMES
11 FIDALGO
12 WHIDBEY
13 CAMANO
14 INDIAN
15 MARROWSTONE

16 BAINBRIDGE
17 VASHON-MAURY
18 FOX
19 MCNEIL
20 ANDERSON
21 HARSTINE

MAP 2
MAP 3
MAP 4
MAP 5
MAP 6

NORTH

Bellingham

Victoria

CANADA
USA

STRAIT OF JUAN DE FUCA

Port Angeles

Port Townsend

Everett
Mukilteo

Port Gamble

Kingston

Edmonds

Seattle

Bremerton

Hood Canal

PUGET SOUND

Shelton

Kamilche

Tacoma

Olympia

MILES
5
10
20

BLACKMER MAPS

Islands of Puget Sound

The San Juan Islands

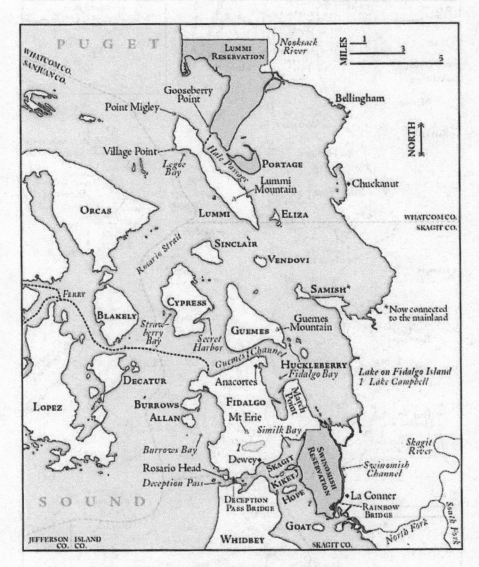

Lummi, Fidalgo, and nearby islands

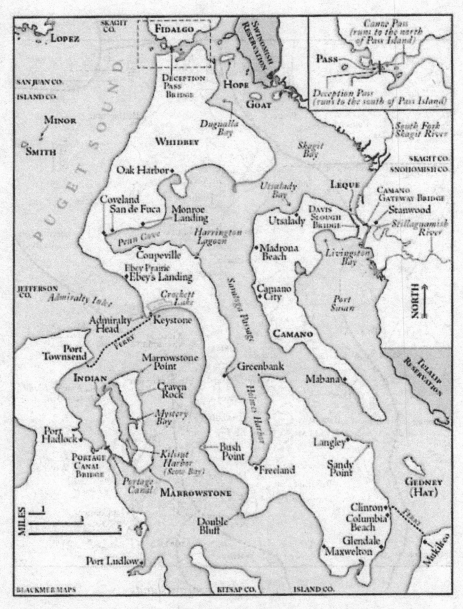

Whidbey, Camano, Indian, Marrowstone, Smith, and Hat Islands

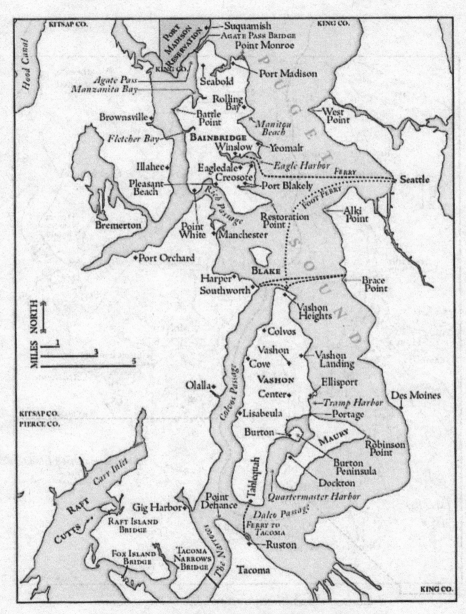

Bainbridge, Blake, and Vashon-Maury Islands

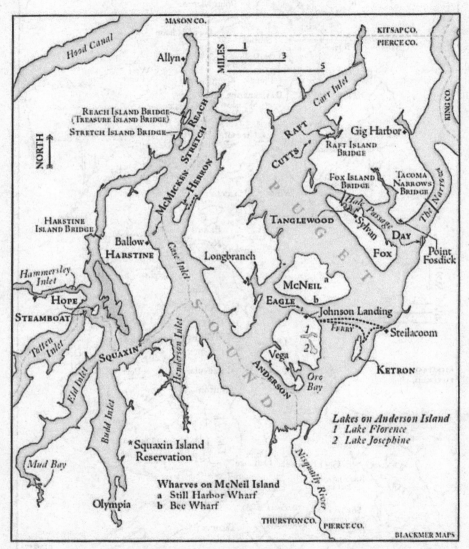

Islands of the southernmost reaches of Puget Sound

Preface

THE ISLANDS OF PUGET SOUND HAVE long fascinated visitors. In 1948, a real estate company held a contest for the best one-hundred-word essay on "Why You should Live in the San Juans." The prize: 3.5-acre Deadman Island, about 150 yards off the southwest shore of Lopez Island. The winner, Mrs. Richard Annibal, had long fancied having an island of her own. Unfortunately, she was too busy raising three children to use her prize. She soon found a buyer, Mrs. A. E. Chamberlain, also of Seattle, who traded a 1936-model car for the island she had never seen. She explained, "We took a trip through the islands recently and I just decided I'd like to own one."[1]

Geological actions shaped these bits of land that Indians long lived upon. Spanish and English explorers were the first white people to see the islands when they sailed into Puget Sound in the 1790s. Since then, especially during these last two centuries when white newcomers have been arriving, Europeans and Americans have brought about developments that have transformed the islands. Widespread logging, agriculture, construction of roads and towns, and more, have altered the islands. This book recounts the changes, telling the story from earliest times to 1948 and the real estate contest and then on into the twenty-first century, until COVID overwhelmed our lives. The story encompasses the southernmost islands in Puget Sound—Anderson, Squaxin and Harstine—through to the San

Juan group and Lummi Island just south of Canada. Here is a look at the common themes of history on the islands and how this history may differ from that of mainland communities as well as from island to island. In some ways, of course, island history and mainland history are similar.

I lived on one of the islands, Vashon, for more than half a century, and recently have been thinking about all the changes that have occurred on my island during these years. Newspaper stories have suggested that other islands have been changing in ways similar to what I have seen happening on Vashon, from increasing tourism to dwindling school populations. Eventually, my musings led me to think about the history of all these islands. No one has written an account tracing the story of this group from prehistoric times to the present. I think it is time to have such a chronicle.

Which islands merit inclusion in this story? Numerous small islands from Steamboat Island in the far south Sound to Skipjack Island in the northern San Juans are well known to boaters but have not played a significant role in Puget Sound history. Not every island's name appears in this work. Many of the incidents that are part of this history exemplify similar events on various islands and illustrate larger historical patterns. Numerous stories and patterns exist. I might highlight something that happened on one or two islands and not mention its occurrence on others. Because this account mentions many islands, towns, and other places, I have included maps to show their locations.

There is no way a book-length history of the islands can recount all the interesting events that have occurred on all of the islands. That would require an encyclopedia. After all, as Canadian humorist Stuart McLean said concerning islands a little farther north, "If the destination was dull, there wouldn't be a ferry."[2] In order to offer a picture of the entire area, this volume must pick and choose. Each chapter stands alone, but together they present a record of island history.

A significant aspect of terminology creates a problem. The Native peoples of Puget Sound are called Indians or Native Americans. Canadian Native people sometimes come into this story and they are known both as Indians and as First Nations or Aboriginals, not Native Americans. Thus, it seems preferable to use "Indian" some of the time rather than "Native American" because "Indian" includes people of both Canada and the United States.[3]

I indicate that all these islands are found in Puget Sound. However, explorer George Vancouver, who bestowed the name, meant it to apply only to the southernmost of these island waters. Today the term sometimes applies to only the waters south of Whidbey Island, and sometimes to the entire Washington State inland sea. A newer term, the Salish Sea, definitively includes all these waters while also extending far into Canada, enveloping many islands that are not part of this story. I use the name that is by far the best known: Puget Sound.

I
ORIGINS

1 | On the Map: The Land and the Water

A GREAT INLET OCCUPIES MUCH OF THE northwest corner of Washington State. It sits almost as far north and west as one can travel and still be in the lower forty-eight states. Inland, the inlet widens into the basin known as Puget Sound, whose islands create an intricate and enchanting landscape. The Sound's geological development is confusingly complex, but, simply, glaciation caused a great ice sheet which extended into the Strait of Juan de Fuca and over the lowland before melting away. Glacial ice had carried rock as it moved, and the rock left grooves in the land, eroding and scraping it to create many north-south valleys and ridges. The result of all the glacial action is the Puget Sound world we know.

Geological forces other than glacial action have also produced Puget Sound scenery. The San Juan Islands are made up of harder rock that predated the glaciers and were exposed above the glacial surfaces. Legend has it, though, that strongman Paul Bunyan threw shovelfuls of dirt into the lake he had just dug, because the men for whom he made Puget Sound did not pay the agreed-upon fee. The shovelfuls are the San Juan Islands.

Two islands, Indian and Marrowstone, deserve special mention because of their unique history. These long, slender islands paralleling one another were once joined at very low tide, but landfill made the connection permanent. These pieces of land were also connected to the mainland, but a canal dug in 1915 to create a channel for maritime use made Indian and Marrowstone the islands (or island) they are today. Just over one hundred years later, the connection between the two islands was replaced by a bridge that allows passage of fish between them.

European and American explorers have written about what the islands were like before white settlers appeared. In 1841, Commander Charles Wilkes wrote that Vashon Island was "composed of rough masses of rocks, and is well covered with timber," rising "to the elevation of 700 feet." Crew member Joseph Perry Sanford of the expedition described "Sinclair's Island" in a similar way. This smaller island in the San Juans, Sanford wrote, "is almost immediately from the water the height of 600 or 700 feet and is extremely rugged but well wooded."[1] (Vashon-Maury's highest elevation is 492 feet, while Sinclair's is 275.)

Like these two islands, many others are far from flat. Much of their land rises precipitously for many feet above the water. Occasionally, one finds an expanse of flat land at sea level. More often, relatively flat parts of the islands sit one hundred feet or more above the Sound, and a boat trip on Puget Sound can bring many of the islands' steep slopes into view. Cruising through Admiralty Inlet west of Whidbey Island provides an excellent view of the extensive cliff along the west side of that island. The highest point on the islands is the summit of Orcas Island's Mt. Constitution, about 2400 feet above sea level. This and other peaks are part of the bedrock around which the glaciers sculpted the land.

Lakes are among the natural features found on the islands. One of the most interesting is Crockett Lake, a lagoon on the west side of Whidbey Island just east of the Coupeville ferry dock. Crockett Lake is a little over a mile long, west to east, and between one-fourth and one-half mile wide. This marshy, brackish lake is separated from Puget Sound by a sand and gravel bank called Keystone Spit. During the 1970s a development plan was in place to build a marina on the lake along with waterfront homes along Keystone's tongue of land. Community members opposed to the plan organized, acted and succeeded in saving the lake and the narrow neck.

Consider 171-acre Cascade Lake and 198-acre Mountain Lake in Moran State Park on Orcas Island. Homesteader Andrew Newhall built a dam of logs and soil at Cascade Lake for a sawmill he operated. Early in the twentieth century Robert Moran replaced the dam with a concrete barrier and built another at Mountain Lake. The two lakes still supply water to Moran's home, called Rosario, as well as to much of eastern Orcas Island. They are centers of recreational activity including boating and swimming. They are beautiful though not being entirely natural.

The islands include numerous streams, but these are narrow and short. Very few warrant a name. Many are intermittent, including all of them on San Juan Island. Among the longest is Whidbey Island's Maxwelton Creek, whose main branch extends for about four miles. Salmon appear in some of the creeks and have been found in waters of Whidbey, Camano, Bainbridge and other islands.

The islands all enjoy a mild, temperate climate, thanks to the warm ocean current from Japan, but conditions can vary greatly, even on a single island. Both the effect of the mountains to the west and the patterns of wind cause variation in rainfall. North Whidbey Island generally experiences only about twenty inches of rainfall annually, about two-thirds as much as the island's far south end. Most Puget Sound winters bring some snow, but rarely does more than three inches collect on the ground, and that hardly lasts longer than a few days. Some years it does not snow at all. At other times, islanders living on the waterfront may experience rain while those on higher ground see snow. During snowy weather, a commuter at sea level learns to contact a friend atop the island to ask about road conditions. Temperatures are moderate in the Puget Sound region. In summertime they usually climb to highs between seventy and eighty-five degrees, while winter lows tend towards the thirties. In the future, climate change may lead to warmer temperatures throughout the year, however.

The waters of the Sound are cold. Some hardy souls brave the frigid sea to swim, but the water temperature ranges from only about forty-five degrees in winter to fifty in summer, though it is warmer near the shore after the tide comes in over shallow beaches. In the winter, winds prevail from the southwest, bringing clouds, storms and rain. North winds bring clear days with the lowest temperatures of the winter and the highest ones of the summer.

Puget Sound has a reputation for rain. In reality, the area's summer days are mostly dry and sunny, especially from mid-July to mid-September. More than three-fourths of Puget Sound's annual precipitation falls during the six months from October through March. The area receives less rain annually than New York City, but on Puget Sound, precipitation usually comes gently and continues in long stretches. Fog is not uncommon around Puget Sound, especially at night and morning in fall and winter.

Like weather, tides affect island life. The farther south one heads through Puget Sound, the greater the daily tidal variation. While the difference between low and high tide is only eight feet at Port Townsend's entrance to the Sound, it can be as much as fifteen feet in the far south Sound. Tides can be very important to island dwellers. For example, the optimal time to dig for clams comes when the tide is low. Exceptionally low tides can halt boat service in some places, and if storms coincide with high tides, damage to structures near the water can be severe. Indicating the importance of the tide, island newspapers at times have included tide tables.

Currents in Puget Sound waters can vary, and one finds anomalies in certain locations. For example, along Colvos Passage on the west side of Vashon Island the current runs to the north no matter the wind or the tide. Further north, currents race through Deception Pass, so boaters time their trips through the pass for slack water. Charles Wilkes wrote in 1841, "This passage ought not to be attempted without a commanding breeze, which generally prevails from the westward. Small, quick-working vessels may beat out with a favorable tide, but it would not be safe for those of any burden."[2] This is still true today.

Some types of natural disasters affect the islands. Major flooding passes them by, but a prolonged winter wet spell can inundate low spots in fields and roadways. Much more seriously, such weather can loosen soil and lead to landslides. Sometimes the worst result is a temporary road closure, but cliff erosion has damaged both property high above the water and buildings on the beach. Homes have been known to slide into the waters of Puget Sound, since the desirability of waterfront property has led to some houses being bult in dangerous places. A local tragedy devastated the Bainbridge Island community in January 1997, when a mudslide from the bluff behind the Dwight Herren home along the southern edge of Rolling Bay killed all four members of the family and destroyed their home, much of which fell into the Sound. On March 27, 2013, a hillside on the west side of central Whidbey Island gave way, sending one beach house off its foundation. An elderly resident inside awoke to find that he, his bed and his home were moving, but he managed to get out safely. Henceforth known as the Ledgewood landslide, this slide isolated several other houses, as it cut off road access.

For island waterfront dwellers, living on the shore means ever-changing views, in rain and wind, sun or shade, featuring boats and ships of all kinds on the water, which itself changes from tide to tide. High water and wind combined can be dangerous, however. A few days after Christmas in 1990, wind and tide pushed strong waves into houses on Point Monroe, a narrow spit at the northeast corner of Bainbridge Island. The waves damaged several homes; two partially collapsed. Storms may be dangerous as well as beautiful.

Plants and animals enhance the islands' landscape. Plant life thrives. Most impressive are the great trees, mainly the Douglas fir and alder, with lesser numbers of western red cedar, hemlock and others. The islands feature many natural forested areas. Old-growth Douglas fir, western hemlock, western red cedar and Pacific yew thrive in large Moran State Park on Orcas Island. As the elevation rises, these trees are replaced by lodgepole pines. Bainbridge Island's Grand Forest also features beautiful, imposing evergreens. Oliver Van Olinda, Vashon Island's first historian, arrived on Vashon in 1891. Coming from sparsely-treed Nebraska, he recalled his awe upon reaching the island, with its "giant fir trees towering three hundred feet above me on either side of the trail in an almost impenetrable wall."[3]

In addition to the dominant trees, another native, the madrona, or madrone, adds interest to the landscape because of its unusual appearance. An evergreen with leaves in place of needles, its reddish, peeling trunks and branches are slender and far from straight. Having never before seen madrona trees, early explorers mistook them for magnolias.

Much of the islands' forest land was cleared in the nineteenth century. Settlers grew crops on a lot of it, but when land is not cared for, underbrush quickly springs up. William A. Peck, Jr. wrote of San Juan Island in 1859 about "a growth of vine maple, blackberries and alders so thick it was impossible to penetrate it without axes."[4] The first major tree that springs up to reclaim the land from the brush is the fast-growing deciduous red alder. Later, the Douglas fir comes to crowd it out. Many island fields once cleared for cultivation have reverted to forest, and these days the trees growing naturally in our forests are dominated by the alder and Douglas fir.

Members of the 1790s around-the-world British Royal Navy expedition led by Captain George Vancouver wrote of the smaller plants they saw. Peter

Puget noted gooseberries and wild roses on Indian Island. On Marrowstone, he found no wild roses, but rather raspberries. Archibald Menzies, naturalist and expedition surgeon, saw Indian women on Bainbridge Island digging lily bulbs (possibly camas) to eat. They also harvested young raspberry shoots for food, he added. Joseph Whidbey wrote that "The Farmer in this place would have nothing to do but put his plough in the ground—being many thousand acres clear appearantly [sic] for that purpose, surrounded by beautiful Parks full of excellent Deer—with Goosberrys—Raspberrys—Currants & Strawberrys, growing in abundance."[5]

Lummi Indian elders have reminisced about going to "the islands" looking for edible wild plants. Agatha Charles McClusky remembered a potato-like root and wild onions, while Isadore Tom noted the berries he and others would pick and the fish they speared.[6] The islands' native flora also includes some beautiful but inedible plants, most spectacularly the Washington State flower, the rhododendron.

The explorers who saw the great growth of vegetation on the islands often did not realize that most of the soil was not very rich and that it would require a lot of nourishment to make good cropland. Instead, they saw the landscape as potentially productive. Vancouver noted its "abundant fertility," and Menzies wrote on Whidbey Island, "The Soil tho in general light & gravely would I am confident yield most of the European fruits & grains in perfection." He did worry about whether fresh water would always be available for cultivation.[7] Settlers came, and after they cleared land and began farming, they learned what plants could thrive, but as twenty-first century farmers on the islands can attest, most island soil is neither rich nor fertile.

Ebey Prairie, the famous natural prairie in the center of Whidbey Island, attracted some of the islands' earliest settlers because it has some of the best agricultural land to be found on any of the islands. Natural grasslands still appear here and there, although land clearing, cultivation and fire suppression have strongly changed the landscape since the days of the explorers. Windswept grasslands on the southern reaches of Spieden and nearby San Juan Island feature few trees.

These days, domesticated animals live on the islands, but so do wild animals. The best-known are deer, about which the earliest Europeans on the islands commented. Thomas Manby, third lieutenant on Vancouver's 1792 expedition, noted that deer "no doubt swim from island to island," but he also speculated incorrectly that the dead deer the explorers saw afloat in the water or dead on the beaches were victims of "the rapid tides." Archibald Fleming noted that when his pioneer family arrived on San Juan Island, "there were many elk, beaver and some wolves." He remembered "seeing twelve or fifteen deer at one time, playing and jumping on a hill side."[8]

The settlers killed off all the elk and many deer, and thus venison often appeared on pioneer tables. Meanwhile, strychnine got rid of the wolves. By the end of the nineteenth century, concern arose that the islands' deer would be totally exterminated. In the last half century or so, however, the deer population has recovered and these animals have become a pest to island gardeners. Waldron Island, however, has no deer to bother farmers. On most islands, an occasional bear or cougar appears, and some islanders see coyotes, which can attack and kill farm animals. In 2019, people on some of the San Juan Islands reported seeing a bear, apparently the same one on its travels. Frequently visible are river otters, beavers, raccoons or squirrels. Moles attack gardens, at least on Bainbridge and Vashon, though some of the islands are apparently mole-free. Slugs and insects seem to be everywhere. Native animals mostly seem to do well on the islands.

Invasive, or non-native, animals also live on the islands. One is the eastern grey squirrel, which has multiplied in the Puget Sound area while the number of western greys has declined. A much more dramatic invasive story is that of the rabbits of San Juan Island. Settlers brought in a few before 1900. Some islanders raised rabbits commercially in the 1920s, but the depression of the 1930s killed the market. The rabbit business folded and people simply released the remaining animals. With few or no natural predators, the rabbits multiplied. Estimates of their numbers on San Juan Island ranged up to one million by the 1970's, though in the 1980's, for unknown reasons, the quantity rapidly declined. The American Camp section of San Juan Island National Historical Park found that rabbits numbered fewer than five hundred in 2010, but the Park Service has worked to curtail the numbers further. The rabbits' extensive underground tunnels degrade the land, and they also destroy native plant growth.

The islands see a variety of birds, from the ubiquitous robin to blue jays and hummingbirds, along with a few hawks and eagles. More bald eagles nest in the San Juans than anywhere else in Washington State, and peregrine falcons also call the San Juan Islands home. Due to the mild climate, some birds are visible year-round. Land birds such as owls and shore birds such as ducks and loons winter in Puget Sound country.

In 1842, Peter Puget noted eagles along with "Crows, Ravens Curlews & some Oceanic Birds" off Marrowstone Island.[9] Islanders overlooking a north-south passage of Puget Sound can see birds in formation on their annual migrations, as these channels are frequent flyways. Seabirds, mainly gulls and cormorants, find ferry docks to their liking, especially the pilings locally known as dolphins, which are driven into the seabed to help guide ferries to a pier. Washington State Ferries has placed spikes atop fixtures at the docks to discourage the birds and what they deposit.

Aside from the land and its creatures, the sea is also an important part of the island environment. Puget Sound's great numbers of fish and other sea animals have helped make life possible for the people who have lived on the islands. While this sea life is still visible today, it no longer thrives in the huge numbers of yesteryear. The creatures of the waters then and now range from the porpoise, sea lion, seal, and orca—or killer whale—to many varieties of fish. On the island beaches, people find many kinds of edible sea life: crabs, clams, oysters and mussels—something for every taste. Not to be forgotten is the giant clam that burrows deep into the Sound's beaches and is known as the geoduck, whose name Puget Sounders pronounce as "gooey duck." By far the most important of the sea animals, however, is the salmon.

Today's Puget Sound landscape and waterscape are beautiful, but they are not what the early Native Americans or pioneers saw. All sorts of development, from logging to farming to housing, have altered the land. Its very shape has been changed, too. Consider the sand spit that once protected the site where Whidbey Island's Oak Harbor grew. Some of the area's very earliest settlers noted the "peaceful harbor protected by a crooked spit."[10] Here was an Indian burial site. After the Navy came to Whidbey Island in the 1940s, government workers removed the remains, destroyed the spit and dredged the area. These days one might never guess that a long finger of land once existed there.

Another man-made landscape change occurs on most of the islands: bulkheads placed along waterfront property. They cover about half of Vashon-Maury Island's shore. These seawalls help protect the land from erosion but harm the beaches and beach life. Normally, winds and storms wash away beaches, which are then replenished with sand from coastal bluffs. If a bulkhead stops the sand from reaching the beach, though, the beach can disappear. These beaches create spawning grounds for fish. Young fish develop here and feed on the insects that live among plants on the beach. Therefore, nowadays efforts are underway to remove bulkheads when possible. These days, too, islanders worry about climate change, thinking about what might keep the sea level from rising and destroying beaches and bulkheads alike.

Here, then, are our islands and their environment. From the days of their formation to the increasing development on them today, the islands have survived. The Native Americans, the early European and American settlers and recent islanders all have lived on and appreciated the islands of Puget Sound. Native Americans and later European-Americans have transformed the landscape, and islanders have been able to see substantial alterations even in one lifetime.

May all the changes yet to come preserve the best of island life so that the islands continue to evoke the response Hattie Swift had in 1864 when she arrived at Coveland on Whidbey Island:

"There is the most elegant and romantic scenery here that I [ever] saw in my life. The mountains are glorious and the forest elegant. I can't begin to describe it for it is beyond description . . . The climate is perfectly delightful."[11]

2 | The Early Inhabitants

NATIVE PEOPLE HAVE LIVED ON THE Puget Sound islands "since time immemorial." We know about the life of these Indians from their traditional teachings and practices passed along by word of mouth from the time Native American languages were unwritten up to the present day. Archaeological work also offers details of the historic Native American presence on the islands. An artifact found on Maury Island shows that humans have populated the Puget Sound area for as long as eleven thousand years, and other study shows that people have lived on the San Juan Islands for about twenty-five hundred years.[1] Explorers and early settlers wrote of their encounters with the Indians on the Puget Sound islands. These sources all include information about life before white newcomers dominated the islands.

The Native people around Puget Sound are part of a large cultural group known as the Coast Salish. In the mid-nineteenth century, white officials classified these peoples into separate tribes, or bands, whose names are used today. These designations are somewhat artificial, because of the extensive intermarriage between people from different bands and the tendency for officials to group small bands together to identify them using one name. With this in mind, let us look at the people that occupied the islands.

South of the border between British Columbia and Washington State, the Lummi come first. They once lived on the mainland, on Lummi Island

and in the San Juan Islands, with villages on San Juan, Orcas and Lopez. Like other Puget Sound Natives, they traveled during the summers and set up temporary camps for fishing and food gathering. Some S'Klallam from the Olympic Peninsula traditionally fished the waters in Lummi territory and, during the first half of the nineteenth century, married Lummi women and settled in Lummi communities.

Two small groups, the San Juan and Mitchell Bay tribes, lived on the San Juan Islands and have shown a relationship to various nearby bands, including the Lummi as well as some of the Native peoples of nearby Canadian isles. Archaeologists have determined that the site on northwest San Juan Island called English Camp housed Native Americans from about 1500 A.D. Evidence also shows prehistoric Indian presence on Lopez, Stuart and Sucia Islands. In 1927, members of the San Juan Tribe described early life on the San Juan Islands, reporting that their band may have had from thirty-five to forty houses, each built for several families and averaging thirty-four by sixty-four feet.[2] In contrast to the typical ten by twelve-foot settler's cabin, these buildings were immense.

The Samish people, who roved the eastern San Juans, including Cypress, Fidalgo, Guemes and eastern Lopez Islands, had winter villages on Fidalgo and Guemes plus the peninsula known as Samish Island. In 1792 Spanish explorers saw a Native village on the southern shore of Guemes Island. It held two longhouses in which several families lived. Even small Kiket Island just off the Fidalgo Island shore once held a longhouse. Either the Samish or the nearby Swinomish lived in these structures. The Swinomish people counted eastern Fidalgo, northern Whidbey and several small nearby islands as their land. Their most important village was located near the present-day town of LaConner.

The Lower Skagit Band occupied the northern and central regions of Whidbey Island. They had many small settlements around Penn Cove, one of the most heavily populated areas in Puget Sound. Native testimony reported that the Whidbey Island Skagits once had "forty-seven substantial wooden houses."[3] A Skagit people called Kikiallus lived on northern Camano Island where they had at least two villages as well as summer camps. On the southern part of Whidbey Island scholars have identified two Snohomish village sites. One of them was at Sandy Point, just east of Langley. They also had villages on South Camano Island and Hat Island. In addition, some Suquamish lived on Whidbey Island.

The Chemakum band and later the S'Klallams dominated Indian and Marrowstone Islands across the Sound from Whidbey Island. At one time the Chemakum had a summer camp on the point at the northwestern end of Indian Island from which they would confront other people traveling by canoe. Eventually, stronger peoples defeated them in several early nineteenth century battles and the S'Klallam took over Chemakum territory. The S'Klallam, found mainly west of Puget Sound, were "formidable," according to George Gibbs, who noted in his 1854 report that there were about seventy individuals in the Chemakum group, but that they were a subsidiary of the S'Klallam.[4]

The Suquamish people dominated Bainbridge Island, though their home base is across a narrow channel from the island at the mainland town now called Suquamish. They had villages on Bainbridge Island at Battle Point, Port Blakely, Port Madison and Pleasant Beach and they had one on Blake Island. Although the Puget Sound peoples did not designate men as chiefs, they did recognize prominent men. The settlers called the Suquamish leader Chief Sealth and they named the city of Seattle for him. He was born on Blake Island and kept a cabin near Agate Point on Bainbridge island, where he spent a lot of time during his later years.

The S'Homamish, today known as the Sxwobabc instead of the older Chinook Jargon name, inhabited the next large island to the south: Vashon-Maury. Puyallup Indian Joe Young said that to other people of the South Sound the Vashon Islanders were the "swift-water people" for their skill in traveling the waters, which could be rough. People portaged canoes over the narrow marshy neck between Vashon and Maury Islands that is still known as Portage.

These people later became part of the Puyallup band, whose people lived on the mainland just to the south, where Tacoma sits today.[5] The Puyallup once obtained shellfish on Vashon-Maury's east side, and now they harvest shellfish in Quartermaster Harbor between Vashon and Maury Islands.

Various bands, including the Sxwobabc, Nisqually, Puyallup, Steilacoom and Squaxin Island people, made summer camps on the island just south of Vashon, Fox Island. The Squaxin Island people, whose homes lined the banks of seven South Sound inlets—Carr, Case, Hammersley, Totten, Eld, Budd and Henderson, used Squaxin Island for ceremonies such as the potlatch.

These Native American people who lived between the Canadian border and the southernmost shores of Puget Sound shared a similar lifestyle.

They carried out similar seasonal activities as they obtained, prepared and ate similar foodstuffs, traveled in similar watercraft and shared similar beliefs. Their life on the islands differed with the seasons. People lived in permanent houses during wintertime but in the summer traveled around to gather food, to visit relatives and to trade. Some permanent villages and houses sat on the islands, while many other sites hosted temporary summer camps. In winter villages, people lived in longhouses built of split cedar, with posts forming the framework. Men split cedar planks to make roofing material. Mats hanging against the walls helped protect families from drafts, while holes arranged in the roof above fire pits let smoke escape. Several families, even as many as ten, could live in one of these longhouses, each family with its own section of the building, divided by mats from other families. Lucy Gurand described a longhouse on Maury Island near the harbor entrance "built by my people as a fort, about two hundred feet long [and] . . . in the neighborhood of fifty to sixty feet wide."[6] For summer camps, people made simple mat dwellings constructed over frameworks of poles sometimes arranged in a rectangle, but often around a tripod. Cedar boughs could replace the mats. Often people slept outside, using these shelters for storage only.

Much of people's activity dealt with building a food supply, and the sea was the most valuable source of food. Men were the fishermen. The most important species they sought was the salmon, which Native peoples caught throughout the region. Some men would fish for steelhead in the winter, but most did not leave their winter communities until the weather was warmer and calmer, and as summer came, so did the earliest salmon. Whidbey Island Skagit would travel about a mile upstream on the North Fork of the Skagit River to fish for salmon.

The Lummi are known for the efficient reef-netting technique they developed for salmon fishing in the Sound. Men would hang a net between two canoes and direct the fish into the net. The nets had to be renewed each year, and men and women both worked at this. A crew helped the owner of a fishing site operate and maintain the equipment. The crewmen would then receive some of the catch. Scholars have estimated that one Lummi reef net could capture a thousand fish daily. Each family or other group had its own reef-net sites where as many as ten or fifteen men hauled in the fish. These important sites were passed down through a family's descendants. Lummi reef nets once appeared at many locations, including points just off Fidalgo, Lummi and the San Juan Islands. Divers have found great rocks used by the Lummi as anchors for their nets. Since the non-Indian fishermen used concrete, not rock, these rocks clearly indicated Lummi sites. Others fished there, too. "I have seen the fish so thick that the beach is all covered; you couldn't walk without stepping on the salmon of every kind," said San Juan Indian Caroline Ewing in the 1920s.[7] Some of the salmon would be smoked or dried for winter use.

Native Americans caught other fish in Puget Sound waters. Among archaeological finds from the English Camp site on San Juan Island are bones from halibut, flounder and herring. Sometimes, people fished from their canoes, other times they used shore-based dip nets. They harvested herring with a herring rake or, in deep water, sometimes speared them. Herring could easily be dried on windy beach sites and preserved for later use. During spring and summer, while men fished, women would gather shellfish to be smoked for winter use. People usually harvested clams during the spring and summer, but they could be dug throughout the year. And when the lowest tides came after dark, people lit pieces of bark for light to make digging possible. The deeply-buried geoduck, which require strenuous digging, were mainly taken in midsummer when very low tides occurred during daylight. Also harvested were Olympia oysters, mussels and barnacles.

By May, women would begin to dig camas bulbs with digging sticks made of wood, or occasionally, antler. Women might then steam the camas. What was not eaten right away would be baked and dried, to be available as winter food. Women also dug onion and garlic bulbs.

Summer was the time when women hunted useful plants to use for food or for fabricating everything from baskets to clothing. Berries were plentiful. By May or June, Native Americans could gather the mildly flavored salmonberries, the earliest of the berries to ripen. Later came thimbleberries, red huckleberries, serviceberries and elderberries along with wild strawberries and blackberries. Women harvested evergreen huckleberries in October.

T. T. Waterman, who studied Puget Sound Indians during the early twentieth century, once bought a picker—a berry-gathering tool fashioned from cow horn—on Squaxin Island. It included curved fingers. If workers combed berry vines with pickers when the fruit was ripe, berries would fall into the workers' baskets. Some berries could be dried for later use.

Lummi Herman Olson noted that blackberries could be dried most easily.[8] Foods also included currants, Indian plum, Oregon grape, salal, rose hips, acorns, hazel nuts, ferns and new shoots of berry plants.

People dug out the tall bracken fern, ground up its roots and baked this as we would flour. Skunk cabbage leaves found use as wraps for food. The women also used plants for brewing tea, either as a pleasant drink or as medicine. Plants used to treat illness included nettles and skunk cabbage leaves. Women harvested Oregon grape, yarrow, thistle and, from the Douglas fir, pitch, for their medicinal properties.

While summer was important for gathering foodstuffs and grasses for weaving, winter was the main time for passing along cultural knowledge, for artistic work and for making useful items. Men fabricated fish nets, spears and canoe paddles, but their most important winter work was canoe construction. First, the craftsmen cut down a suitable cedar tree, split the trunk and used wedges to remove chunks from the halves. The men would burn away unwanted wood and then, with an adze, do the final shaping. To create a canoe's curved shape the men steamed the wood, both from fire below and hot water and hot stones within. These craftsmen could make canoes up to forty feet long for use in Puget Sound waters.

Archaeologists have found and analyzed many objects that Indians made in earlier times, among them fishing materials, digging sticks, adzes, arrows and arrowheads, dishes, baskets, bracelets for decoration, combs, even carvings of human figurines. Obtaining, preparing and storing materials before there was time to use them could be as much work as the process of spinning, weaving, or carving the final product. The local trees produced both firewood and construction material.

The Coast Salish had many uses for cedar—from clothes to baskets and fishing nets, as well as building material for houses and canoes. People made rope and string from willow bark and nettle fiber. Women sometimes cultivated nettles to use for net making. These nets, dyed with alder or Douglas fir, would be invisible to fish. Tule and cattails were good for making mats to be placed in canoes or houses. Non-plant products included wedges made from antler. The Coast Salish did not make pottery and used almost no metal. Thus, some of the baskets the women wove had to be watertight, to use for cooking or for carrying liquid or wet items. Other woven containers, such as clam baskets, had a purposely open weave to let water drain away.

Women kept dogs for their wool to be used in making blankets and garments. So that the animals would not run off the owners sometimes took them to tiny uninhabited islands which acted as enclosures without fencing. While anchored off Bainbridge Island in 1792, explorer George Vancouver noted blankets he thought were made from hair of the Indians' dogs, because the dogs he saw were closely shorn.[9] Coast Salish women also wove with mountain sheep wool received in trade from the Cascade Mountains to the east. Duck down, cattail fluff or fireweed fluff might be added to the wool.

Native Americans used animal skins and the inner bark of cedar trees for clothing. A poor man might have had only a blanket in winter and would be almost naked in summer while poor women might have had cedar bark skirts to wear. At the other end of the spectrum, women made ceremonial attire including fur robes from bear or lynx, along with feather capes. Tightly-woven basket-fashion hats offered protection from the rain. Women made fur hats for wintertime, too. Decorations, perhaps beads and shells, often graced the garments.

Native American women prepared meals every day. Most food had to be cooked, and this was done either in pits or on spits and racks above a fire. People dug pits with digging sticks. Stones that could hold heat would be placed in the pits. The next step was to build and then tend a fire above the stones. Finally, when the stones were hot and ready, one could brush away ashes left by the fire. Now the food, wrapped in leaves, ferns or seaweed, could be laid atop the rocks and covered with mats, branches and possibly soil. Cooking would begin. Rocks heated in firepits were also used to boil water. If placed in a basket filled with water, heated rocks could bring water to a boil and thus simmer food. Barbecuing on racks or spits would generally be done over hot coals. When meat or seafood was smoked, people built a fire using green wood, which would smolder, not burn.

Puget Sound peoples hunted land animals, mainly deer. Interestingly, archaeological study on San Juan Island has shown that the people there had apparently been harvesting plants and using land animals long before they began to eat sea products. The people on the islands hunted and trapped land animals for food in a number of ways. They caught certain kinds of birds in nets. At sites including Pole Pass between Orcas and Crane Islands, people hung these nets across the narrow channel to snare waterfowl. Men also hunted with bow and arrow, crafting points from bone, mussel shells or stone and fletching arrows with feathers—from eagles, if possible. Native Americans sometimes trapped deer in pits or nets. In 1848, a Native American leader invited nearby peoples to Whidbey Island for a deer drive. People built a fence of brush and seaweed from Penn Cove across the very narrow neck of the island, then used dogs to drive deer up to the fence, catching up to sixty animals in one hunt. Hunters could also chase deer off some of the cliffs that line island beaches, as the carcasses could be retrieved easily from below. Farther north, because San Juan Island was so thick with deer, said Caroline Ewing, "we had to go and drive the deer just like a sheep."[10]

Coast Salish people did not farm the land, but they did make efforts to help it produce the plants they wanted, burning off an area to stimulate growth of useful plants. On Whidbey Island, for example, pioneers found great numbers of bracken ferns and camas, plants that Indians had encouraged and whose abundance suggested that their growth had followed these fires. Bracken tended to be among the earliest of plants to reappear after a fire, and Indians dropped camas bulbs into the soil of burned-over land.

Native American life was not always tranquil. Different groups claimed specific areas for hunting, gathering and fishing, requiring other people to obtain permission to use these areas. War could ensue from poaching on another band's traditional hunting, fishing or gathering area. Tribal groups sometimes raided each other's settlements or camps and some bands were traditional enemies. George Gibbs reported that the Skagit and S'Klallam were long-time enemies.[11]

Puget Sound Native Americans also feared and suffered from raids by people known as "Northern Indians" who came in huge canoes from Canada or the Alaskan islands. The Northern Indians appeared in "flotillas of vast dug-out cedar canoes, filled with large numbers of men armed with guns and other weapons," Douglas Deur has written.[12] People would flee to nearby forest or even the mainland when the great canoes came in sight. Lummi tradition preserves an account of a Northern Indian incursion when the interlopers killed several hundred Lummi, and perhaps others, on Eliza Island. Sometimes the local people prevailed, as the Lummi did when these invaders later returned. Also, Battle Point on Bainbridge Island's west coast may have this name because the local Suquamish defeated northern raiders there.

The white people who came to the islands could understand that Native Americans sometimes used violence to protect themselves against enemies in different bands, but Native American life included beliefs and customs foreign to Europeans and Americans. These varied from occasional pastimes to seasonal ceremonies such as welcoming the first salmon of the year. Others include forms of individual spiritual development or enlightenment.

One custom that dismayed the white explorers and settlers was the funerary practice involving placing the deceased in trees. Indians would wrap their prominent dead in blankets and arrange them in canoes to be lifted onto posts or tree branches. This offered protection from wild animals that might dig up what, or who, was buried in the ground. This practice occurred in various places, including Tanglewood Island, the tiny island just off Fox Island's north shore. Also, in 1792, Peter Puget and other explorers noted a "Sight so truly horrid" on Indian Island: poles upon which skulls complete with hair were exhibited.[13] These memorial methods did not long survive the coming of the outsiders, as was the case with some other traditions, including relative nudity, flattening the heads of babies by binding them tightly while the child was confined in a cradle, and slavery.

The Northwest peoples practiced slavery. While Indians from north of the U.S.-Canada border captured Puget Sound people to use as slaves, peoples of the Sound followed this practice themselves, purchasing people, capturing them in warfare, or obtaining them to satisfy a debt or a gambling loss. Oftentimes the slaves came from distant tribes. An 1844 report estimated that almost three percent of the Squaxin Island people were slaves, while the number among the Lummi was more than nine percent.[14] The mother of Suquamish Chief Sealth was reportedly a slave, and her son apparently held several slaves himself.

Native American life in the Puget Sound area was not all work, warfare and practices the white people found uncivilized. Native people had, and still have, games, songs and dances: the dance of the sacred mask, the salmon dance, wolf dances and many others. A widespread gambling game called slahal, played with bones, includes singing and drumming. The Lummi people's festival, the Stommish—meaning warrior—was held in earlier times to celebrate victory over the Northern Indians. Lummi people revived it in 1946 to celebrate the return of tribal warriors—that is, the men who had fought in World War II. Today, the Stommish continues in the summer.

Puget Sound Native Americans held ceremonies for various occasions. The First Salmon Ceremony, observed annually when the first of these fish swam back from the ocean, occurred throughout the region. It was a way to offer thanks to this fish so important to the Puget Sound peoples. This observance takes place today, too. Other ceremonies were held during healing rites or to celebrate marriages. A wealthy man could have several wives at once, as did Chief Leschi of the Nisqually.

The potlatch was very important to these tribes. A prominent person could schedule one to mark a significant occasion such as birth, marriage, or death. At the gathering, the host presented gifts, which could be very valuable, to all the guests. The host would invite people—often from many communities—and would give them various items, blankets, beads, food, and possibly even canoes or slaves. Potlatch celebrations included danc- ing, singing, storytelling and spiritual rites. A potlatch served to strength- en ties within a community as well as with the neighboring bands who were invited to the ceremony. Significantly, this tradition indicates that to the peoples of Puget Sound possession of material goods was not so im- portant. Instead, sharing with others took precedence. Squi-qui, a leader of the Skagits on Whidbey Island, constructed a building for hosting pot- latches on the north side of Penn Cove. In 1855, the frame of a building constructed for potlatches forty years earlier at Bainbridge Island's Port Madison was still erect and showed that the building had been about sixty feet wide and about one-tenth of a mile long.

Too often, outsiders have tended not to understand that there is a spir- itual meaning in the potlatch, the First Salmon Ceremony, and other ob- servances. These express the importance of spirits in traditional Native American life. People could inherit or earn spirits; each individual had his or her own. Adolescents could undertake spirit quests, which includ- ed fasting in lonely places. Some spirits were more powerful than others. Different spirits conferred different powers or abilities, including the pow- er to cure illness or gain skill at hunting, fishing, weaving, or even warfare.

People with strong powers to cure became shamans, or healers. Lummi Isadore Tom's father told his son to seek his own spirit on Portage Island, just south of the Lummi reservation. It was the middle of the night, during rain, lightning and thunder. The young man fasted, walked alone for a long time, and swam, as his father had told him. While in the water he had his vision, and heard his spirit, who taught him healing songs and said he could begin healing people when he was older. In Tom's fifties, the same spirit returned and told him it was time to begin healing. Thus, Isadore Tom took up his gift, becoming a healer.[15] Healers could offer cures in several ways, including prescribing medicine, group singing, and partici- pating in a ceremony. The rituals included helping a patient experience a trance and singing a particular song with him when he awakened.

Along with religion, ceremony, and healing, came narratives. For a people not literate, these accounts taught the band's history and would be recounted to generation after generation. The recitations describe the origins of the world, its natural features, its resources, and its people. One account describes creation, starting with a featureless earth and powerful people who did not follow the teachings. The Changer—in different form according to different bands—came and created mountains, rivers and the other natural features of the world. He destroyed or changed the people who were not living in a good way. He also made sure plants and animals would always be useful to the people who came later.

One Lummi account tells about Whateth, one of Mt. Baker's, or Kulshan's, two wives. After an argument, the mountain made his wives leave. He bade the animals dig a channel to help Whateth on her way. This channel now holds the Nooksack River. Whateth traveled to Puget Sound, taking along food for her lunch and stopping to eat at tiny Clark and Barnes Islands, which are between Lummi and Orcas. Because she ate there, the Lummi could henceforth find food on these islets. Further on, Whateth stopped at Matia Island, where she ate some camas and thus camas continued to grow on Matia. On the Sucia Island shore she found mussels, so Lummi people later harvested mussels there. Turning south- west to Waldron and Orcas Islands, she ate devil fish—octopus—at Flattop Island, where the sea creatures were afterward available for the Lummi. Finally, because her tall figure and the great winds blowing around her led the waters to envelop nearby people in deadly whirlpools, Whateth lay down so no longer would she attract the winds. She became an island, and thus saved the people. To the Lummi people, the place where she lay was Whateth Island, and its shape does bring Whateth's story to mind. We know this island as Spieden, named for a member of the Wilkes expedition to Puget Sound country in 1841.[16]

A Fox Island story explains the origin of clay babies, tiny, rounded clay rocks of many shapes, some looking like miniature animals. They rather resemble cookie dough rolled out not too thinly and cut into shapes, baked and just taken from the oven. Many clay babies have been found on the island's westernmost beaches. Long ago, the daughter of a chief liked to play on the beach and amused herself shaping mud into many forms. An unknown young man came to woo her. One day, deciding to find out where he came from, she secretly followed him and saw him walk into the water and disappear under the waves. When she told her parents of this, they feared that he was "the old man of the sea," and that if the girl did not accept his proposal, he might retaliate by causing all the springs on the island to grow dry. This happened and so the girl's parents were forced to give their daughter to the man in the sea. The pair disappeared under the water as the girl slowly turned into a sea creature before her parents' eyes. When she was homesick, she would return to her treasured beach and mold more clay babies. Some of these natural works of art can be seen today in the Fox Island Historical Museum.[17]

The Native Americans on the Puget Sound islands forged a lifestyle that met their needs. The people had food, medicine, heat, homes and camps and boats. They developed a yearly round of activities that kept them physically healthy while their traditions and beliefs sheltered their spirit. The feeling of these Native Americans toward their homelands, including the islands, is exemplified by Judy Wright, a Puyallup who speaks thus of her people's land, including Vashon Island: "It is our belief that our people's feet touched the shores, breathed the air, felt the peace and serenity of silence, witnessed our beloved Mt. Takoma and were thankful to the Creator for providing the abundance of nature. These were legendary times of happiness and fruitful living. The people took care of one another, remembered the long-departed souls of their relatives, and cherished the land and the burial places of those gone to the other side.[18]

3 | The Explorers

Voyagers came to North Pacific waters late during the world-wide age of exploration in ocean-going ships. These vessels first penetrated Puget Sound in the 1790s, nearly three hundred years after the 1492 journey of Christopher Columbus. Several nations' explorers, first the Spanish and the British and later Americans, came to Puget Sound. Their journeys took them to mainland sites as well as islands, but this account includes only their encounters with the islands, and it uses today's names to identify locations. Russians also appeared along the Northwest Coast of North America, but never in Puget Sound.

Two expeditions carried out extensive exploration of Puget Sound. The first, commanded by George Vancouver for Great Britain, came in 1792. Charles Wilkes led an American survey into the Sound in 1841. Other outsiders came, too, especially the Hudsons' Bay Company which established trading routes through Puget Sound in the early nineteenth century. It was Vancouver's and Wilkes's journeys, however, that studied and charted Puget Sound waters. Both men led expeditions meant to solidify their nation's claims to the region.

In 1791, European vessels came to the islands for the first time. Two members of a Spanish expedition, Jose Maria Narvaez and Juan Pantoja y Arriaga, took a schooner and a longboat around the San Juans. Pantoja first came to Patos Island, where he and his crew spent the night. In the next few days, they saw many islands. He wrote, "Having proceeded for two days among different islands, at times under oars and at other times under sail, we found ourselves in another great archipelago of great and small islands. This we could not explore and see to what point the arms of the sea extended on account of a heavy rainstorm."[1] It was June, and the abundant rain lasted for four days. Later, Narvaez sailed along Lopez and Guemes Islands and even to Hale Passage between Lummi Island and the mainland.

Led by Alcala Galiano and Cayetano Valdez, Spaniards sailed to the San Juans again in 1792, this time east to Guemes Island, where they traded with the Indians they met. They landed on one of the San Juan Islands to take an instrument reading before heading through Guemes Channel and then Hale Passage on their way north. In Hale Passage they met some English explorers, including George Vancouver. Here the Spanish and the English had a chance to examine each other's charts. It became apparent that the Spanish explorers had not entered the waters south of the Strait of Juan de Fuca.

Soon, Captain Vancouver led the first detailed exploration of Puget Sound. Part of his duty was to chart the coastline and to locate the western entrance to the Northwest Passage for which the Europeans were searching, hoping it would be a convenient route from Europe across the Americas to Asia. Vancouver and his crew spent about a month surveying Puget Sound. On April 30, 1792, Vancouver's armed sloop *Discovery* entered the Strait of Juan de Fuca accompanied by William R. Broughton in the armed tender *Chatham*. When the party reached the eastern end of the strait and came to Puget Sound waters, the captain sent Master James Johnston of Broughton's crew southward in a small boat. Johnston headed between Indian and Marrowstone Islands and discovered that at high tide small boats could sail on between these two pieces of land to the bay beyond them. Meanwhile, Vancouver headed around Marrowstone Point, but he had difficulty making southward progress thanks to a strong and unfavorable tide. After midnight, wet and uncomfortable, the crew landed near the southern point of Marrowstone Island and built a fire.

Soon the commander ordered Broughton in the *Chatham* to the north, where he and Johnston in a small boat explored San Juan Archipelago waters. Someone in their crew, probably Edward Bell, clerk, or William Walker, surgeon, kept an unsigned journal. Writing about the islands they sailed among for five days, the author noted that "the land is delightful, being in many places clear and the soil so rich that the grass in several parts grew to man height."[2] Because the expedition was to look for the Northwest Passage, careful mapping of the San Juan group would be both time-consuming and unnecessary, and therefore the expedition's chart for this area is less accurate than those detailing the waters in the south Sound. But the Broughton party learned what the San Juans were like. Broughton's men reported Indians in an Orcas Island village. The explorers also spent a day in May fishing from Cypress Island and eating wild strawberries they found there.

After dispatching Broughton north, Vancouver and his party headed south through Admiralty Inlet and continued toward Bainbridge Island. One of *Discovery*'s spars was "in a defective state," Vancouver reported, and while the ship lay off Bainbridge the men replaced the spar. The commander felt lucky that this occurred in a land abounding with tall timber affording "thousands of the finest spars the world produces." Also abundant was a supply of twigs and branches from which the men brewed "spruce beer,"[3] whose Vitamin C would prevent scurvy.

Vancouver looked for an anchorage when he passed Bainbridge Island. On the southeast corner of the island, he saw "a projecting point of land, not formed by a low sandy spit, but rising abruptly in a low cliff about ten or twelve feet from the water side. Its surface was a beautiful meadow, covered with luxuriant herbage. On its western extreme, bordering on the woods, was an Indian village, consisting of temporary habitations."[4] The commander named the spot Restoration Point, commemorating the seventeenth-century restoration of the English monarchy on the same day in 1660 after the interlude of rule by Oliver Cromwell.

After a few days, Vancouver and Joseph Baker took a small boat to explore westward through narrow Rich Passage, which divides Bainbridge Island from the southern Kitsap County mainland. Legend suggests that Vancouver met Chief Kitsap of the Suquamish people at Manzanita Bay while exploring the channel heading north beyond Rich Passage, but this seems unlikely. Vancouver's writings do not mention it. Moreover, if any of the Vancouver party had ventured as far north as Manzanita Bay, they surely would have learned that Bainbridge was an island. The expedition maps, however, show Bainbridge as a peninsula whose northern part is connected to the Kitsap County mainland.

Thinking the *Discovery* too large to penetrate some of the channels he felt should be examined, Captain Vancouver sent small boat parties to explore them. On May 19, 1792, he dispatched two boats, captained by Puget and Whidbey, to investigate the southern passages. Expedition naturalist Archibald Menzies was also in the party. The men had a week's provisions with them.

Directed by Vancouver to depart at four o'clock in the morning, May 20, they left, "well Armed" according to Puget. The tiny fleet headed south through the passage between Vashon Island and the mainland to the west. Vancouver's orders specified that the boats should follow the starboard, or right-hand, shoreline, and thus they headed on through The Narrows— better known as the Tacoma Narrows today—toward Fox Island, then westward against a strong tidal push, making camp for the night on the mainland in view of Fox Island.

The next morning, they turned toward the northwest, joining wide Carr Inlet and landing on an island small enough that it was obviously an island at first glance. They named it Crow Island, Puget noted, for "its only Inhabitants, an astonishing Quantity of Crows," some of which they breakfasted upon.[6] This was probably Cutts Island, just two acres in size, and now a state park accessible only to boaters.

Exploration farther up and then down Carr Inlet ensued. The boats next traversed the passage to the west of McNeil Island, then turned eastward between Anderson and McNeil Islands and pulled up at a luncheon spot on what Puget described as a "long, flat Island," known today as Ketron.[7] Though the morning weather was lovely, just after noon a storm blew in. Thunder, lightning and rain compelled the men to find a campsite early, and they settled on Oro Bay, the lovely protected inlet on the southeast side of Anderson Island. Here, the exploring party spent the night. Some of the men took a boat in search of fresh water and established that the camp was on an island. On that dismal evening, friendly Native Americans visited, traded a few items, and brought vegetables and some greatly appreciated fresh salmon to the British visitors.

Dreary weather continued. Fog delayed the morning's hoped-for early departure. Accompanied by more Native Americans desiring trade, Puget's party finally headed northwestward from the southern shore of Anderson Island into Case Inlet. About two in the afternoon they stopped, however, due to a fierce storm. Weather in Puget Sound in May and June can be unsettled, and the party in the two small boats, unprotected from rain, saw the worst of it. They had now reached Herron Island, a little over a mile long and half a mile wide. Puget dubbed it Wednesday Island because the party spent much of Wednesday afternoon and night camped there as the rain continued.

The morning proved dry, though the sky was far from clear. After paddling north to the head of the inlet, presumably beyond today's community of Allyn, the men turned around and followed the starboard shore southward, seeing Reach and Stretch Islands and stopping to camp on Squaxin, or possibly Harstine, Island. Whichever it was, Menzies wrote that they "found the country exceeding pleasant, & the Soil the richest I have seen in this Country—The Woods abound with luxuriant Ferns that grow over head."[8] After exploring inlets to the south, the party returned to the *Discovery*'s anchorage near Bainbridge. Puget's expedition had taken three days longer than Vancouver had specified, but the trip led to charts of the southernmost parts of the Sound that show the islands in reasonable accuracy.

Without waiting for Puget's party to return, Vancouver, Johnston and Baker also set off in small boats, steering southward between Vashon Island and Seattle, eventually stopping for the night on Ketron Island. They spent the next day exploring some of the southern passages before heading back to the *Discovery*. This time they sailed their small boats northward up Colvos Passage west of Vashon Island, proving to Vancouver that Vashon was indeed an island, and furthermore, he wrote, "the most extensive island we had yet met with in our several examinations of this coast."[9]

It was time to head north. Therefore, at the end of May both the *Discovery* and the *Chatham* sailed up the bay between Camano Island and the mainland. A combination of miscommunication and a seaman's inattention led to the grounding of the *Chatham* in this shallow bay named Port Susan, but when the ship floated off on the high tide it proved undamaged. Vancouver took a small boat farther up the channel and wrote that "the upper part of the inlet had appeared to be perfectly closed," but he was unsure. What he found at the north end of the bay was "a flat sandy shoal" where "the land . . . seemed of a swampy nature. He spied "a shallow rivulet falling into the sea" which is the southern mouth of the Stillaguamish River.[10] The two mouths of this stream cut off tiny Leque Island from the mainland, and, just west of Leque, Camano Island.

Joseph Whidbey and Lt. James Hanson headed northward along Saratoga Passage between Camano and Whidbey Islands in two small boats. These men probably became the first white men to set foot on Camano Island—which to the expedition did not appear to be an island— as they paralleled the long island Vancouver would name for Whidbey. Vancouver had given Whidbey and Hanson explicit instructions to avoid trouble with the local people. Heading north along Saratoga Passage, Whidbey and party prepared to land on Whidbey Island, but seeing a village, Joseph Whidbey turned and headed for the opposite shore, on Camano. Several large parties of Native Americans joined them here for a time and the explorers found them cordial.

Whidbey's party continued along the long eastern shore of Whidbey Island but turned back to the south near small Hope Island. More than two hundred years after Vancouver's visit, when Sam McKinney was recreating the expedition's travels, he noted that a sailor heading north along Saratoga Passage could reach Hope Island and have no inkling that a nearby channel to the northwest—through Deception Pass—led westward into Admiralty Inlet.[11]

The next morning saw the Whidbey party visiting Penn Cove. Vancouver himself never sailed into the cove, but based on Whidbey's description of the inlet the commander wrote, "A very excellent and commodious cove or harbour," adding that the shoreline featured "spacious meadows, elegantly adorned with clumps of trees; amongst which the oak bore a very considerable proportion, in size from four to six feet in circumference. In these beautiful pastures, bordering on an expansive sheet of water, the deer were seen playing about in great numbers." Vancouver added, "The country in the vicinity of this branch of the sea is, according to Mr. Whidbey's representation, the finest we had yet met with, notwithstanding the very pleasing appearance of many others."[12]

On June 4, King George's birthday found the expedition reunited, and Vancouver officially claimed the entire Puget Sound region for the King and his country. The ships sailed south around Whidbey Island, stopping that night along its west side. Meanwhile, Vancouver sent Puget and Whidbey off in two small boats. Heading north, they came to the western entrance of Deception Pass. While traveling through it and beyond, Whidbey realized they had come to the area he had earlier explored. But their orders were to go north. They went back through the pass and camped uncomfortably on the west side of Fidalgo Island. Insects harassed them during the night, but the two explorers felt better in the morning when they found plenty of wild onions and strawberries. Continuing to travel mostly northward, they passed through Guemes Channel and set up camp on June 10, on or near a "Long Sandy Spit," most likely the narrow peninsula now called Samish Island. During the day they explored Vendovi Island. That night, "An animal called a Skunk was run down by one of the Marines after Dark & the intolerable stench it created absolutely awakened us in the Tent." The marine's clothes retained the offensive odor even after they were boiled, so he disposed of them.[13]

Meanwhile, Vancouver's party journeyed on towards isolated Smith Island, where Vancouver, Broughton and Menzies briefly stepped ashore. Next, they sailed to Rosario Strait, coming to Cypress Island and, on its west side, Strawberry Bay. As Vancouver observed Cypress and nearby San Juan Islands, he decided that this land was much different from what he had seen while in the southern part of the Sound: "The shores now before us, were composed of steep rugged rocks, whose surface varied exceedingly in respect to height, and exhibited little more than the barren rock, which in some places produced a little herbage of a dull colour, with a few dwarf trees." When he arrived at Strawberry Bay, there were no more berries, but not far away the men made spruce beer and found wild onions. Vancouver reported that Cypress Island was "principally composed of high rocky mountains, and steep perpendicular cliffs," with "low marshy land" along the shore of Strawberry Bay. Puget and Whidbey returned meanwhile, affirming that the island we know as Whidbey was indeed an island. They also described the powerful current through Deception Pass, which Vancouver reported as "navigable only for boats or vessels of very small burthen."[14]

The expedition continued northeastward, passed Lummi Island without pause, and proceeded to waters belonging to Canada today. As for the waters which would later be part of Washington State, Vancouver and his men produced charts, soundings and diaries that form the basis of our knowledge of them. The English explorers also spoke highly of the area. Whidbey even suggested that it would be a good location for a penal colony. Prisoners could live on the land in the Puget Sound area after finishing their sentences in Australia.[15]

Except by Native peoples, the Sound was probably next visited in the 1820s, when the Hudson's Bay Company appeared. The company's goal was fur-trading, not exploration. The vast British firm explored Puget Sound hoping to find a route between the Columbia River and Canada's Fraser River that was safer than the treacherous ocean waters. In 1824, the HBC dispatched a party to explore the possibility. During their journey they camped overnight on Vashon Island, where John Work wrote that they saw signs indicating that Indians had brought horses to the island. This apparently was the first time anyone except for Native people had set foot on Vashon Island.

During 1832 and 1833 the HBC established Fort Nisqually on the southern shore of Puget Sound. From here, ships could sail through protected inland waters to the company's Fort Langley on the Fraser River. The Puget Sound islands did not play a large part in HBC operations, though, serving mainly as places to obtain resources. Company records report deer-hunting excursions to islands, probably including Anderson Island, which is located directly across the channel from the mouth of the Nisqually River. In addition, Native Americans brought fish and meat from some of the islands to trade. After the HBC had established the two forts, Chief Trader Francis Heron, looking for a better site to erect a permanent fort, suggested Whidbey Island as a location that could replace both forts. But the company's Chief Factor, John McLoughlin, disapproved, thinking that most of the Indians who appeared at Forts Langley or Nisqually to trade salmon would not go to Whidbey, as it was out of the way for them.

In 1835, John Work was a member of a party traveling from Fort Langley to Fort Nisqually. Heading south from Port Townsend, the men faced a portage which Work's description indicates was where Portage Canal was dug in 1915 to create Indian Island. Work noted that "It was still only about half flood when we crossed the Clallam portage and we had to carry the baggage & drag the canoes about 200 yards," adding that "At high water the portage would be only 100 yards."[16]

While the HBC operated in Puget Sound, the United States Government sent out the second great journey of exploration that came to these waters. After almost three years exploring the Pacific Ocean, the United States Exploring Expedition led by Lieutenant Charles Wilkes on the USS *Vincennes* and accompanied by the brig *Porpoise* reached the Sound in May 1841. On May 7, Acting Master George T. Sinclair described an area we know to be at Indian and Marrowstone Islands as "a very good harbour just to the S^d of Port Townsend and nearly communicating with the Head of that bay, only a narrow strip of land connecting an extensive Island, which forms the Eastern shore of Port Townsend with the mainland. This Island itself is almost divided into two. Gap in the Island forms a beautiful & deep cove communicating with the water of Port Townsend to the N° & only prevented from opening to our present anchorage by a narrow strip of land." After heading south for several days, the mariners anchored for the night off Bainbridge, stopping at Port Madison Bay. After he and his men had surveyed the bay, Wilkes found it to be another "excellent harbour, affording every possible convenience for shipping."[17]

Puget Sound clearly impressed the men. They sailed on southward, "taking the passage to the right of Vashon's Island," Wilkes noted. Soon the expedition came to Fort Nisqually, and about this time, Wilkes suggested that nearby Ketron Island would be a good location for a town. Reading Wilkes' description and looking at a map, though, suggests that he was thinking about Anderson Island instead. He wrote that Ketron was "about a mile and half to the north of Nisqually anchorage, where the shore has a considerable indentation. There, although the water is deep, vessels would be protected from the winds." This sounds more like Anderson Island, given the location, Ketron's tiny size and Anderson Island's extensive Oro Bay.[18]

Surveying continued, and just as Vancouver had, Wilkes sent out parties in small boats to examine some of the narrower passages. He assigned two small boats to study the extensive harbor on Vashon Island, which Wilkes later named "Quartermaster Harbor" to honor members of his crew. The harbor extended around the piece of land we call Burton Peninsula, George Sinclair noted, and men in his party discovered the portage between Vashon and Maury: "It is a mere strip of sand so that Vashon is nearly two islands," Sinclair wrote. Joseph P. Sandford described the portage as a "very narrow isthmus of white sand." Midshipman Augustus L. Case also made notes of his time on Vashon. On May 18 the men camped on the island, where they "[found] plenty of water." Native Americans appeared with fish to sell. The next morning, Case went ashore on the north end of the island. Here, he commented that "This end of the island on its western side is steep to 7 fathoms within a boats length, but shoals to the northward & should not be approached to close in that direction."[19]

Later that day, Case and his boat left Vashon and sailed on to Bainbridge Island, where they "found on the island three houses & two potato patches belonging to the Suquamish Indians. The largest house measured 45 by 70 feet built of logs & roofed with boards." The party then surveyed Hood Canal for some days, finally returning to Bainbridge where they camped and Case noted that a party of Suquamish visited the camp bringing "fish, &c. for sale," but it would have been trading, not selling. On May 25, some of the men traveled through Agate Pass on the west side of Bainbridge Island. Thus, the Wilkes Expedition discovered that Bainbridge was an island.[20]

Surveying continued around Camano and Whidbey Islands and farther north. Among the crewmen who praised Whidbey Island's Penn Cove was Lieutenant James Alden, who wrote "This is one of the most delightful places my eye has rested upon during our sojourn on the coast. The cove is beautiful in the extreme. good anchorage all about. undulating country, hills & valleys interspersed just right to make it agreeable &c &c &c." Case noted "finding good anchorages all along the shores of Whidbys Island," on the island's west side, with "banks generally fifty or more feet high of stratified clay." Wilkes wrote that Deception Pass was "intricate and narrow." The expedition found Strawberry Bay, off Cypress Island, still a congenial place to stop, with strawberries growing on the island just as Broughton had found so many years earlier.[21]

Meanwhile, another of the expedition's ships, the *Peacock*, was sailing in the Columbia River region. After hearing that this ship had been wrecked on the river's bar, Wilkes cut short the surveying in Puget Sound and adjacent waters and proceeded out through the Strait of Juan de Fuca to sail south towards the Columbia.

The Wilkes Expedition charts include an odd anomaly, for they include two non-existent islands in the northern San Juans. Seven of Wilkes' boats took part in surveying that area. One of the surveyors on them recorded seeing two small islands between the northern coast of Orcas Island and Sucia Island farther north. The supposed pieces of land, designated Gordon and Adolphus Islands, were duly produced on the expedition's charts published six years later. John Frazier Henry, writing in 1982 about these islands, has speculated that a disgruntled crewman may have invented them to tarnish Wilkes' reputation. Some crewmen had been unfairly and egregiously punished by the commanding officer and most of the men resented his capricious moods. Another possibility, as Henry notes, is that lack of time meant not enough care had been taken while surveying. Wilkes apparently never did discover that two imaginary islands existed on his map. At least he never mentioned anything about these two islands.[22]

Except for the two fictitious islands, the explorers recorded the Sound and its environs more accurately than the Vancouver expedition had been able to do. This expedition deduced from tidal action that Camano, as well as Bainbridge, was an island. In addition, thanks to Wilkes, the United States government came to realize the importance and potential of the Puget Sound region. Wilkes' United States Exploring Expedition thus played a consequential role in American history.

The men who explored Puget Sound and its islands were the precursors of the European Americans who came to the islands to make their fortunes and to create homes. From the explorers we have the earliest written descriptions of the islands. Thanks to these visitors by sea, the islands were as accurately known, if not more so, than was the mainland surrounding the Sound. What these men wrote indicated that the Puget Sound region possessed qualities that could make life fruitful for future settlers. Thanks partly to the explorers, pioneers would soon be arriving in the islands.

4 | The Pig War

THE BORDER CONFLICT CALLED THE PIG WAR dominated events in the San Juan Islands and nearby areas for several decades in the nineteenth century. Because of this conflict, the story of European-American settlement in the San Juan Islands is unique. At first, British settlers came, sent to confirm their nation's sovereignty over the area. This was the era when many Americans felt that territorial expansion, including the San Juan Islands, was the Manifest Destiny of the United States. Overlapping claims to these islands meant years of contention and has become known as the Pig War.

In 1846, the British and Americans adopted a border treaty for the northwest. It stated, "The line of boundary between the territories of the United States and those of Her Britannic Majesty shall be continued westward along the said forty-ninth parallel of north latitude to the middle of the channel which separates the continent from Vancouver's Island; and thence southerly through the middle of the said channel, and of Fuca's Straits to the Pacific Ocean."[1] The treaty paid no attention to the existence of the San Juan Islands, which are in the middle of the specified channel. Both British and American officials notified their governments of the agreement's ambiguity, but despite this, the governments accepted the treaty.

Because of concern about the international boundary, the British soon worked to secure a claim on the San Juan Islands, establishing a Hudson's

Bay Company outpost on San Juan Island. As the HBC was a fur-trading enterprise, the company did not want people to settle in company territories, for when settlers came, animals disappeared. James Douglas, in charge of the HBC's Fort Victoria (later the city of Victoria, British Columbia), carefully discouraged settlement on the San Juans, but hoped to solidify the British claim to them. In 1850, he dispatched a man to San Juan Island to establish a fishing camp. Several men returned the next year and built a small structure at the camp for salting fish that Indians brought to them. While the British set up this operation on San Juan Island, several Americans unsuccessfully tried to operate a lumber business on Lopez Island.

Douglas, now governor of Vancouver Island while he remained regional head of the HBC, took additional action in December 1853. He sent Charles J. Griffin with 1,369 sheep and a few Hawaiian men, known as Kanakas, to establish a sheep farm near Eagle Cove on San Juan Island. Griffin and crew created a ranch he called Belle Vue Sheep Farm, built six log cabins, cleared land for pasture and planted some to oats. The men cut a wide passage called a sheep run to the open land in the center of the island, brought in a few other farm animals and created three additional sheep farms on the island. Six years later, the flocks had grown to 4,500 sheep.

Of course, an official American response followed. In 1854, the Washington Territorial Legislature designated the San Juan Islands as part of Whatcom County. (San Juan County was not created until 1873, after the matter of sovereignty was finally settled.) Colonel Isaac N. Ebey of Whidbey Island, the recently appointed customs collector for Puget Sound, gave British rancher Griffin a bill for customs duty because imports to the United States were subject to this tax and the HBC farm had indeed imported animals to San Juan Island. Griffin ignored the bill, and Governor Douglas appointed a British customs collector.

Meanwhile, Whatcom County Sheriff Ellis Barnes went to the Hudson's Bay farm to collect the tax. Of course, no HBC man would honor this request. On March 30, 1855, Barnes returned with about six armed men to force payment, without result. Barnes and his men therefore went looking for sheep and eventually found a herd that included expensive rams brought for breeding. The sheriff immediately auctioned the sheep off to his associates for a pittance, and then the men struggled to get the animals onto their boat, finally managing to leave the island with thirty-four sheep. The subsequent British claim for the sheep was never paid, but the dispute may have helped encourage the British and American governments to agree in 1856 to appoint boundary commissioners to settle the sovereignty dispute. The commission never made a decision regarding the San Juan Islands, however.

Adding to the concerns of people in the San Juans, Indians continued to appear from the north now and then, sometimes frightening settlers. The Indians did not threaten HBC camps, however, because the company had worked with Native people for many years, employing and trading with them in the search for furs and food. James Douglas ordered two British ships to patrol the waters. Meanwhile, two United States Army companies arrived in the area out of worry about possible Indian attacks. Captain George E. Pickett, later a famous Confederate general, led one of them.

All of this was the opening act of the long and mostly peaceful conflict between the two nations known as the Pig War. As the 1850s approached an end, about twenty people worked on San Juan Island for the HBC, three of these being U.S. citizens. About ten other settlers could be found on the island. Such was the situation when the pig incident occurred.

Lyman Cutlar of Kentucky came to San Juan Island in 1859 and began farming on an inland site near Belle Vue Sheep Farm. He planted a patch of potatoes without adequately fencing the plot, and soon a Hudson's Bay pig discovered it. On June 15, 1859, the pig rooted among the potatoes, and Cutlar shot the offender, a Berkshire boar. He told the HBC's Griffin that he had killed the pig and that he would pay for the animal. He later claimed that he had shot the pig only after its repeated visits to the potatoes, while Griffin charged that Cutlar offered shockingly inadequate compensation. Griffin was already frustrated, as some of the other Americans on the island had settled on land he had been using in his sheep operation.

At this time, Brigadier General William S. Harney, who commanded American army operations in the northwest, was on an inspection tour of military forts in the area. On July 9, his ship, the USS *Massachusetts*, appeared just off San Juan Island. Historian Michael Vouri has written that Harney had "an active imagination, occasionally bordering on paranoia," and that "he hated taking orders from superior officers because he believed he had no superiors."[2] Once among the San Juans, Harney heard about the pig dispute, perhaps embellished in the telling. Soon, twenty-two American settlers signed a petition asking him to provide protection against the Northern Indians, one settler later asserting that Harney had suggested submitting such a request to him. In response, Captain Pickett and sixty-eight men landed on July 27 and set up camp near the HBC Farm. Pickett then proclaimed American authority over the island. Governor Douglas in Victoria, who was also rather hotheaded, sent Royal Marines under Captain Geoffrey Hornby on the HMS *Tribune* to the island. Hornby, not wishing to provoke hostilities, kept the men on shipboard. Soon, three British ships lay offshore and their captains conferred with Pickett, suggesting a joint military occupation of the island. The American commander did not agree but proposed that he contact his superior, Harney.

During these troubled days, Lt. Col. Silas Casey arrived with more United States troops. He arranged that the American camp be moved to a better-protected site while remaining near Belle Vue Farm. Additional soldiers disembarked, and soon over four hundred men were at work fortifying the camp area. William A. Peck, Jr., who came with the Army Corps of Engineers, recorded his experiences in a journal. He admired the setting, with the Cascade peaks in the distance, good weather, blackberries and raspberries and plenty of timber, noting "the enchantment of the scene . . . one of the most beautiful locations imaginable." He saw Indians camping on the island and fishing for salmon and he estimated that some two hundred Indian women, mostly prostitutes, he said, were on the island. The British had from eight thousand to ten thousand sheep on San Juan Island, he thought. American inspectors judged that perhaps 4,500 sheep could be found there.[3]

As construction on the American Camp progressed, British response awaited orders from London. In Washington, D.C., when President James Buchanan learned of the military activity on San Juan Island, he ordered caution and sent out another military man, General Winfield S. Scott, to investigate. Scott had been active in the War of 1812 and had led an invasion force in the Mexican War. By 1859 he was the most prominent military officer in the United States.

General Scott arrived at the Strait of Juan de Fuca in October 1859 and met with Douglas, each one polite but ready to support his nation's position. Scott ordered that many of the troops and the heavy guns be withdrawn. Soon, work stopped on the American fortress. American officials agreed to reassign Pickett to Bellingham because of British antagonism towards him, but a few months later, Harney sent him back to San Juan

Island. Soon, the two governments agreed that each could station up to one hundred men on the island to keep the peace while diplomats settled the sovereignty issue. The peace held, and men from each camp became friendly with one another.

Orders arrived in January 1860 for creation of a British camp on San Juan Island. The officers considered several possible locations for it, including the site of the future town of Friday Harbor, but instead chose a site on the island's northwest coast, about eleven miles north of the American camp. The British site was pleasant, spacious and well-watered. Lt. Richard Mayne of the British party maintained that this location was much too far from the American camp, but he was not the decision-maker, and building the camp began in the spring. Although the camp was a *British* installation, its name, "English Camp," has endured. Captain George Bazalgette, commander of the British, arrived with eighty-six men on March 21, 1860. In taking over the area, the British soldiers destroyed a longhouse, perhaps built by the Lummi.

From 1860 to 1872, American and British troops occupied San Juan Island. On and off, Captain Pickett commanded the American troops stationed there, but he resigned his commission in 1861 to fight in the Confederate Army. After the Civil War began in April that year, some U.S. Army officials considered abandoning American Camp, but because of the significance of the border question in this possibly strategic region, the camp stayed open. With the camps established, civilians drifted to the island to meet the troops' necessities and desires. In 1860, only seventy-three civilians had lived on the island, but by 1870 there were 457.

The soldiers, both British and American, found their days on San Juan Island dull. Life was hard at first, as the men had to work to establish the camps. Soon the officers had pleasant living quarters. Both camps housed everyone else in barracks and both camps included small hospitals. English Camp facilities, which even included a reading room for the men, were superior to the poorly heated and inadequately maintained American barracks; the U.S. government did not appropriate funds for upkeep. English Camp featured a blockhouse on the shore which has been restored, as though standing guard for today's visitors.

With the two camps in place, military life settled down to routine activities. For most of the next twelve years, the two small military detachments on opposite sides of the island had little to do except keep peace

among the settlers. Most of the activities on the island by both nations' soldiers involved controlling illicit liquor and prostitution. Many of the men
on the island, soldiers and civilians alike, became quite friendly with the
Indian women, who were the only women available at the time. A few of
these liaisons led to marriages, which produced some of San Juan Island's
pioneer families.

For the men in both armies, occasional celebrations, often including
men from both camps, broke the tedium. Foot soldiers from both nations
no doubt marched from one camp to the other, but the British officers had
horses, while the Americans depended mainly on mules. Queen Victoria's
May 24 birthday and America's July 4 Independence Day offered reasons
for holiday festivities in which settlers, as well as soldiers, took part. The
U.S. soldiers held Fourth of July celebrations even through the Civil War
years. Many social events also featured horse races. In one particular year,
British horse Bessie beat American Siwash, while Captain Pickett was
thrown by his mount. Dances and special dinners also dotted the camp
calendars. Such fraternization helped pass the time.

The settlement called San Juan Village was the island's commercial center, such as it was. Deserted today, it sat on the south shore of Griffin Bay
near American Camp and Belle Vue Sheep Farm. As more people came
to the island, this hamlet emerged to serve the needs of settlers as well as
the troops. San Juan Village soon boasted the island's post office and shops
that specialized in fruit, meat, baked goods and other groceries. People
could buy liquor in the post office building and at many other nearby
establishments.

The abundance of alcohol helped fuel violence, even murder, and San
Juan Village came to have a reputation for depravity. The unsettled jurisdiction of the island encouraged immorality, for no one was sure what the
law was. Military authorities and civilian officials did not always agree on
the legal authority regarding the civilians. Ungovernable, lawless characters
appeared to drift to San Juan Island because of its indeterminate status.
The lack of taxation also drew various sorts of people to the island. Pickett
charged that San Juan Village was "a depot for murderers, robbers, whis-
key-sellers; in a word all refugees from justice." In 1862, Lyman A. Bissell,
newly in command of American camp, banished tough customers from the
island, though he had questionable authority for this action. He created a
small military police force and ordered the men to search all arriving boats

to prevent liquor from being smuggled on to the island. He also arranged arbitration in cases of civilian quarrels. E. T. Hamblett, the island's justice of the peace, who held office in one of the saloons, led a protest by some of the settlers. "Major Bissel [sic] had forbidden the Government mail carrier from carrying any mail for the citizens," wrote a settler. Bissell also made decisions regarding land ownership, perpetually causing controversy. Ironically, Americans who had called for troops to come and support their nation's claim to the island now disliked military authority. Island residents and American officials alike chafed at some of the actions.[4]

In October 1865, Thomas Grey replaced Captain Bissell. Grey's arbitrary decisions led to more confrontations. He even turned away the men from English Camp who came to join the Americans' Fourth of July celebration. Some thought Grey's regime almost amounted to martial law. Civil authorities protested, and the Washington Territorial Legislature responded by petitioning Congress for relief from Grey's arbitrary rule. Secretary of State William Seward ruled that civil authorities were subservient to the military officials on the island. Grey was soon relieved of duty, yet civilians on the island remained subject to military decisions.

Some civilians who came to San Juan Island despite its uncertain future assumed roles that a pioneer community needs in order to be successful. Stephen and Lucinda Boyce arrived on the island in 1860, making Mrs. Boyce the first white woman to live there. As the island did not have a doctor, she worked to treat illness and injury. Her husband was justice of the peace, liquor inspector, and, after sovereignty was settled, the first sheriff of the new San Juan County. Another early settler, Edward Warbass, arranged provisions for the American Camp, claimed land at the site of today's Friday Harbor, served in the Washington Territorial Legislature for a time and played a significant part in establishing the new county for the islands. He then became county auditor.

The military occupation of San Juan Island finally ended in 1872. In January 1871, the two governments agreed to submit the question of San Juan Islands sovereignty to arbitration. German Emperor Wilhelm I agreed to be arbiter, and he was to decide whether the international boundary was meant to be Rosario Strait, east of the San Juan Islands, or Haro Strait, west of the group.

The emperor appointed a three-man committee of experts to consider the question. Two were eminent judges and the third a leading German geographer. The United States and Great Britain each submitted detailed arguments. One of the judges felt that although some factors favored the British claim, by comparison the Americans had the stronger case based on records and correspondence cited in the testimony. These showed that British motivation in the 1846 treaty had been merely to confirm that Vancouver Island was British, and, moreover, that Haro Strait, not Rosario Strait, was the main navigable waterway. The geographer announced his concurrence with these views. The other judge, however, vehemently held that the proper decision would be to run the boundary down the middle of the archipelago. Thus, San Juan and nearby small islands would be British, while Orcas, Shaw, Lopez and the islands to the east would be American. Directions submitted to the emperor for arbitration, though, had asked that the emperor choose between only two alternatives for a boundary: Rosario and Haro Straits.

One might wonder why a division of the archipelago was not included as a possibility. Secretary of State Hamilton Fish had made clear that the United States would not accept this, probably because San Juan Island could be strategically significant. Therefore, its loss to Britain would be "a disaster which they could never risk," historian James O. McCabe concludes. The British, in turn, had worried about the possibility of Americans fortifying San Juan Island, threatening the approaches to Victoria and the Canadian mainland. On the other hand, both nations were anxious to settle the question. Britain had concern about the balance of power in Europe and wanted the United States as an ally should the need arise. Finally, in comparison to both Rosario and Haro Straits, the middle channel is very narrow. Imagine the ease of smuggling everything from people to illicit drugs across the passage between the south ends of Lopez and San Juan Islands, about a three-quarters-of-a-mile canoe paddle. Haro Strait, which became the border waterway, varies in width, but on average is about seven miles wide. Since a decision for the middle channel could not be considered, the emperor awarded the islands to the United States. The date was October 21, 1872.[5]

Joint occupation of San Juan Island therefore ended and the two forces disbanded their military camps. The end of the conflict set the stage for the creation of San Juan County and Edward Warbass picked the location of his claim in Friday Harbor to be the county seat. Its only building at the time was the simple, hastily erected structure designated to be the courthouse. San Juan Village slowly began to die as activities deserted the locale, moving to Friday Harbor and nearby Argyle. The United States Army sold most of the American Camp buildings at auction, and at English Camp the commandant's house eventually became the property of pioneer William Crook. Quickly, most of the British who settled began procedures to obtain American citizenship, perhaps figuring wrongly that they could otherwise lose their property. More than half the British who stayed on the island became United States citizens. Unfortunately for them as well as other settlers, taxes could now be collected.

Among the settlers were members of the two occupation contingents who decided to stay. Robert Smith, of the Royal Marines stationed at English Camp, is notable, as some of his descendants, members of the Chevalier family, still live on the island today. Members of the Bill Mason family, whose direct ancestor Patrick Biegin served with Pickett at American Camp, also continue to live on San Juan Island. The future seemed settled for British and American families on the other islands in the San Juan archipelago, too. Consider James and Amelia Davis, who made their home on Lopez Island in 1869. Davis filed papers with British officials to claim the property where the family lived. After the Kaiser's decision, James Davis traveled to Port Townsend to apply for United States citizenship.

As for the Hudson's Bay Company and Lyman Cutlar, both left San Juan island. HBC Agent Robert Firth leased Belle Vue Sheep Farm from the British firm. He homesteaded on the property and became an American citizen. American farmer Robert Frazer took over Lyman Cutlar's land. Cutlar meanwhile remained on the island for a few years and in 1860 became a partner in a firm formed to extract lime. Apparently, he later left for the nearby American mainland and died there in 1874. Meanwhile, San Juan Island, along with the rest of the archipelago, could be officially opened for settlement.

The San Juan Islands today attract many Canadian visitors as well as Americans. Among the places the tourists see are English and American Camps. Interest in the Pig War and the increasing number of visitors to the sites of the two camps led to the creation of San Juan Island National Historical Park, encompassing both camps.

For many years, the Crook family lived on land they owned at the English Camp site. They resisted selling land for a park but finally allowed Washington State to purchase it in 1963. Three years later, Congress approved creation of the national park. Interested visitors had already been inspecting the sites where English and American Camps had once existed, and now preservation work and restoration began. The work uncovered a treasure—money William Crook had hidden. In over sixty years his son Jim never found it, but it turned up in a pot hidden behind the hatch cover leading to the attic of the English Camp barracks. It was given to Jim's sister, ninety-one-year-old Rhoda Anderson. The park service originally planned to build campgrounds for visitors in both the English Camp and American Camp sections of the park, but later dropped the idea.

The two portions of the park differ markedly. American Camp sits on a wide, open, windswept plain featuring distant views and a nearby lighthouse. English Camp, on the other hand, is in a pleasant green cove, surrounded by trees. In addition to its blockhouse, it includes a reconstruction of the small formal garden created during the British occupation. Perhaps one-third of a mile inland and uphill is a small cemetery enclosed by a white picket fence. Here lie one civilian and five of Britain's seven Marines who died during the occupation—none in battle, for relations had remained good throughout the years of occupation.

With settlement of the Pig War, "For the first time in the history of the United States there was no boundary dispute with Great Britain," noted President Lyndon Baines Johnson on September 9, 1966, when he signed the bill to create the park.[6] In 1976, one hundred years after Kaiser Wilhelm's decision, Friday Harbor businesses closed so that all islanders might attend a commemoration at English Camp.

When British and American people first came to the San Juans, no one imagined that a disagreement about the islands' sovereignty would lead to years of uncertainty. After an American killed a British pig, commanders for both nations brought troops to the island. Higher officials decided that only small numbers of them would stay, to prevent war while maintaining a claim to the islands. Thus, the Pig War was a war that did not happen. As a reminder of what might have been, however, as well as of the friendship that continues between the two nations, the only place in the entire United States National Park System where a British flag now flies is on San Juan Island.

Puget Sound's islands come in all shapes and sizes. McMicken Island, shown here, is just east of Harstine Island and at low tide is connected to the larger island by a sand bar. The entire eleven-and-one-half acre island is a state park accessible only to boaters. *Courtesy of Deborah Hoy.*

The most isolated of the islands is fifteen-acre Smith Island located about six miles west of Whidbey Island. The Smith Island Lighthouse built in 1858 protected mariners for almost a century. Erosion doomed the structure and by the end of the twentieth century every bit of it had been claimed by the sea. Today an automatic light and an unmanned weather station operate on the island. The sand bar shown in the 2011 photograph appears during low tide, connecting long, skinny but minuscule Minor Island (also equipped with a light) to Smith Island.

Along Whidbey Island's west shore is a prominent bluff left after the last Puget Sound glacier slowly disappeared. A trail ascends from Ebey's Landing State Park and proceeds northwestward along the top of the bluff for a mile or more before switchbacks bring one back to the beach. From the bluff the hiker has views of Ebey's Prairie as well as the island's coast and the distant Olympic Mountains. This is a 3.7 mile hike well worth every step one takes.

Sailing south just after passing between San Juan and Lopez Islands one approaches rocks where sea lions and cormorants are oblivious to tourists.

An August 2014 morning found whales cavorting in Rosario strait between Decatur, Blakely and Cypress Islands. This view looks northeast towards Cypress.

A tiny Native American cemetery in the woods west of Coupeville commemorates Chief Snatelum of Whidbey Island's Lower Skagit Tribe. Snatelum supported good relations with the Hudson's Bay Company and welcomed missionary activities in Penn Cove. He organized action to repel Northern Indians and won respect from Native Americans and whites alike. He died about 1850.

Captain George Vancouver's ship *Discovery* anchored off this southeastern point of Bainbridge Island in 1793 and Vancouver named it Restoration Point, to commemorate the restoration of royal rule in Great Britain more than a century earlier. Here the captain saw a Native village; he went ashore and some of the local people later visited the *Discovery*.

During the Pig War no one died in battle but the British established a small cemetery in the forest on the hillside above their camp. Seven men are buried here, four of them after drowning.

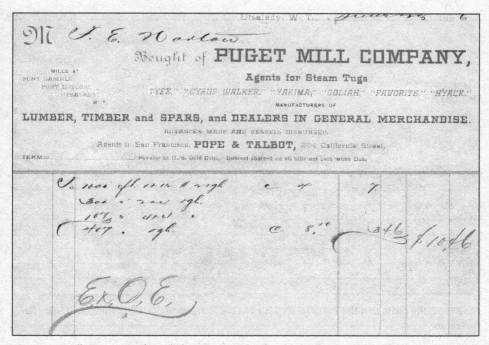

The Puget Mill Company of Utsalady, Camano Island, sold this lumber in 1886. Notice the prices: 2x4s sold for $8.50 per thousand board feet.

William Renton opened his mill at Port Blakely in 1864. For years the harbor saw ships like this come in to load lumber.

Blakley Mills Largest Saw Mill in the World near Seattle, Wash.

For a time, the claim that the Port Blakely Mill was the "Largest Saw Mlill in the World" may have been true.

ATTENTION!

Madrona Point is

SACRED GROUND LEAVE NOW

By authority of the Lummi Nation

In recent times, more and more forested land is being protected from development. Orcas Islanders worked in the late 1980s to secure the future of Madrona Point, located next to Eastsound. Thanks to U.S. Government help, the Lummi Tribe was able to buy the land and people could enjoy its forest and beach. Early in the twenty-first century, though, the Tribe closed it to outsiders, citing misuse, and many Orcas Islanders resent this.

This building several miles from Coupeville in Ebey's Landing National Historical Reserve is known today as the Ferry House. It sits on the plain just above the landing where people arriving by ship would land on Whidbey Island's west shore. About 1860 the structure was built as a tavern meant to refresh travelers before they made their way to Coupeville. By the late 1870s it had become an inn, serving meals and welcoming overnight guests. The nearby landing was moved away before the end of the century. For awhile the building was a boarding house and in 1917 it became a private home. Today it is managed by the National Park Service as part of the Historical Reserve, but Ferry House is not now open to visitors.

Both pioneer Jacob Ebey's house and the nearby blockhouse still sit on Whidbey Island, as this 2012 photograph indicates. Islanders constructed eleven blockhouses in the mid-1850s to protect white settlers from possible Indian raids. Four of the defensive structures survive on Ebey's Prairie. To reach this blockhouse and cabin, take Cemetery Road past Sunnyside Cemetery, park at the end of the road and walk along the trail for about two-tenths of a mile.

PUGET SOUND INDIAN RACING CANOE. WASHINGTON.

Early in the twentieth century these Native Americans posed by their narrow racing canoe; note its decorative bow. They men are standing on the LaConner shore across Skagit Bay from the Swinomish Reservation on Fidalgo Island. *Postcard courtesy of Cherie Christensen.*

Native Americans introduced reef net fishing to Puget Sound waters. Here are fishermen in 1943 preparing to raise the net between their boats. *Courtesy of Cherie Christensen.*

The wine industry in Puget Sound country started on Stretch Island, a 300-acre isle just north of Harstine Island in South Puget Sound. Wine-making began here in the late nineteenth century, and when prohibition ended in the United States in 1933, a Stretch Island vintner received the first Washington State license to produce wine. This 2008 photograph shows a vineyard remaining on this land so important in Western Washington's viticulture history.

Starting in 1888, first the Harrington and then the Beall family operated these greenhouses on Vashon Island. In its heyday, the farm had fifty-nine greenhouse buildings. Specializing in flowers, Beall's became prominent for the quality of the roses and orchids grown. Eventually, changes in the world economy made it more profitable to grow flowers elsewhere and the Bealls sold this property in 1989. *Courtesy of Bruce Haulman.*

Built in 1904 near Langley as a Norwegian Lutheran Church, this has been the Deer Lagoon Grange Hall since 1926. From its earliest years it has served as a community center for South Whidbey Islanders.

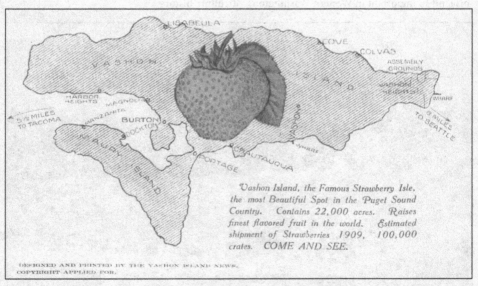

Vashon Island, the Famous Strawberry Isle, the most Beautiful Spot in the Puget Sound Country. Contains 22,000 acres. Raises finest flavored fruit in the world. Estimated shipment of Strawberries 1909, 100,000 crates. COME AND SEE.

DESIGNED AND PRINTED BY THE VASHON ISLAND NEWS.
COPYRIGHT APPLIED FOR.

Advertising was alive and well on Vashon Island in 1909, as this postcard suggests. For several decades afterward these berries were an important part of Vashon's economy. The name "Vashon" appears on the map at the location we now call Vashon Landing and Burton was then the main community on the island. The original postcard shows the island in light green while the strawberry is vivid red with darker green leaves.

This rural scene shows northeast Whidbey Island just south of Dugualla Bay. The barn indicates the importance of agriculture in this area. Goat and Ika Islands appear eastward, to the right of the photo, across Skagit Bay, while Fidalgo Island appears to the left. The distant hills are on the mainland.

Featuring the longest-established vineyard in San Juan County, Lopez Island Winery has been cultivating vines since 1987. Wine is bottled from several varieties of European grapes grown on the island.

7-Sockeye Salmon at Anacortes, Wn.

The writer of this postcard, sent in July 1915 to a Montana acquaintance, reported that "This is a fine place, beautiful scenery & fine climate. We visited the fish cannery here. Buy your salmon in flat cans." Salmon canning played an important role in the Anacortes economy at that time.

Loading Lumber at Port Blakely, Washington.

In 1902, Bainbridge Island's Hall Brothers Shipyard at Port Blakely built the four-masted schooner *Blakely* to haul lumber for Capt. William Renton's Port Blakely Mill Company.

This postcard, based on a photograph by Oliver S. Van Olinda, was mailed on Vashon to a recipient in Pullman, an Eastern Washington city, in 1911. Its message describes supposed transportation on Vashon Island before automobiles became common. "This is the Vashon Railroad in disguise. There are four cars. You only see two. There is also a fleet of Indian ships around the wharf. Some place this." Vashon Island had no railroad line; rail cars on barges were filled with berries to be taken to the mainland. And might the "Indian ships" have been canoes?

VIEW OF WHARF AT RICHARDSON, SHOWING FISH PACKED READY FOR SHIPMENT.

In the 1890s and the early twentieth century, Richardson, on the south coast of Lopez Island, was a leading community in the San Juan Islands. Fishing, then canning, brought prosperity. The photo appeared in the September 1903 issue of *The Coast*, also known as *Wilhelm's Magazine*.

The largest dry dock on the west coast of the United States sat at Dockton on Maury Island from 1892 until 1909 when it was moved to Seattle. A sign in Dockton today indicates the dry dock's location and tells its history. *Courtesy of Bruce Haulman.*

This 2015 photo shows part of the Jefferds family's Penn Cove Shellfish mussel-growing operation near Coupeville on Whidbey Island. Suspended from the rafts shown here are thousands of rope lines upon which tiny mussels attach themselves. Commercial mussel production includes several steps, but after about a year the mussels are ready to harvest.

This nineteenth-century lime kiln sits in Lime Kiln State Park on San Juan Island. Visitors should look for the short trail in the park that leads to the kiln for which the park was named. While the kilns at Roche Harbor are better known, they are built into a hillside while this one stands alone.

Walking around the kiln at Lime Kiln State Park brings one to this furnace entrance. Imagine life as a stoker feeding wood into the fire in order to bring the temperature up to about 2000 degrees, enough to extract usable lime, or quicklime, from the stone.

The community on Eagle Harbor's northern shore, Winslow, began to grow when the Hall Brothers moved their shipyard in 1902-03 from Port Blakely to this other Bainbridge Island inlet and a creosote plant opened across the bay. By this time, steamships were more prominent than sailing vessels, but tall ships continued to carry freight on Puget Sound. *Courtesy Michael Maslan Vintage Posters and Photographs.*

An early twentieth-century view of Dockton from Quartermaster Harbor shows that the dry dock is gone. The town never did grow much, if any, after 1900. Perhaps more interesting than the distant community in the photograph is the offshore ship, launched in 1900 as the USS *Wyoming*. Reconditioned in 1910 as a submarine tender, the USS *Cheyenne*, she appears on this postcard mailed in 1911.

II
DEVELOPMENT

5| The Forests

THE LAND AND THE FORESTS CAME BEFORE THE PEOPLE, and before new settlers could develop farms or towns on the land they had to confront the trees. From the very beginning of white settlement, using the trees came before using the land on which they grew.

While the Wilkes expedition's ships poked around the inlets of Greater Puget Sound and rival nations claimed the San Juan Islands, the westward march of Americans across the continent was gaining strength. In the Puget Sound region, entrepreneurs and pioneers cleared the forests, harvested the wood, and settled the land. Population grew, ways of life changed, and eventually attitudes shifted, so by the twenty-first century many islanders had grown concerned not about exploiting land and forest, but about conserving them. Here is the story.

When white people first came to the islands, entrepreneurs appeared to make their fortunes from that natural resource which all who approached the islands could see: trees. Steamers, homes and local businesses all needed wood—for building material and fuel. A lot of the wood went into constructing and powering the steamboats that were becoming more and more common in Puget Sound after the mid-nineteenth century. The Hudson's Bay Company's *Beaver*, for example, could consume as many as fifty cords of wood in a day of travel. The new wood-burning, steam-powered vessels brought both people and goods to the islands and shipped away some of their lumber.

The 1849 California gold rush created a market for lumber in rapidly growing San Francisco and Sacramento, among other places. The huge trees of Puget Sound country were not so far away, and great logs from these trees on the islands could be transported fairly easily, having been felled near the shore. The men who actually cut the wood and the businessmen who organized the timber and shipping industries were true Puget Sound pioneers.

Harvesting lumber was a necessity for settlement of the islands. Except on a few natural prairies, the people who came to live could not farm until they cleared the land. Many Puget Sounders know the song "Acres of Clams," which tells of a one-time gold miner who decided to try farming and thus headed for Puget Sound. But he found that the land was "covered all over with timber thick as hair on the back of a dog." Thus,

> I staked me a claim in the forest
> And set myself down to hard toil.
> For two years I chopped and I struggled,
> But I never got down to the soil.

As for the song's title, the settler eventually came to love this area, where settlers were "surrounded by acres of clams."[1]

Early travelers to this region found that cedar and western hemlock trees common to the islands could have a three-foot diameter and a height of 150 feet. The greatest of all, the Douglas fir, can grow to three hundred feet, with a six- to eight-foot diameter. The early loggers used hand tools—axes and two-man saws—to fell these giant trees and cut the timber. Thick undergrowth and trees' huge roots and swelled butts made the job more difficult, but oxen or bull teams could pull the logs to the beach.

Most of the settlers who came to live in Puget Sound country became loggers by necessity to clear their land for farming. Some found the effort lucrative enough that they continued to log despite the dangerous and strenuous work it meant in those days. For example, John James Eden settled on Guemes Island in 1872 and cleared twenty acres for a home and an orchard, but continued logging, with up to two dozen men working for him. Throughout the islands one could find similar small operations. Some communities held logging bees, an example of neighbors helping neighbors.

As Puget Sound country developed, more and more entrepreneurs came, as did more and more steamboats. They burned wood, lots of it, and island timber stoked the ships' boilers. The entrepreneurs wanted the wood, not the cleared land. Speculators, too, acquired land for the wealth they could amass from timber sales, and sometimes harvested wood they had no right to cut. Mill companies acquired land once surveying was complete but also often bought logs from independent loggers. When the larger companies wanted to buy land, sometimes they bent the law, hiring people to file claims which they would then sell to the mill owners.

Heavily forested land dominated the islands, though there were exceptions, especially Ebey Prairie near the center of long, narrow Whidbey Island. People logged in and near this extensive prairie and as early as 1853, ships picked up timber at Coveland, at the head of nearby Penn Cove. Much of the island's timber went to a mill at Utsalady, on Camano Island.

Among the most prominent nineteenth-century sawmills in Western Washington were three built on Puget Sound islands. At Utsalady, Thomas Cranney and Lawrence Grennan founded Grennan and Company in 1856. With some help from the local Native Americans, this business prospered. At the end of the year, the company even sent a shipload off to France. Grennan and Company soon became the first large-scale operator on nearby Whidbey Island, too, harvesting timber there for their mill. It would be shipped from Utsalady, some going on to the American east coast or Europe.

The 600-by-124-foot Utsalady mill building opened in 1858 may have been the largest one in the world at that time,[2] and the mill operated profitably until a company steamer, the *Pacific*, sank on November 4, 1875, killing some 275 people and causing great financial loss. As a result, the Puget Mill Company bought the Utsalady mill. Two of the new owners were men named Pope and Talbot, whose later forest products company carries their names. Under these men, about forty-five people worked at the mill in the 1880s, but it temporarily closed in 1891 for renovation and never reopened, largely due to the national economic crash of 1893.

Two great mills and the towns they generated arose on Bainbridge Island in the nineteenth century. George Anson Meigs opened the first mill about 1855 at Port Madison. The busy mill brought residents to the community and the business flourished despite a boiler explosion and a later fire that destroyed the plant. Ships carried products to markets.

The company harvested timber from Bainbridge Island and nearby Blake Island, where in 1861, Meigs bought two-thirds of the land. During the mill's heyday, Port Madison was the leading town in Kitsap County, in 1857 becoming its first county seat. Here, too, the county's first school opened in 1860.

Captain William Renton built his Bainbridge Island mill in the bay called Port Blakely in 1863, about a decade after serious logging began on the islands. A company town grew, with a road of sorts connecting it to that other mill town, Port Madison. In 1875, six separate logging camps operated on the island, selling to both mills. Nearby mainland camps also supplied lumber to these Bainbridge Island mills. Renton's company built a seventy-five-room hotel in Port Blakely and together with the Port Madison Mill made Kitsap County the industrial leader of Washington Territory in the 1880s. Renton's mill burned down in 1888, but he built an even larger one in its place. The company continued to thrive. Its executives acquired inland tracts of forest and built logging railroads to facilitate log transportation. On an 1890 tour, United States President Rutherford B. Hayes stopped at Port Blakely, but he skipped Port Madison because of political differences with Meigs.

George Meigs' finances were shaky. His Port Madison mill became involved in legal battles and closed in 1892. Almost everyone left the once-bustling town, and county voters moved the courthouse to the mainland. At Port Blakely, a 1907 fire destroyed most of that mill. A smaller facility replaced it, and World War I orders helped keep it in business, but the end came in 1922 when the mill closed for good because the market could no longer support it. At both Port Madison and Port Blakely, a visitor today sees no indication beyond interpretive signs that either of these lovely inlets ever featured a great mill and all the supporting services of such an enterprise. Late nineteenth-century photographs do, however, document the existence of these mills and the towns they supported.

Timber, not settlement, was the reason for the earliest land purchases on Vashon Island, as elsewhere. The first non-Native enterprise on the island, according to Oliver Van Olinda, involved wood. It began in 1852 when crewmen of the ship *Leonesa* loaded spars aboard to take to the east coast. By the early 1870s, more loggers worked on the island. In 1863, Andrew Pope and William C. Talbot claimed eighty acres above Cove, and in 1864 and 1865, George Meigs bought about one hundred acres, almost two-thirds of it on the Burton Peninsula.[3]

By the 1870s, small logging camps could be seen scattered through the islands. More and more of the land being harvested for timber was in the interior of the islands and on the mainland, away from the shore. Therefore came the logging roads known as skid roads, wide cleared tracks with small logs placed crosswise about every six feet. Oxen, and later horses, would pull the harvested logs, greased with oil from the dogfish—a small shark harvested in those days for its oil—along this track until they reached the shore. Once on the beach, men would construct rafts of logs to send to a mill elsewhere on Puget Sound.

Late in the 1870s, William and John Coffelt built a mill on Blakely Island's Thatcher Bay. Above this bay is little Spencer Lake, and water-power ran the small firm's first saw. William Coffelt and his brother-in-law William Vierick later installed a steam engine to run a more powerful saw. Logging uncleared land supported the mill into the 1920s, and thereafter, mill operators bought logs and salvaged others from previous logging operations. Henry Hoffman has written about harvesting logs from the beach to take to this mill during the depression years of the 1930s. Finally, in 1942, the mill ceased operation.[4]

San Juan County became recognized as a good source of limestone, and wood was the fuel used to operate lime kilns on the archipelago's islands. When lime extraction at Roche Harbor on San Juan Island was at its height during the first few decades of the twentieth century, seven kilns ran all the time, each consuming about three cords of wood daily. The company used additional lumber to build barrels in which to ship the lime. By the beginning of the twentieth century, the Roche Harbor barrel factory could manufacture some four thousand barrels each day. Many island settlers made money cutting wood to feed the kilns and make the barrels. Local legend held that the islands were denuded to feed the company's fires, but recent study has estimated that loggers cut only about 8.7% of San Juan County's forested acreage to supply kiln wood.[5]

The development of railroads strongly influenced island loggers and mill companies. The big firms, which were buying land for the trees on it, constructed railroads to reach timber far inland. For example, the Port Blakely mill acquired many acres on the west side of Puget Sound. During national railroad construction, the Puget Sound mills found a ready market, especially for railroad ties. The coming of the railroads meant that an island location became a disadvantage, for railroads could be built well into mainland foothills. Once a transcontinental line reached Puget Sound, mainland timber suppliers were more conveniently located than island mills.

Not all the wood found a useful role. Forest fires destroyed some of it. In August 1890, an Anacortes newspaper noted that "a great curtain of smoke hanging over Admiralty Inlet and the great peninsula, shuts the country beyond from our view." At the beginning of the twentieth century, one reason for siting a lighthouse on Burrows Island, just west of Fidalgo, was the need to protect maritime traffic through Rosario Strait because, according to a congressional report, during certain seasons of the year fog and smoke from forest fires prevail[6] Forests on the islands have burned, too, but the islands' relatively small size limits possible damage.

Logging continued on the islands in the twentieth century, though many of the largest trees had already been harvested. Mechanization began making the job easier if not safer. For example, with cables and winches, donkey engines moved logs to the watercourse or railroad track from which the timber could be shipped. Camano Island had twenty-two logging camps in 1901. On Marrowstone and Indian Islands serious logging did not start until about that time. Before then, the few settlers cleared only enough land for their farm fields and buildings. Scow Bay, between the islands, made a perfect log pond from which logs could be taken to market. Soon, though, no longer was logging on the Puget Sound islands a major activity, though local firms selling to the large mills carried out smaller-scale logging. In the first half of the twentieth century, views toward the shore showed much mostly denuded land.

Only in Anacortes on Fidalgo Island did forest industry remain important on the islands. It survived because of the rail connection between the island city and the mainland, and because Anacortes mills could conveniently ship products throughout the world. The first mill on Fidalgo Island opened its doors in 1878. By the end of the 1920s, more than one thousand people worked in the city's mills and wooden box factories, and in 1929 nine Anacortes mills were in production. Only one or two remain today.

Not until after World War II were many parts of Orcas Island seriously logged, for its mountainous terrain had made harvesting wood on the slopes too expensive. A market for housing construction after the war plus technological innovation meant that where logging could be done safely and profitably, Orcas hillsides were tackled. At the same time, oil refineries opened in Anacortes, attracting workers and leading to land on Fidalgo Island being cleared for housing.

Logging left the land behind, though. Too often logged-off land remained an ugly mishmash of stumps and weeds. Logged-over lands are ideal for brush picking, and Western Washington rural residents have earned money gathering brush. In earlier days, this found a market as a component of fill material, and more recently, selectively chosen brush appears in flower arrangements. Meanwhile, acreage on some of the islands has been converted to tree farms. Christmas trees thrive on tracts that once held fruit orchards or strawberry fields.

Forest cover has increased considerably since the mid-twentieth century. The trees have grown tall partly due to the decline of agriculture. Some beautiful distant views of several decades ago are now gone as the trees have grown—for example, obstructing some views from the Deception Pass highway. Much, perhaps most, of the islands' acreage is now forested, and some is logged profitably. Today, though, islanders rarely see the great rafts of logs lashed together that were guided by tugboats through Puget Sound waters until about the end of the twentieth century.

Over the years, islanders' attitudes toward use of forest products have evolved as land and forest conservation have become important to Puget Sound area residents. A conservation movement can be traced back many years—America created the world's first national park in 1872—and in the twentieth century, concerned islanders began forming organizations to protect their farmlands, forests and beaches. Land use regulations now restrict what trees can be cut. The forests are there, as air views of the islands show, and many wooded tracts are protected from development. A number of examples of land protection campaigns on the islands might be cited.

Active land conservation organizations have been busy in the San Juans for half a century. In 1971, the Nature Conservancy, a national organization, purchased 256 acres of land including waterfront on Waldron Island to keep it from becoming a subdivision. Nine years later, public contributions and supportive landowners enabled the Nature Conservancy to buy Yellow and Sentinel Islands, both in the San Juans. Eleven-acre Yellow Island is especially treasured for the splendor of its wildflowers. In 1999 county voters authorized a one percent real estate excise tax to conserve more land by purchase, thus creating a land bank.

Another early effort at land and forest preservation occurred on Cypress Island in the eastern San Juans. Settlers here were always few, as much of the island's land rises steeply from sea level to peaks over 1500 feet high on an island only six and one-fourth square miles in area. In the 1970s and 80s came a battle over Cypress Island's future. Developer R. A. Hanson of Spokane purchased almost half of the island in 1978 and acquired more land a year later. He had some timber harvested and an airstrip put in. He planned to build seven hundred houses plus two hundred condominium units, a resort and a marina, but this scheme drew increasing protests. The firm proved unable to get needed permits and eventually, in 1989, sold its Cypress Island land to the state. By 1990, Washington State owned eighty percent of the island, and has acquired more since then.

In 1979, the first land trust in Washington State, the San Juan Preservation Trust, began its efforts, arranging with landowners for conservation easements, acquiring gifts of land for protection, and working with individuals and other conservation organizations, such as The Nature Conservancy, to raise funds for land purchase. The Preservation Trust's activities also include research and education.

For a time, timber giant Georgia Pacific held some four or five thousand acres on Blakely Island as a tree farm. Subsequent owner Thomas Crowley gave almost one thousand acres of this land to Seattle Pacific University in 1976, and the university has operated a field station there. Meanwhile, most of Blakely Island remains undeveloped today. There have been unsuccessful efforts to establish a state park on the island and the Nature Conservancy has been involved in efforts to curb development. Though all of Blakely's land is privately held, much of it has been protected, for example through conservation easements with the San Juan Preservation Trust.

In November 2006, several land conservation groups came together to buy some 1,500 acres on Orcas Island's Turtleback Mountain at the center of the island's western lobe. A foundation established by Norton Clapp, one-time chairman of timber giant Weyerhaeuser, owned the acreage, but because the foundation wanted funds for its charity work, the mountain was up for sale. Price was the only question in this case. Eventually the conservation groups paid seventeen million dollars for the property. People may visit the preserve now, but only on foot.

Guemes Islanders saved a significant piece of real estate from development in 2009, raising more than two million dollars for the Skagit Land Trust and San Juan Preservation Trust to buy seventy acres of the highest land on the island, which rises to almost seven hundred feet above sea level. The alternative would have been division into ten acre lots for housing. After completing the purchase, environmentalists began work on building a trail to the summit of Guemes Mountain, where people can now enjoy lovely vistas of the northern Sound. Note that the San Juan organization thus works beyond San Juan County. Whatcom County's Lummi Island and Skagit County's Sinclair, Guemes, Cypress and Fidalgo Islands are in its purview. The Preservation Trust also raised funds to complete the purchase of 220-acre Vendovi Island, between Lummi and Guemes. Lummi Island also has its own organization, the Lummi Island Heritage Trust, which has seen several areas on the island set aside as preserves. One features a trail leading to a scenic viewpoint high on Lummi Mountain.

In the late 1970s, Whidbey Islanders fought a land-clearing battle to prevent logging on a 255-acre tract abutting South Whidbey State Park. These woods were a mixed old-growth and second growth expanse of University of Washington land known as Classic U. When the contractor started building logging roads into the site, demonstrations began, protesters blocking access. Opponents of the logging filed a lawsuit, a judge issued a temporary injunction against the logging company and later the court ruled the sale of the timber invalid because no environmental impact statement had been filed. But negotiations continued, and in 1981, the state government and Whidbey environmentalists agreed on a compromise that would see some of the tract logged but the oldest trees preserved for at least ten years, until a final plan could be worked out. Finally, in 1992, Washington State Parks acquired the contested land by trading Eastern Washington acreage for it and added it to South Whidbey State Park. In 2006, citizen effort helped add another 7.3 acres of old-growth forest to the park, which is revered for its forest perhaps as much as for its beach, and many visitors now hike through the once-disputed land.

The Whidbey-Camano Land Trust, founded in 1984 to protect Whidbey land, carried on for almost twenty years with volunteer participants and managed to conserve 438 acres of land on Whidbey Island. In 2003 the organization acquired professional staff and expanded to include Camano Island in its mission. More recently, the Land Trust has purchased additional land under threat of clear-cutting, including the Trillium Community Forest southeast of South Whidbey State Park. The Trillium Corporation had owned the property, sold it, and the buyers wanted to divide it into 124 ten-acre homesites. After development of a few acres, the housing market contracted, the company went bankrupt, and the Land Trust raised enough money to buy the rest of the property. Well more than one thousand people contributed a total of more than four million dollars to acquire the tract. The forest is now available for public use.

Land preservation sometimes takes the form of wildlife refuges, as in the San Juan Islands. Some of these areas are open to the public, with anchorages for pleasure boaters. An example is Turn Island. Also, worried that future government philosophy might change and offer similar islands to developers, some San Juan Islanders urged that protected islands be designated a national monument. In 2013, this happened. The new San Juan Islands National Monument offers more permanent protection to pieces of land already held by the federal Bureau of Land Management on various islands. Among the areas in this monument are all of Patos Island, the Cattle Point site of the lighthouse near American Camp on San Juan Island, and on Lopez Island, Iceberg Point and Watmough Bay. The national monument accomplishes some of what a United States government study suggested in 1970, the establishment of an "island trust" for the San Juan Islands, with the federal government having a role in planning along with state and local governments.

Some mostly forested tracts found on the islands are maintained as parks. On Bainbridge Island is a unique forest-dominated park, the Bloedel Reserve. The Bloedel family grew wealthy in the logging industry, and in 1931, Prentice and Virginia Bloedel bought Bainbridge property to be their home. On 150 acres they maintained an extensive forest as well as lawn and garden. Years later, the Bloedels turned the property over to a foundation, and for a fee which helps maintain the property, the public has been able to visit the garden since the late 1980s to enjoy the trees, the flowers and the views, all in a serene retreat.

Residents concerned about overdevelopment created the Bainbridge Island Land Trust in 1989, at a time when island population was growing about eight percent yearly, while real estate values were increasing between one and two percent monthly. In its first twenty years, the Land Trust protected more than one thousand acres of land, including the island's majestic

Grand Forest, three acres centrally located on the island. Bainbridge voters agreed to buy the acreage, which gained the name "Grand Forest" after school children named it.

The Vashon-Maury Island Land Trust has worked with the Vashon Park District, the King County Department of Natural Resources and Parks, and the Vashon-Maury Island Audubon Society to preserve and manage island lands. On Anderson Island, Forterra, formerly known as Cascade Land Trust, has helped acquire park land for preservation. The Capitol Land Trust works to protect islands in South Puget Sound, while the Jefferson Land Trust includes Marrowstone Island, which lies in Jefferson County. Other organizations, of course, are also interested in forest and land preservation, for example the Anacortes Friends of the Forest on Fidalgo Island.

People of all ages use the various islands' forest trails for exercise, nature observation and, simply, relaxation and pleasure, while students learn about nature in protected pieces of forest, such as the Elger Bay Preserve on Camano Island, which abuts the Elger Bay Elementary School grounds.

Despite efforts at land protection, the results sometimes can be frustrating, as at Orcas Island's Madrona Point. Late in the 1980s, Norton Clapp and a company of his were ready to develop or sell this small peninsula at Eastsound. The Lummi Nation wanted to buy it, as the area was part of their historic homeland and probably the burial site of some Lummi. Two of San Juan County's three commissioners opposed sale to the tribe, however, citing the possibility of future activities such as "bingo halls and cigarette sales."[7] The county did not have funds to buy the property, and the state would not be able to appropriate funds for purchase until after the planned development, including perhaps as many as eighty-eight residences, would be underway.

The controversy simmered for some time. Archaeological excavation at a small site on the property found no signs of burials. Consultations and negotiations continued, and, in an election, voters replaced one of the commissioners who had opposed Lummi ownership of the land with one who supported it. The local congressman, Al Swift, worked for protection of the land, and in 1990, with Swift's urging, the federal government appropriated funds for the Lummi to buy the land. The final accord specified that the county would provide law enforcement. The site remained undeveloped and was open to the public, but in 1998, Lummi Tribe Land Use

Planner Todd Tucker described "increased visitation and transient use" which threatened "significant cultural, spiritual, archaeological and environmental resources,"[8] and later the tribe closed off access.

Some islanders feel that visitors had caused no harm and that the Lummi action closing the peninsula was arbitrary. Efforts have been made to mend the fissure between islanders and Lummi and reach a settlement on maintenance of the site that would both preserve it and open it to the public. Groups working to protect the land succeeded in stopping development of the area, but the result has caused bitterness.

On Vashon Island, controversy arose in 2010 about whether to allow hunting in Island Center Forest, a 363-acre preserve open for hiking, mountain biking and horseback riding. Much of the forest's county-owned land is classified as "working resource land," however, and hunting has gone on there for years. But nearby homeowners as well as many people who frequent the forest have wanted an end to this hunting, despite the problems deer create for gardeners all over the island. Also, this was the only county-owned property in all of King County where hunting remained legal. In 2011, officials tested a compromise, allowing an extra-short hunting season of only three weeks. King County continues to open the forest to hunting for up to three weeks each October.

For perhaps a century after white entrepreneurs and settlers came to the Puget Sound islands, forests were there to be cut down, with their wood used for fuel or construction. These uses continue today, but forest land is protected now in a way that Puget Sound country's pioneer settlers could not have imagined.

While many pieces of forest have been saved from development, is their protection adequate? In January 2013, news emerged that thieves had cut down twenty-one large maple trees in Jarrell Cove State Park on Harstine Island. The perpetrators chose a distant section of the park where they did not expect to be discovered. Perhaps they wanted only relatively short but prime sections of the trunks to use in guitar construction, for they left the forest ground littered with most of the timber. On the other hand, each year one reads of new parcels of island acreage that land trusts and similar organizations are working to save or have recently acquired.

Questions abound. Will our descendants find the islands a world dominated by forest, looking more like land the explorers saw? Would this be a positive development? The demand for houses keeps growing, so should the islands be kept as preserves or are they places where people may live? Can we sustain both? The islands were among the earliest places in Puget Sound country to be logged, though today they are among leading areas in land and forest preservation.

6 | The Settlers

NON-NATIVE PEOPLE HAVE COME TO LIVE on the Puget Sound islands since about the middle of the nineteenth century. The pioneers
cleared the land, used or sold the wood they chopped down, built houses,
farmed—in other words, built a life. Settlers came from areas all over the
world, found work and raised families. And even though life in the United
States has changed immeasurably since the pioneers came, newcomers
have never stopped coming to make their homes on the islands.

Over the years, settlers have come for different reasons, but a common pattern for the earliest settler families was for a man to establish a
small island farm, first clearing land and using or selling the logs, then
planting crops, raising animals, fishing, and harvesting clams and other
sea life. Family members might come with him or arrive later. Often, a settler wrote to the folks back home and described the virtues of Puget Sound
country. Relatives, friends and acquaintances would follow the first settler,
so island communities could grow to contain a number of people from the
same eastern or midwestern community. People from one country, or a
region of that country, also tended to congregate in one place.

Records do not identify the first settlers on all the islands. The earliest
one who came probably was Thomas W. Glasgow, who came arrived on
Whidbey Island in 1848. Glasgow built a cabin and planted some crops,
but due to fear of Indian depredations, soon left. Soon Whidbey Island

also saw the earliest permanent settlement, partly because of the fertile prairie that beckoned. Isaac Ebey, perhaps the most famous of all the early settlers, arrived in 1850. The U.S. government adopted several policies in the mid-nineteenth century so prospective settlers could acquire land, and Ebey filed a claim for 640 acres. His family became the island's first lifelong settlers, and the area where they settled bears their name today: Ebey's Prairie. By early 1853, settlers had claimed most of the island's prairie land, and by 1860, seventy-four families lived on the central Whidbey plain.

Retired sea captains were prominent among Whidbey's early residents. These men had seen and admired the island as they sailed along the Sound. One of the captains, Thomas Coupe, came in 1852. Another mariner, Captain Howard Bentley Lovejoy, came to Penn Cove in 1853 and became the first Puget Sound ship's pilot. His sons built boats in Coupeville and ran the Island Transportation Company, operating vessels to connect Whidbey Island and various other Puget Sound ports. Not only Whidbey Island attracted mariners. Captain James Griffiths' wanderlust took him from Wales to the sea and around the Horn, then north as far as Alaska before he bought land in Port Townsend and Marrowstone Island in 1855.

Various islands saw settlers in the 1850s. Some came to Camano's logging settlement, Utsalady, in 1853. Throughout the islands, squatters and drifters also appeared, and some settled without formal land titles. Two men came to live—and fish—at Bainbridge Island's Agate Point in the early 1850s, but the island's first settlement, Port Madison, centered on logging. An 1857 census showed 58 people in the town, and in 1860, 192. In 1864, Captain Renton established the Port Blakely mill, attracting people to the southern part of the island.

One of Washington Territory's most prominent pioneers, Ezra Meeker, briefly lived on McNeil Island, though he apparently never filed a claim on land there. He came in 1853 and he and his brother Oliver built a cabin. Then Ezra Meeker brought his wife and tiny son to the island. Their eighteen-by-eighteen-foot cabin featured a "stone fire-place, cat-and-clay chimney its lumber floor, real window with glass in it, together with the high post bedstead out of tapering cedar saplings, the table fastened to the wall, with rustic chairs," he wrote.[1] Meeker sold his McNeil land in 1862 and settled permanently in Puyallup. Ezra Meeker gained national prominence, mainly for his efforts to keep alive the story of the Oregon Trail and the pioneers it brought west.

Permanent settlers first came to McNeil Island in 1884 and by 1890 about ten families lived there. In 1870, though, the United States government had bought some land on the island and in 1875 established a territorial prison. At first, rowboats brought inmates to the island. The prison became a real settlement, complete with a shipyard that opened in 1911. Meanwhile, the settler families farmed, harvested timber, repaired boats and fished. In 1936, however, the government took over the entire island and ordered the remaining settlers to leave. Many moved to nearby Anderson Island. Farther north, Indian Island families lost their land when this island became a military base in 1940.

Other islands first saw settlement in the 1860s. During that decade, a few settlers appeared on both Cypress and Blakely Islands, and at about the beginning of the decade, Amos Johnson became the first settler on Guemes Island. In 1872, the John James Edens family came to Guemes. Edens once claimed that he could always spot Guemes Islanders because their arms were so long, thanks to all the rowing they had to do to cross the channel from Fidalgo Island—often against the tide.[2]

William Munks was the earliest Fidalgo settler who stayed on the island. His wife noted that for $60 and a watch, he bought "a squatter's right—from this tree to that tree" in January 1861.[3] Munks and a friend, Eric Compton, made their living by rowing to Bellingham and selling what they grew and hunted. In 1870, the census on Fidalgo Island counted sixty people. Nineteen of the residents were Native American women who were housekeepers, and often wives, of settlers. Two large refineries now dominate the land on Fidalgo Island's March Point, where Munks settled.

Vashon Island saw its first claims for land filed in 1861, though the island's first settler, Matthew Bridges, did not arrive until 1865. He and his Native American wife lived on various parts of the island while he logged the land there. At least ten families who had arrived by 1885 still had descendants connected to the island in 2013.

The earliest pioneers on the San Juan Islands usually arrived as single men, and according to the 1870 census, forty-nine Indian women on San Juan Island had married men not of Native blood. Some had made their living trapping for the Hudsons' Bay Company and some had been members of the small military contingents stationed on San Juan Island. Karen Jones-Lamb, in *Native American Wives of San Juan Settlers*, wrote that most of the men in those islands who married early on took Indian wives.[4]

One might think of this as the women marrying members of an occupying power, as did war brides when American soldiers were stationed in Japan and Germany after the defeat of these countries in World War II.

Later in the nineteenth century, more and more white women came west, and they and their families often looked down on the interracial families. In 1879, the Whatcom County prosecutor charged nine white men with illegal—if any—marriages with Native women. The men included Henry Barkhousen of Fidalgo Island, then part of Whatcom County. The other eight men soon arranged legal marriages, but Barkhousen fought the charges, and won acquittal. Peyton Kane, who has written about the case, noted that more than half the voters in Whatcom, Skagit and San Juan Counties in the period from 1860 to 1880 came from mixed families. A desire to decrease the political influence of the large number of men with Indian wives probably motivated the original charges against the men, but Washington State's northern island communities owe a debt to these founding families of mixed heritage. They were respected people despite the attempt at denigration.[5]

By 1880, more and more families were appearing on the islands, but in 1883 Shaw Island had only twelve residents, ten of whom were bachelors. Settlement came slowly to Lummi Island, as people considered this to be Indian land, though it was not included in the Lummi Reservation. The first non-Indian family, headed by Christian Tuttle, did not arrive until 1871. He and his wife did their bit to populate the island, though, raising six children.

Residents of the San Juans often moved from island to island during their lives. Note the story of Caroline, or "Toots," Chevalier Mills, born on Spieden Island in 1908. Like so many San Juan Islanders, she had an Indian mother. She grew up on Spieden but went to different schools on Waldron, Stuart and San Juan Islands. Married on San Juan in 1937, she and her husband Norman Mills lived successively on Johns and Lummi Islands, then in Bellingham, and finally on Stuart Island.

In those nineteenth century days when small boat transportation was the norm, settlers established homes on some of the lesser-known San Juan Islands which today are uninhabited or harbor only a few families. Pennsylvanian John Reed and his Indian wife, Tacee—also known as Mary—were the first permanent settlers on Decatur Island, tenth largest of the San Juans. They came before 1870 and settled on "the finest place and the largest area of good land in San Juan County," according to a correspondent to the *Anacortes Progress* in 1889. They produced shingles and also farmed. Decatur Island has never been widely populated, though. A 2015 report estimated that only eighty-four people lived there.[6]

Small Sinclair Island, north of Cypress and Guemes Islands, is just one and one-half square miles in area. Three settlers established themselves on Sinclair before 1875, and by 1892, newcomers had claimed all of the island's land. Skagit School District #28 enrolled eighteen children in 1891 at the Sinclair Island school. The district included Cypress Island too, so children from Cypress sometimes boarded with Sinclair families. The 1900 census listed twenty-one residents on Sinclair: seven fishermen, including their cook, and five families totaling fourteen people. In 2015 Sinclair had sixteen residents according to Washington State's report, but some people may stay there only or mostly during the summertime.

A few settlers came to Cypress Island in the 1860s and 1870s, though without taking official possession of any land. Using the 1880 census, Christopher White has estimated that perhaps four or five people lived there, at three different inlets around the island. By 1890, the population, including homesteaders, had risen to twenty-nine. People came and went, most not staying long. Before the turn of the century island families had enough children to support a one-room school. Its terms lasted only three to five months, and some families had their children go to school on Guemes or Sinclair Island for an additional term. After 1906, Cypress had a school only during a brief period in the 1920s. Cypress Island never did have many settlers, as it proved hard to make a living there by farming, logging and fishing. An estimated seven people lived on the island in 2015. The state's Department of Natural Resources has suggested that perhaps the island these days provides a scenic reminder of "conditions in western Washington prior to European settlement."[7]

Waldron Island is the San Juan outlier to the northwest and is only about four and one-half square miles in area, but by 1863 eight settlers had arrived. That year a young Waldron couple were wed in the first marriage to be celebrated in the San Juan Islands. Six years later, though, the bride and her father were found murdered, and people assumed that Northern Indians killed the two. Waldron Island had a post office as early as 1880. Mail came first by canoe, then steamboat three times a week, and eventually, in 1975, by small plane—though in the mid-1980s, the mail once again began arriving by boat. In 1876, the island received its own election precinct and nowadays Waldron Island even has its own zip code (98297). The island's population is about one hundred, with perhaps twice as many during the summers.

Then there is Henry Island, just off northwest San Juan Island. Shaped somewhat like a capital H, it is barely over a mile and a half in area. In the early days of settlement August Hoffmeister, a German who ran a store for the English garrison on San Juan Island during the Pig War years, pastured sheep on Henry Island. For a while, a lime kiln operated on the Island. A bay on the island's west side is called Smuggler's Row, describing its use as a refuge for lawbreakers in the 1890s. When June and Farrar Burn stopped there in 1946 as they cruised through the San Juan archipelago in a rowboat outfitted with a sail, they found that only one family appeared to live on Henry Island.[8] In 2015 there were twenty-seven residents, and docks scattered here and there around the island serve their homes and also those for summer people. Finally, according to the 1900 census, Blakely and Stuart Islands each had more than fifty residents, while in 2015 Washington State estimated that forty-one people lived on Blakely and thirty-three lived on Stuart.

Pioneer life thus began on the islands in the second half of the nineteenth century. People built their own cabins and made many of their furnishings, although settlers could soon find manufactured goods, from dishes to fabrics and clothing, available in Victoria, Port Townsend and Olympia. Finished furniture came around the horn of South America. Islanders traveled by farm cart or wagon when not on foot or horseback, on trails often widened only by usage. One early popular route was across the narrow waist of Whidbey Island from Ebey's Landing to the Coupeville vicinity. People made their own entertainment in pioneer homes and communities. As more settlers came, schools, churches and, of course, taverns appeared.

Many different sorts of people from many different places have come to settle in the islands, and here are some of them. Among Whidbey Island's settlers in the 1850s were a fair number from Ireland. Irish families settled in the central part of the island, the area now dominated by Coupeville and Oak Harbor, as well as here and there on other islands.

Sizable Norwegian communities grew on various islands. By 1890, Norwegians were beginning to come to Marrowstone Island, some by way of Minnesota. Peter Nordby acquired 187 acres of Marrowstone land in 1891, leading to the dedication in 1892 of a townsite called Nordland. Nordby himself never lived on the island, but many Norwegian names appear among the settlers of that era. A number of Norwegians also settled on Vashon Island, especially on the west side around Cove and Colvos, where most stayed busy fishing and farming.

Poverty and the wish to avoid religious persecution brought many Dutch to America and the first ones to come to Whidbey Island arrived in 1894, in response to advertising seen in midwestern states. Perhaps two hundred had arrived by 1896. These, and the Dutch who followed, were mostly farming people. The largest number settled in and near Oak Harbor where some went into business and many farmed nearby. Dutch names are still to be heard on Whidbey Island. In the mid-twentieth century, though, some Dutch farmers lost their land when the U.S. Navy built Naval Air Station Whidbey Island.

Croatian communities also emerged on some of the islands in the late nineteenth and early twentieth centuries. Their homeland was along the east coast of the Adriatic Sea in what was then the Austro-Hungarian Empire. After the First World War, this Croatian region became part of the new nation later called Yugoslavia, and, finally, in 1991, an independent Croatia. Croatians had left for America, hoping to escape both poverty and political oppression. In the old country and on Puget Sound islands they worked in shipbuilding and fishing. Croatians reached Dockton on Maury Island by way of a few other communities in North America, the first of these migrants, including John A. Martinolich, arriving in 1896. He got a job at the Puget Sound Dry Dock Company, worked his way up and began to run his own shipyard in 1904. Some of the Croatian families remain on Maury Island to this day, some continue in the fishing industry. After a few years, some of these families began moving to Bainbridge Island. They mostly settled around Eagledale, on the south side of Eagle Harbor. Many of the men found jobs in the Hall Brothers Shipyard, which had recently relocated to the north side of the harbor. Thus, these workers rowed across the inlet to and from their homes. Other Croatian men joined the Bainbridge fishing fleet. Meanwhile, a third large Croatian community took root in Anacortes. The earliest known of these settlers was John Padovan, who came about 1901. The Babarovich brothers homesteaded on Sinclair Island around the beginning of the twentieth century but relocated to Anacortes a few years later. Other Croatians soon joined them. Fishing brought them to the Fidalgo Island city just as their compatriots had come to Maury and Bainbridge Islands.

Chinese men looking for work to send money back to their families facing hardship in China also arrived in the islands in the late nineteenth century. They came to various islands—Bainbridge, Whidbey, Maury and some of the smaller islands. Some appeared on San Juan Island while it was under joint occupation.

On Bainbridge Island, Chinese came to earn a living in those thriving mill towns, Port Madison and Port Blakely, and they worked as cooks and laundrymen—just as the stereotypes of early Chinese in the United States have us believe. The mills also employed some Chinese as fishermen, and on the docks they loaded and unloaded ships. In 1876, after someone found a Chinese man murdered in his bed, all the Port Madison Chinese workers were fired, essentially being run out of town. At Port Blakely, the Chinese all lived in one house, separate from other employees, and the mill owner's wife rented them a garden plot. They even raised hogs until a county official stopped this, but the mill discharged all the Chinese in the mid-1870s. Perhaps the national recession known as the Panic of 1873 and the mill's financial troubles were the underlying reasons for this, but the general prejudice towards Chinese in the United States at that time surely played a part.

After the salmon canning industry started in the 1890s, many Chinese found employment in canneries located on the northern islands, especially Lummi and Fidalgo. These men were not welcomed on fishing boats, but cannery owners prized the Chinese for their quick work. Other people expressed little interest in the seasonal cannery jobs and owners often found it hard to locate workers—but the Chinese wanted jobs. However, newly-invented machinery in the twentieth century called the "Iron Chink" replaced the Chinese, whose jobs thus disappeared.

Chinese could also be found on Whidbey Island. Because nearby Port Townsend was a port of entry to the United States and farmers on nearby Whidbey needed help, Chinese went to the island starting in the 1870s and found work, often as sharecroppers. Many lived together in a building on Ebey's Prairie and worked on farms, while others served as houseboys for white families. Almost half the hired men working on Whidbey farms were Chinese. After a time, farmers began renting land to Chinese rather than employing them. However, anti-Chinese feeling grew, partly through a concerted movement by Coupeville merchants who complained that the Chinese bought little from the town's shops. The storekeepers wanted white families on the land instead, figuring they would patronize the shops and thus add to the town's prosperity. Threats against the Chinese and the white farmers who employed or rented to them plus federal exclusion laws led to a decline in Whidbey's Chinese population. The highest count of Chinese on the Island, seventy-six, appears in the 1890 census, but probably many more remained uncounted. Afterwards, the Chinese on Whidbey decreased bit by bit, to a census number of twenty-eight in 1910 and only eight in 1920.[9]

In the American West, non-Chinese resented the Asians mainly for the jobs they took and the low wages they accepted. This resentment helped lead to the 1882 Chinese Exclusion Act, which made Chinese entry into American territory illegal. Chinese workers continued to be smuggled into the United States from British Columbia, though, and the islands played an important role in this smuggling. Note places called Smugglers' Cove on San Juan, Lummi and Whidbey Islands as well as on Patos, the northernmost island in Washington State. Legend has it that when government agents approached a smuggler's vessel too closely, the smuggler might jettison his illegal load overboard, even when that load was human. It is certain that smugglers occasionally abandoned Chinese passengers on uninhabited islands somewhere in the northern Sound.

Maury Island had a small Chinese community, the men fishing, then drying their catch and selling it. Late in 1885 and in the early months of 1886, hordes of angry people drove most, if not all, of the Chinese from Seattle and Tacoma, and suddenly, on September 11, 1885, the Chinese community on Maury Island disappeared too. Years later, Oliver S. Van Olinda wrote that after the immigrants fled, "the wharves were in a few years battered to pieces, the mass of squalid shacks were burned as forest fires reached them, but numerous hogs, which the Chinese abandoned, remained and roamed the woods for years, until the early settlers gradually gathered them and made good use of them."[10]

Hawaiians came to the San Juans in the nineteenth century, brought by the Hudson's Bay Company. In 1872 when San Juan Island sovereignty became settled, the British troops left. So did most of the Kanakas, many merely going to the Canadian islands just on the other side of the new border. Two Kanakas stand out in San Juan Island history, though for very different reasons. One, Joseph Friday, had settled with his family, raising sheep on the spot that was later picked to be the county seat of newly-formed San Juan County. This location, well-protected by nearby Brown Island, became known as Friday's Harbor. The other Hawaiian, Kanaka Joe—or Joe Nuanna—murdered two white men and a woman. Convicted in 1871, he claimed he and a friend had planned to kill all the white settlers. Joe, only half-Hawaiian, was hanged, and because of this crime, Kanakas on San Juan Island became so distrusted that all of them except Joe Friday left when the British did.

Other peoples, often identified by national origin or culture—mainly Japanese, Filipino and Hispanic—have also come to the islands. After United States law banned Chinese from entering the country, Japanese immigrants dominated immigration from Asia. Even before the beginning of the twentieth century, some came to Puget Sound country. At first, by far the greatest number of Japanese who came to the islands gravitated to Port Blakely to work in the mill. Most of these men toiled six long days each week for little money, while they lived in a bunkhouse. One of them, Kihachi Hirakawa, arrived in December 1890 and went to work moving lumber and piling it up. For ten hours' work he got one dollar and three meals. The company later allowed the Japanese workers to build a village up the hill beyond the end of Blakely Harbor. The workers and their wives and children built a small community, called Yama: the Japanese word for mountain. Many of the women knew no English and kept to Japanese customs. At Yama were a small store, a barber shop, a Buddhist temple, a church, and even a hotel. By the twentieth century, some three hundred Japanese lived at Port Blakely, but with the mill's closure in the 1920s, the families drifted away and many of the people turned to agriculture, as some of the other Japanese on Bainbridge already had done.

Vashon is the only other island that had a sizable Japanese community, but it was never as large as the one on Bainbridge. The Vashon Japanese farmed, and there may have been as many as sixty Japanese farm families on the island in the first decade of the twentieth century, though the 1940 census counted only thirty-nine families. In the heyday of the large and prosperous lime company at Roche Harbor on San Juan Island, Japanese worked there, too, housed in "Japan Town" at the edge of the larger settlement. Company owner John McMillan employed a Japanese, Sukeichi

Nagaoka, as his chief steward. Some Japanese families remained at Roche Harbor until World War II.

Some Filipinos arrived at Port Madison on Bainbridge as early as the 1880s, but in the 1920s, when times were hard in the Philippines, more came. During World War II, with all Japanese forced off Bainbridge Island and so many other men in the armed forces or defense jobs, Filipinos kept the farms going. Some eventually bought their own farms. Few Filipino women had come to Bainbridge Island, for they had no money to pay for passage, while employers had financed the men's journeys. Some of the island men thus married Canadian Indian women whom they had met when the Canadians arrived to work temporarily in the strawberry harvest. Thus, a new population has grown on Bainbridge Island: the Indipino community.

Filipinos did not always find a welcome on the islands. In 1934, Vashon Island Deputy Sheriff Finn Shattuck ordered all Filipinos to leave the island, because islanders complained that the pickers' "irregular conduct" caused conflict.[11] But Filipino Andy Monsanto, who worked for Masa Mukai for a long time, leased land for his own Vashon farm in 1949 and farmed until 1954, when changes in the postwar economy made the challenge too difficult. On Whidbey Island after World War II, a large Filipino community developed in the Oak Harbor area, mainly including employees of the Naval Air Station established there as World War II began, plus families and retired Navy men. In addition to the groups already mentioned, Hispanics have recently come to the islands in greater numbers. People from Southeast Asia, Russia and other lands also make their way to the islands, and some Blacks, too, have come.

Settlement on the islands has never stopped. The first settlers arrived because in those days before the automobile they found the islands convenient, with available land, trees and sea life. The era of settlement came in the late nineteenth century, while the twentieth century saw a more stable, slower growing population and a changing economic base as forestry gave way to fruit production which tourism in turn replaced. People have continued to come, though some only stay for a few years. Perhaps these folks find ferries too inconvenient or too expensive, or perhaps they miss the city lights. An economic downturn after the end of World War I in 1918 and the worldwide Great Depression of the 1930s took its toll on the islands, with population barely growing, even decreasing on some islands. Only 731 more people lived on Whidbey Island in 1940 than in 1920.

Island newcomers during the Depression of the 1930s included young men brought to Orcas Island and the Deception Pass area on Whidbey and Fidalgo as members of the Civilian Conservation Corps, or CCC. This federal program created jobs during those hard times and the results of what the men did can be seen to this day in the infrastructure of the area's parks at Deception Pass and Mt. Constitution. The men came from many parts of the country and a few stayed. One young man from Brooklyn, John Tursi, joined the CCC when only sixteen. Hired because he said he was twenty-one, he soon arrived at Deception Pass. He met and married an Anacortes girl, served in Europe during World War II and returned to Anacortes for good.

Some people discovered Puget Sound country after having been stationed in the area during World War II, perhaps on Whidbey Island. Since then, many other people have come, perhaps planning to commute to a nearby city for work while their children can enjoy what life on an island has to offer. Some new residents wanted more land than they could afford to buy on the mainland yet still be able to commute to a city job. They may have wanted to garden or raise a few animals in their spare time. Some people have preferred island schools to city schools for their children. Some, with money, have come for life on the waterfront or in a spacious home with a view of mountains and water. The ambiance of an island is what all of these people have sought.

In the late 1960s and the 1970s, islands attracted hippies, young laid-back folks searching for peace and inexpensive places to live. Young people's drug use made the news. Not all longtime residents welcomed these newcomers, and in 1970 and 1971 the presence of hippies on Vashon Island precipitated talk of an informal posse, the Vashon Vigilantes, to keep hippies off the island. Soon, two young men firebombed the building that housed the local court and the insurance office of District Court Judge Phil Schwarz. One of the men said they did this to provoke the establishment. The Vashon posse did not materialize and worried islanders soon calmed down.

Other people without nearby mainland jobs have come to the islands to find local work, perhaps because a job is open in an island supermarket or small office or a local school. These days, many more people are visible commuting on the morning ferries *to* Vashon Island than could be seen a generation or two ago. Many people employed on Bainbridge Island live on the relatively inexpensive Kitsap County mainland and help cause a rush hour traffic problem on the island.

Who moves to the islands to settle these days? Most people who come to Orcas Island to settle first saw the island as tourists, wrote Joe Symons in 2009. Rising housing costs suggest that many recent residents are wealthy people, most often retirees. Some of their homes have great views or face the waterfront. These structures can include the megamansions that many other islanders scorn. When asked about the greatest change she had seen on Orcas Island, the late Virginia Jensen, who lived her entire life on the island, promptly replied, "The houses built on Buck Mountain."[12] At night, anyone looking up from sea-level Eastsound, the island's commercial center, can see lights in these houses poking out of the forest high on the hillside surrounding them. Today's land-use regulations mean that these homes are on five-acre plots, and their views can be spectacular. Given island living costs, the owners of such properties sometimes rent them out and live in more modest houses themselves. Meanwhile, to someone driving around one of the islands such as Fox or Harstine, the land can look surprisingly empty, with many of the early homesteads gone and the land returned to forest. However, a trip around these islands in a small boat shows that people live on the waterfront wherever the terrain makes this practical. On the San Juan Islands not served by Washington State Ferries most residents these days also live on the waterfront, but many are part-timers.

The islands attract artists, authors and musicians. Some of those talented people are homegrown, too. Bainbridge Island High School teacher David Guterson attained national recognition with his first novel, *Snow Falling on Cedars*, which brings to life a ficticious Puget Sound island of the mid-twentieth century.

In past years, visionaries would predict rising populations and increasing development on the islands. In the early 1950s, when bridges crossing Puget Sound were under serious consideration, the King County Planning Commission predicted that were the bridge built via Vashon Island, Vashon-Maury Island population would reach 56,000 people.[13] The 1950 population was 2,889; in 2010 it reached 10,624. Population growth on other islands has been relatively modest, too. The growth of Naval Air Station Whidbey Island and, elsewhere, better ferry service, have brought a sizeable increase, though. This happened after Guemes Island received a larger boat in 1979 and on Vashon as bigger boats came to the island in the 1980s and 1990s.

Future population trends are hard to predict. Given stricter land use rules, it is difficult to picture island population increasing much, but each generation will bring newcomers. This is so different from the early days of settlement when land acquisition was simple and logging and farming attracted settlers. In those pre-automobile years, the islands seemed to be at the center of development in Puget Sound country. Now, more and more, they are a refuge from development.

Finally, note that descendants of some early settlers still live on the islands, such as the Shermans on Vashon, the Munk family on Fidalgo, the Grangers on Lummi and the Boyce clan on the San Juans. While many settler families have come and gone because living conditions, transportation, employment, education and other aspects of island life have changed over the years, these four families represent the many families who enjoy life on the islands and want to stay.

7 | Meeting of Cultures

IN 1792 PUGET SOUND INDIANS SAW WHITE PEOPLE for the first time but had no idea how much these new men would affect them. Americans, who gained control of this land, introduced diseases, confined Native people, and interfered with their traditions. But first, the Puget Sound Native Americans saw Spanish and then British explorers. Northern Indians also threatened Puget Sound Native people and sometimes challenged them.

Britain's Vancouver Expedition brought the first non-Native people to enter the southern Sound, and the explorers who penetrated these waters felt anxious about possible encounters with the Native people. Vancouver expressed a lack of interest in them. Like Vancouver, Joseph Baker of the expedition did not think much of these people, describing them as "rather ill favored than otherwise & most excessively dirty."[1]

In Puget Sound country it was Hudson's Bay Company men who first had continuing contact with the Native people. The HBC felt that trading with them was crucial, because Indians provided many of the pelts which the HBC collected. The company employed some Native people who hunted for them, transported HBC men and goods by canoe, brought needed wood and helped in additional ways. Many other Indians came to trade or visit, for example Chief Challicum from Whidbey Island. Hudson's Bay men sometimes asked Challicum to deliver messages between Fort Nisqually and Fort Langley. During these years, the Native people and HBC officials generally got along well, partly because the Indians did not expect these trading people to stay permanently.

Native Americans in Puget Sound country began planting potatoes sometime in the first half of the nineteenth century, possibly after learning of this useful tuber from HBC men. In 1840, missionary Father Francis Blanchet saw Indians' "potato fields planted in rows much too close, although the vines appeared sturdy to me." In 1854, Indian Agent Michael Simmons reported that the native peoples in Puget Sound country were producing more than eleven thousand bushels.[2] Members of the Wilkes Expedition met Indians in 1841, and, while not admiring the Native way of life, apparently collected thousands of their artifacts for the Smithsonian Institution.

Troubles came after Americans began settling in the area. During the nineteenth century, many, many white settler families moved westward across the American continent. Some newcomers homesteaded land even if an Indian community complete with buildings sat there, as happened at San Juan Island's Mitchell Bay. Native Americans wanted to maintain and farm small plots, but too often the white settlers' animals would cause havoc with the plantings or settlers would take over the land in ever greater numbers. In 1858, Simmons noted that white settlers were, reported anthropologist Wayne Suttles, "taking over the good potato prairies."[3] It is not surprising that most Indians became discouraged with growing food. Some of the newcomers also enclosed plots of land to keep Indians away from accustomed fishing spots.

Indians and settlers alike could be victims of the warlike tribes from across the northern border. For protection against them, Whidbey Island tribes built forts some four hundred feet or more long, strong and difficult to attack. Despite this, they later found themselves driven away from their potato patches by the Northern Indians. Throughout the area, settlers sometimes helped local Native Americans fight off the invaders, as did Lopez Island pioneer settler Hiram Hutchinson about 1850.

Northern Indians ventured elsewhere, too. A particularly strong attack came in 1858, destroying a Lummi village at the head of West Sound on Orcas Island. The bay at the innermost part of this sound has become known, therefore, as Massacre Bay, and the small island near the head of the bay as Skull Island. In the long run, though, the white settlers rather than the Northern Indians destroyed the Native way of life in Puget Sound country.

More and more whites came west, and in 1853 part of the very large Oregon Territory became a separate entity, Washington Territory. Isaac I. Stevens, the new territory's first governor, received orders to make treaties with the Native people living in the territory, creating reservations for them. Stevens was not a calm, deliberative person but rather an ambitious young man who did not know enough about Western Washington geography or the peoples whose future he had to determine. Richard White has described him as "tireless, ambitious, talented and not a little dictatorial."[4]

Under Stevens' leadership, the Treaty of Medicine Creek, signed by tribal representatives on December 26, 1854, officially designated certain tracts of land as Indian reservations for South Sound peoples. Negotiations took place in an imprecise language—Chinook jargon—and there is no doubt that many of the Native people attending the meeting at the creek near Olympia did not understand the implications of what was happening.

The Treaty of Medicine Creek made 2.2 square mile Squaxin Island an Indian Reservation. The Native Americans assigned to it had lived along seven inlets of the South Sound and officially they became the Squaxin Island people. Though living in different communities, they spoke the same language—Southern Lushootseed—and had intermarried and come together on their "gathering place," the island.[5]

Squaxin Island was meant to be the headquarters for three new reservations in the South Sound region: Squaxin Island, Nisqually and Puyallup. At first, the American negotiators considered the small island as a possible home for all these peoples, but once the governor's commission formed to draw up treaties establishing reservations realized exactly how small Squaxin Island was, the commissioners planned separate—but also small—mainland areas for the Nisqually and Puyallup bands and assigned Vashon Island's people to the Puyallup Reservation along with the Puyallup. Over the years, the term "Puyallup" came into use to represent both groups. Meanwhile, a few of the Vashon Island people went to the Squaxin Island or the Nisqually Reservations instead.

Next, Governor Stevens headed north to make treaties with other bands. The Point Elliott Treaty, signed January 22, 1855, created the Lummi Reservation on the mainland just north of Bellingham and across a narrow channel from Lummi Island. Earlier, when smallpox appeared on the San Juans thanks to European visitors, Lummi there had fled and joined their compatriots on the mainland. The Point Elliott Treaty also established the Swinomish Reservation on Fidalgo Island and assigned Swinomish, Kikiallus, Samish and Lower Skagit people to live there. Not until 1859 did Congress ratify this treaty, and the reservation's boundaries remained undefined until 1873. Many official reservation maps had included March Point, where the Anacortes refineries now sit, and Native Americans thought the reservation was meant to include this land, but by 1873 white settlers had appeared there. President Ulysses S. Grant therefore ordered the boundary be drawn to exclude the point from the reservation.

Though some Samish attended the Point Elliott Treaty Council, no Samish representative is listed and these people did not receive a reservation of their own. Samish people therefore stayed where they were or went to the Swinomish or the Lummi Reservation. Strife arose on Lummi land between some Samish and Lummi, so the Samish left. Later, they learned that the Swinomish Reservation did not include land for them either, because the 1873 demarcation left their homes outside reservation boundaries. Many Samish thus decamped to Guemes Island where some Samish had earlier lived. Here they constructed a new longhouse and in the 1880s held at least two potlatches. Because the government prohibited potlatches on reservation land, the Samish non-reservation on Guemes could be a perfect place to hold these celebrations. Early in the twentieth century, though, the Samish left the island due to pressure from white residents, most going to the Swinomish Reservation.

The Samish finally received federal recognition as a tribe 123 years later, in 1996. In 2010, the Washington State turned over Huckleberry Island, a one-acre spot east of Guemes Island, to the Samish people. Though it is not a reservation, the Samish now have an island they can call their own. Meanwhile, tribal headquarters sit on Commercial Avenue in Anacortes. Another band, the Mitchell Bay Indians of San Juan Island, has not yet been recognized, though a 1919 census listed 250 Mitchell Bay members. The Swinomish community has taken in these people.

By the terms of the Point Elliott Treaty, the Suquamish people would no longer be able to live freely on Bainbridge Island. Their new home, the Port Madison Reservation, sat across Agate Pass from the island, but Chief Sealth kept summer quarters on northern Bainbridge for years thereafter. While the Port Madison mill on the island operated, forty or more Native Americans lived nearby, some working in the mill. Meanwhile, on Whidbey Island, the many Lower Skagit people in the Penn Cove area did not want to leave their home area. Officials worried about tense feelings growing in Puget Sound country and decided to create the temporary Penn Cove Special Indian Agency, which administered tribal affairs on Whidbey island from 1855 to about 1861.

On January 26, 1855, Governor Stevens, forty-seven S'Klallam, four Chemakum and a few other prominent Native Americans signed the Treaty of Point No Point. The S'Klallam, who counted Indian and Marrowstone Islands within their land, found themselves assigned to the Skokomish Reservation on the far southwest corner of Hood Canal. A ship towed the people and their canoes to the site. This small area was far away, and the S'Klallam and the others there were not friendly. Most S'Klallam instead trickled back north to the area of their homeland—where officials had destroyed their villages. The tribe's leader, Chetzemoka, led them to Indian Island, where they settled. Eventually, in 1938, the government established the Port Gamble Reservation for them on the mainland in the far northern part of the Kitsap Peninsula. The tribe also has gathering rights in Mystery Bay between Indian and Marrowstone Islands thanks to their historic use of these waters, and today the S'Klallam help protect and harvest sea life there.

Estimated numbers of members of some of the bands when Natives signed the treaties were Lummi, 656; Whidbey Island Skagit, 1356; Swinomish, 246; Kikiallus, 300; Suquamish, 441; Samish, 200; Squaxin Island, 250. These figures, "gleaned from the reports of the Indian agents and others at about the time the treaties . . . were entered into, and at the time the depositions were taken in 1927" represent the remnants of the various peoples who did not succumb to diseases inadvertently introduced by Europeans. Federal officials heard testimony from Indians in 1927 and believed that these numbers were somewhat smaller than the actual population in the mid-nineteenth century.[6]

Not until the white newcomers to the land tried to enforce the provisions of the treaties which white and Native leaders had signed did the Native peoples fully understand the treaties. For example, the Puyallup and Nisqually complained that their tiny reservations did not even include river access. White settlers were taking up more and more land. They wanted protection but Native Americans wanted treaty changes. Confrontations arose and angry Natives killed a few white settlers. Life in Washington Territory became more and more unsettled, and the various brief clashes in Western Washington became known as the Puget Sound Indian War. Because of the tension between settlers and hostile Northern Indians, Whidbey pioneers built eleven small blockhouses starting in November 1855. Four of these still stand in central Whidbey Island. Meanwhile, Port Madison residents also built a blockhouse, now long gone, on Bainbridge Island.

In late 1855, during this tense time, Indian Agent Michael Simmons tried to prevent rebellious Indians from influencing "friendly" ones. He ordered the peaceful ones to gather in designated locations and subsequently assigned them to fewer and more isolated places, mostly away from reservations: Squaxin Island, Fox Island, two Whidbey Island locations, Fort Kitsap on the Kitsap mainland, and Bellingham Bay. More than one thousand Skagit people, including ones who lived along the Skagit River, gathered at Penn Cove and some 1,400, including Snohomish members, farther south on Whidbey Island. Squaxin Island would now hold more than 350 members of the South Sound tribes. These isolated places offered poor living conditions, including not enough water for the interned people. As Cecelia Svinth Carpenter has pointed out, "any Indian away from an assigned location was fair game" but some young men swam from Squaxin Island across the channel to the mainland for supplies.[7] People interned on this small island noted that troops, meanwhile, brought many coffins to the island. At least seven hundred Native Americans spent about a year on Fox Island. They probably built mat shelters for their homes, but their internment started late in the year and they had to go to the island without any stored food. Agents had to furnish food, clothes and medicine. The Native Americans found the clothing strange and the unfamiliar food dreadfully inadequate. Illness ran rampant. Tuberculosis, especially, led to many deaths.

Farther north, the Native Americans suffered badly, too. On Whidbey Island, Indian Agent Robert Fay reported much disease and inadequate food supplies for the people under his care. Due to this, and because the Treaty of Point Elliott had not yet been ratified, Fay did not object when people left Penn Cove temporarily to go to the places where they usually gathered food, whether by fishing, hunting or foraging.

In those years, "hostile" Indians and settlers remained at loggerheads, especially in the South Sound area. Chief Leschi, a leader whom whites looked upon as the Nisqually chief, was among those still free. On January

5, 1856, with many of his people interned, Leschi sought an end to the tension between Native people and settlers. He secretly canoed to Fox Island with thirty-some men. He planned to meet with his friend John Swan, the agent in charge there. When Leschi reached the island, Swan, who had no authority to negotiate, notified the American commander at nearby Fort Nisqually of the Native leader's arrival. An officer made plans to capture Leschi, but the Nisqually leader stole away along with some of the men interned on the island who decided to join him. Nothing thus came of Leschi's peace effort, and Governor Stevens characterized Leschi's foray to Fox Island not as an effort to bring peace but as an escalation in the conflict between Native Americans and settlers.

Finally, in August, Governor Stevens met with some Native leaders on Fox Island and consented to a few changes in reservation lands, expanding the Nisqually and Puyallup reservations somewhat and creating river access. As fighting waned, officials released Native people from internment and expected hostiles and non-hostiles alike to go to the reservations. Many hesitated, but to encourage reservation use, militiamen and settlers burned tribal longhouses.

Chief Leschi paid the ultimate price for the troubles. Governor Stevens had grown to hate him and hold him responsible for all the violence. Washington Territory tried and convicted him of murder and executed him in 1858. Over the years, Chief Leschi has been both reviled as a war leader and praised as a peacemaker. Recently, he has been unofficially exonerated, seen not as a criminal but as a victim of the clash between settlers' aspirations and Native people's rights.

Subsequent years saw no Indian wars in the Puget Sound area, although occasional conflicts did occur—even murder. In 1856, some Northern Indians had been killed in a fight with American troops from the USS *Massachusetts* near Port Gamble. A military steamer returned the Indians to Canada, supplied them with provisions and warned them not to enter American waters again. Northern Indians continued to seek revenge, and what came was a crime that has gained enormous attention: the murder of Colonel Isaac N. Ebey near Coupeville on August 11, 1857. An informal leader of the settler community on central Whidbey Island and a United States Collector of Customs, Ebey was an unwitting victim of the quarrel. He had in no way been involved, but upon hearing that he was a prosperous, influential man, the Indians killed him, taking his head with them back to Canada. Ebey's family and their neighbors fled to a nearby block-house. Note that Chief Leschi's execution came *after* Col. Ebey's murder.

The northern threat faded over the next few years, and by 1864, Louise Swift, living at San de Fuca on Whidbey Island, could write to her Massachusetts family, "I suppose you think the Indians must be wild and savage but they are far from that. Most of them are harmless. They never come to the house except to trade."[8]

Meanwhile, white officials were organizing reservations. Some 250 people had to move to Squaxin Island. One wonders how much planning went into choosing this island for a Native American home. Obviously, sending Indians to an uninhabited island would move them away from white settlers and thus minimize confrontation. This island had very little fresh water other than rainfall. A few springs appeared, but the people were not able to dig successful wells. There was no drinking water. Governor Stevens had promised to get water to the island through "waterworks, put the water under the bottom of the bay and across to Squaxin Island so that they could have water over there," Squaxin Indian Johnnie Scalopine said some years later, but the water never came. Scalopine noted that Governor Stevens had also promised that some territory on the mainland would be added to the reservation. This, too, did not happen.[9]

Officials planned for a school, medical services, and agricultural in-struction on Squaxin Island. According to an 1858 report, only "a few old women and children, and about a dozen men" were on the island during an official visit in September. Inspector J. Ross Browne estimated that the tribe had 350 to 375 members, but, he wrote, they were "mostly absent lay-ing in their supplies for winter." The government employees stationed on the island—the agent and a teacher—had a house to live in. Seven houses, each costing $215 but whose size we do not know, awaited Native people as did a blacksmith shop.[10]

Classes at the school had not yet started, the teacher "having found it impracticable to procure the attendance of the children." Instead, the teacher kept busy acting as a clerk for the reservation superintendent. Officials had paid Indians to clear and fence a twenty-acre field planted to peas and potatoes. Another ten acres was fenced but not yet cultivated. However, "the land is barren and unfit for cultivation, and the expense of fencing and cultivation will never be returned by the result in crops," reported Browne.[11]

The reservation could not have been less successful. Little by little, people returned to their traditional pattern of life, foraging for berries, roots and vegetables, fishing for salmon and moving from place to place to find these sources of food. They sold fish and shellfish to nearby settlers. By 1862, only fifty people still lived on Squaxin Island and officials relocated the headquarters and school to the Puyallup Reservation. Squaxin Island member Julian Sam Simmonds testified in 1927 about the promises tribe members understood the Treaty of Medicine Creek had made to them, "that each and every old Indian, their children, their grandchildren, and great-grandchildren and so on, that they were to have each an allotment at any reservation that they can come into, being an Indian. . . . They were promised the farm implements, tools of all kinds to use on their lands, the money that was to be furnished them to clear their lands, to get whatever needful things they should have for their schools, and lots of needful other things that were promised the Indians, which they never got."[12]

Meanwhile, the different bands assigned to Fidalgo Island's Swinomish Reservation who became members of the confederation called the Swinomish Indian Tribal Community also found government promises unfulfilled. Lower Skagit member Charley Sneatlium said his family went to the reservation about 1858 to receive the allotment they were to get—but they did not receive any land. He told the Court of Claims that this was "because there was . . . no reservation set aside large enough."[13]

The different bands assigned to the Swinomish Reservation tended to cluster in separate communities there. These settlements held to the shorelines, and fishing and clamming continued as before. Men continued to hunt and sometimes sold meat to nearby white residents, while some of the women worked for white families. Indian Agent O. C. Upchurch wrote, "the reservation is of poor soil, barren except for a poor quality of timber and of value chiefly as a base from which to go fishing, clam digging, and to any field of labor that offers livelihood."[14] Because the people traditionally migrated to different sites during the summer, staying in one place all year long caused stress. Logging brought in some income, but farming proved unsustainable on most reservation land. In 1897, the government arranged for a school to be built on the reservation, just across Swinomish Slough from the white community called LaConner, and the neighborhood near the school became the center of reservation activity. Though life included many frustrations for residents, the fifteen-square-mile Swinomish Reservation—unlike Squaxin Island—remains a Native American dwelling place.

Over the succeeding years, Native life in Puget Sound country continued to change. Traditional practices evolved. Potlatches became more common, though government officials strongly discouraged them. One potlatch was held in 1891 by a Squaxin Island Indian called Old Patsy.

Old Patsy attracted people from tribal groups all over Puget Sound. Celebrations at Patsy's potlatch lasted for a week, in conjunction with the Fourth of July holiday. Because government officials frowned upon potlatches, Indians scheduled them to coincide with national holidays, which would provide an ostensible reason for such a gathering.

Individual Indians acquired wealth in early years through exchanging goods with HBC men and settlers. Class distinctions among Native Americans, previously minimal, grew, as some tribespeople became rich through this trade. For a while, Northern Indians raided more frequently and fighting between local bands, rare in earlier times, increased. Many Native American children had to live at special boarding schools, often far from their homes, where they had to speak English and faced punishment for using their own language. They were supposed to live as white people lived.

The most destructive aspect of Native American contact with white people was probably accidental, though some have believed it was deliberate. From the days when the newcomers first appeared, tribal members succumbed to diseases new to them, to which they had no immunity. Population of all the tribes fell drastically as syphilis, smallpox, and tuberculosis attacked them. Even measles and influenza killed many. At the end of the eighteenth century, Samish Indians who lived along Mud Bay on Lopez Island had been hit hard by smallpox, and as a result the survivors fled to Guemes Island. Another Samish village, at Olga on Orcas Island, was nearly wiped out by the disease, said Ruth Shelton, recounting what she had heard from her family. Indians have reported similar catastrophic impacts of disease among other tribal bands. Because of the diseases introduced by the newcomers, by 1840 the native population in Puget Sound country had dropped perhaps by half.[15]

Native Americans were especially susceptible to disease because many people would live in one longhouse and thus an illness could spread very easily. Boarding schools, too, became breeding grounds for disease.

Hudson's Bay Company men did vaccinate many Indians in the nine-teenth century, but some of the Native Americans thought that disease was a weapon the newcomers were using in order to destroy the native bands. Since so many people died, few were left to pass on traditional teachings to the children.

The presence of white people also affected native peoples' health through the introduction of liquor. On the mainland, across the water and within sight of Squaxin Island was a whiskey shop whose proprietor would blow his horn when he received a shipment. The Indians could then canoe to the shop and buy alcohol. The agent found it impossible to stop the practice, for when he tried to punish people, they simply ran off.

As the government worked to turn Native Americans away from their traditional beliefs and activities and have them adopt the white man's ways, officials arranged that missionaries could introduce Christianity. Among those involved, the Congregational Church would have responsibility for the Squaxin Island tribe and several others, while Catholics were to estab-lish missions and churches on some other reservations.

The first Catholic missionaries had already appeared in Puget Sound country, after the Hudson's Bay Company established a presence. Father Blanchet visited and baptized some Nisqually in 1839. The Whidbey Island Skagits already knew about the Catholic Church from HBC men. Father Blanchet went to Whidbey in 1840 and stayed about a year. The priest assured the Whidbey people that he could help them by both in-troducing his religion and by bringing them helpful goods. Catholic mis-sions opened at Penn Cove and at various mainland locations. To Native Americans, Whidbey Island became the Island of the Cross, because of the cross Blanchet had erected at Penn Cove. The mission on Whidbey lasted for not quite a decade, and afterward, Catholics served Native Americans at the reservations.

Later in the nineteenth century, a new Indian-inspired religion emerged: the Indian Shaker Church. A Squaxin Islander named John Slocum, who was living on the mainland near the island, became ill in 1881 and ap-peared to die. Before his coffin could arrive, however, he revived. Slocum reported to his mourners that he had indeed died but had had a vision, telling him to return to life and lead Indians to a sin-free life. Some of his friends built a church and Slocum preached, but after a while he and his followers lost interest. A year after his illness, however, Slocum once again got sick—very sick. His wife Mary, while praying over him, began shaking uncontrollably. Slocum again recovered and Mary Slocum's shaking received the credit. With shaking an aspect of religious expression, the new worship practice grew, and various tribal groups adopted it. Around the beginning of the twentieth century, the Indian Shaker Church became a legal entity. It continued to gain many new adherents and in the early years had a church on Squaxin Island. Subsequently, Squaxin Island members have attended an Indian Shaker Church at Mud Bay, on the mainland a few miles from today's tribal headquarters. Perhaps the church has survived because its practices contain elements from both Christianity and Native traditions. An example is the spirit dance, during which men dance around a sick person to encourage recovery. Because the church counsels abstention from intoxicating liquor, it addresses an issue that has harmed Indian society ever since the appearance of the white man.

Over the years, native peoples on the reservations lived not much above a subsistence level, often picking berries for commercial growers and creating goods to sell to whites. Despite the restrictions imposed by the reservation system, they tried to continue traditional patterns of life. Some Indians never did go to a reservation. Some went but later returned to their home community. About four Native American families returned to Vashon Island in the early twentieth century.

From the time the settlers arrived, many Indians found work with them, the men in logging, fishing and construction and women in the home and garden. Theresa Trebon has noted that those who stayed on Whidbey Island did so with little interference from white settlers, probably because the Native people lived along the water on sites that did not interest settlers in early days. The Indians meanwhile traded with the newcomers, worked on the settlers' farms, and provided them with transportation, using fast canoes—Trebon calls this "rapid transit."[16] Lower Skagit member Susie Kettle, or Kittle, was a housekeeper for a settler family in Coupeville. On Bainbridge island, Mary Sam, a Klickitat who had been captured in a raid by the Suquamish, lived at Port Madison and did domestic work there. She died in 1923, after spending many years on the island.

On Squaxin Island, people lived in cedar buildings, sometimes on floats they anchored in the inlets. They traversed the island on its many footpaths. Different bands would come to Squaxin Island for an annual Fourth of July celebration or potlatch, but the island population continued to decrease. Non-tribal members bought some reservation land, as a federal law, the Dawes Act, had allowed since 1887, and by the mid-1960s no Squaxin Island Indian lived on the island. For a time, a state park, open to camping but only accessible by boat sat on the south end of Squaxin Island. Washington State had a twenty-five-year lease on the tidelands but could not reach agreement with the tribe on extending the lease, and the park closed in 1994. Starting in 1965, the tribe has bought nearby mainland property in the area called Kamilche. Daily life takes place there, but the island remains a site for fishing, hunting and ceremony. For the people, it is the bond that unites past, present, and future generations. In the 1970s, the tribe constructed a longhouse on the island for meetings and ceremonies.

Over the years, one practice that devastated Puget Sound Native American society was non-Indian encroachment upon fishing practices. The new people took more and more of the sea's resources for themselves, while restricting Native Americans' fishing. Though the Lummi reservation sat on the mainland, Lummis intended to continue fishing in their traditional grounds. Now they had to compete with non-Indian commercial companies and, once salmon canneries were opened in the northwest late in the nineteenth century, the Lummi found their main reef net sites blocked by fish traps installed by the companies. One example was at Village Point on Lummi Island, where the Chicago Fish Company placed a net. The Lummi went to court to assert the rights to their fishing grounds, but the United States Supreme Court did not hear their appeal, instead dismissing it in 1899. Some Indians got jobs in the canneries, though usually the owners preferred to hire Asians instead.

Indian fishing rights finally received recognition in 1974 in the Boldt decision. This is the most important government action since World War II regarding Puget Sound Native peoples. Until then, Indians who had been fishing in off-reservation waters—a right they had been given in the treaties—had found their fishing gear confiscated and themselves subject to arrest by Washington State authorities. Nisqually and Puyallup people were at the center of the controversy. Confrontations grew more serious, including physical attacks and police intimidation. Eventually, legal actions led to the case upon which Federal Court Judge George Boldt ruled. His decision declared that Native peoples had the right to catch half the salmon harvested each year. Due to angry opposition by white fishermen, though, it took Washington State more than a decade to agree to implement this ruling. Tension remained, and in December 1981, the longhouse built by tribal members on Squaxin Island burned down in an arson fire.

The Boldt decision has allowed a few Native Americans to become wealthy, while small-scale tribal fishermen do not find many fish. But today just as centuries ago tribes celebrate the return of the salmon to the rivers each year. Moreover, thanks to legal action following the Boldt decision, Native Americans have been harvesting shellfish, too, for another judge affirmed this right in 1994. The Lummi Indian Nation maintains an active aquaculture operation, raising many varieties of shellfish.

Native American activism continued, too. In 1978, reacting to possible congressional action that would drastically overhaul policies regarding Native Americans, and which could abrogate all treaty rights, groups held protests nationwide. On Puget Sound, members of the Lummi tribe blocked the Lummi Island ferry from landing at its mainland dock, which is on reservation land, but only for an hour.

The opening of casinos on reservation land has helped create tribal prosperity. State law has not allowed casino operation, but Indian reservations are not subject to this because Indian tribes are sovereign nations. Only one Puget Sound island—Fidalgo—houses a casino, though the Squaxin Island band has a mainland casino. Meanwhile, poverty continues to be a problem for many Native Americans.

Most Native people in Puget Sound country now live away from the reservation. Few live on islands today except for those on Fidalgo Island's Swinomish Reservation. Squaxin Island's symbolic importance remains, though, and ceremonial events do take place there. On Whidbey Island, Native Americans participate in canoe races during Coupeville's annual Penn Cove Water Festival.

A celebration of Native culture available to the general public takes place now throughout the summers on small Blake Island. The entire island is a state park, and on its east coast is Tillicum Village, a commercially run tourist site where Coast Salish culture is on display for visitors with crafts, traditional dancing and a salmon dinner. While many Indian reservations have museums or displays of artifacts for visitors to view, Tillicum Village highlights these in a program that begins when the visitors' boat leaves Seattle or Bremerton. Because of COVID, this site has closed.

These days, Native American historical items are carefully preserved, and many are shown at museums throughout the Northwest as well as farther afield. In 2012, the Suquamish opened a beautiful and informative museum at their reservation on the Kitsap County mainland, near Agate Pass. Though Native American dominance of the land is long, long gone, artifacts, art objects at museums, and presentations such as the one at Tillicum Village help us remember that the islands and the mainland did not always belong to the European-Americans. For islanders, another reminder that their homes lie on land the Indians once considered theirs comes when one rides a ferry, for the state's ferryboats honor Native American names. One of the newest vessels, the *Chetzemoka*, commemorates an important S'Klallam chief. Meanwhile, Native American names for locations on the islands have almost all disappeared. Only a few, including Utsalady, survive.

Far more important than names are the Native Americans themselves. Their life on the islands began long ago. After the white man appeared, the subsequent clash of cultures brought poverty and tragedy, but Native Americans are survivors, and their bands continue traditional practices. For example, in most years, Puget Sound area tribes participate in a Canoe Journey, which a different tribe hosts each year. In 2012, participants canoed from their home areas to the South Sound, where the Squaxin Island tribe welcomed them to a celebration. Thus, a tradition lives on as different bands come together to revive the custom of journeying by canoe, an example of how life in the twenty-first century can be fulfilling.

8 | Farming

NINETEENTH CENTURY NEWCOMERS TO PUGET SOUND country built their lives around farming along with the extractive industries of logging, fishing, and mining for clay or limestone. Early settlers farmed. Even ones busy with commerce, education or other such pursuits probably had garden plots. Soon, people planted fruit trees, for Puget Sound country proved eminently suitable for raising apples, pears, plums and more. "With a little work outside the farm a family could make a comfortable, though not a luxurious, living."[1] Betsey Johnson Cammon wrote about McNeil Island, but the sentiment could fit all the islands. Over the years, agriculture has become much less important on the islands, but many small farms and productive garden plots continue to feed both islanders and mainlanders.

On Whidbey Island, the first settlers noticed that Native Americans grew a few potatoes. The settlers traded with the Indians for this familiar food and soon began planting their own crop. Farmers depended on hand tools—scythes, rakes, etc.—and used oxen to pull the plows. Whidbey Island's earliest farmers tried to cultivate crops that thrived on farms in the eastern United States but found the Puget Sound weather uncooperative for some of them. Melons, eggplant and sweet potatoes did poorly, as modern hobby growers can attest. Other crops flourished, and Territorial Governor Isaac Stevens called "Whidby's" Island "the garden of the Territory" in 1856.[2]

When Isaac Ebey began farming, he first raised wheat and potatoes. Other early Whidbey farmers raised mainly potatoes, wheat and oats, crops that today are not ones agriculturists feel make the best use of Puget Sound terrain, but these crops would grow, and they made a familiar life possible: potatoes because they were an easy-to-grow staple, wheat for bread and oats for a farmer's animals. The pioneers brought in sheep, pigs, horses, cows and chickens, and some island acreage became pasture for the animals.

The farmers with cattle fed them mostly native grain at first, but soon this became inadequate, and farmers sold off their animals or began raising feed grain. As time passed, farming patterns on Whidbey Island changed, for a time emphasizing sheep raising instead of grain crops. Potato cultivation continued for years. Many potatoes went to San Francisco for victims of the 1906 earthquake. Also, orchards and truck farming increased, for as cities in the Puget Sound region grew, so did the market for fruits and vegetables.

Isaac Ebey's land is now part of the Ebey's Landing National Historical Reserve, the first such reserve created in the United States. Administered by the National Park Service, the reserve aims to maintain the historic aspects of the area, which include keeping farmland as farmland and maintaining the buildings. Most of the land in the reserve is privately owned, and some of the farms located there are open to visitors. In the reserve, farmers now grow wheat, grain, hay crops, many kinds of vegetables, fruit and flowers as well as raising animals including cows, chickens, and turkeys.

Many of the people who came to farm on the islands found it hard to establish themselves. Trying to farm forested land meant long, hard work, sometimes resulting in stump ranches where trees had been felled but the stumps never removed, cultivation taking place between them. Like farmers and gardeners today, the early farmers found wild animals a problem. Deer abounded on the islands and the early Whidbey settlers thought wolves were a menace. From 1855, Island County officials offered payment for killing wolves and, after people applied strychnine to deer carcasses that would tempt wolves, the county was soon free of them.

The Hudson's Bay Company's Belle Vue Sheep Farm on San Juan Island was another of the very early agricultural establishments on the islands. The farm operated from 1853 until the island officially became part of the United States about twenty years later. In establishing the farm, Charles

Griffin brought in sheep, a few other farm animals, and seed for crops as well as some Kanaka herdsmen. By 1859, HBC had some eighty fenced acres planted with oats, potatoes and peas.[3]

More settlers came to the islands in the late nineteenth century. On various islands of the San Juan Archipelago farm families grew grain—some hay—as well as potatoes. Sheep grazed wherever they wanted. Especially on Lopez and Orcas, one could find many thriving orchards, too. By 1900, some of the farms on Lopez were already large, their proprietors raising grain, cattle, thoroughbred horses, chickens, sheep and hogs, fruit, and vegetables. Dairying and egg production prospered, with a creamery established on the island early in the twentieth century. Farms cover much of Lopez Island and central San Juan Island to this day.

Life on the farm was difficult. James Tulloch came to Orcas Island in 1875. He was not much of a farmer, but he observed that "the methods of farming were extremely crude and most of the work was done with oxen." Only the wealthier farmers even had carts, he wrote, and these had wooden wheels. Some farmers made do "with a crude sled with wooden runners made by bending a fir pole and pinning it to the framework," he noted, adding that "dragging this sled on bare ground with an ox team over rocky trails was slow work and tedious." Tulloch reported that a pig got into his potato field, just as at Lyman Cutlar's place, but the Orcas pig caused no hard feelings and, in fact, provided meat for the Tulloch wedding dinner.[4]

Even the smaller San Juans featured agricultural operations in the early years. On Sinclair Island, Zeno Doty raised about four hundred hogs, but their meat tasted strange, a story goes, because they dined too much on clams they found on the beach.

The earliest white men who came to Camano, as to other islands, came for the timber, not to farm, but the 1870 census described five residents as farmers. Three of them living in the island's northeast may have made the earliest attempts to drain and dike some of the tempting marshland on the east side of the island. Camano Island has not seen as much agricultural development as the other islands, partly because most of its land, like so much land on the Puget Sound islands, is not particularly fertile, while the very rich delta soil on the nearby mainland beckoned prospective farmers. Two goat-raising enterprises did begin on Camano in the late 1920s, and a nearby cheese plant processed the goat milk. Some Camano farmers raised strawberries. Most of the farms on the island in those days could be described as subsistence farms, and many of them no longer existed by 1950.

Picture early farmers on islands throughout the Sound raising many kinds of fruits and vegetables, using some themselves but selling what they could. Islanders who hoped to make much profit from farming had to transport products to the mainland. Some of the early Anderson Island settlers, the Camus, Miller and Bollen families, would load their produce in a small boat and row offshore to intercept a steamer, which would take the goods to a city market. Once the mainland boasted streetcars, Anderson farmers could run their small boats across the channel to Steilacoom, sell their produce and meat nearby or board the streetcar to Tacoma with their goods. For many years, farmers from some of the islands have taken their products to Seattle's Pike Place Market and other mainland locations. When cars and trucks became ubiquitous, though, island agriculture suffered, since mainland farmers could get their products to market more quickly and easily than could islanders.

Not all early farming enterprises on the Puget Sound islands succeeded. Cypress Island homesteaders found life difficult, and few stayed. In 1917 Dr. H. D. Parker of Arizona tried raising goats, keeping the animals for their milk. He brought several hundred to Cypress and began to build a health resort at which the patients—guests?—would receive a "Goat Milk Treatment" when this was advised. The enterprise did not take root and the goats ran wild. By the mid-twenties, the animals were gone, shipped off the island or killed. In the 1920s, a few people leased all of Hat Island to start a fox farm. The plan was for the animals, raised for their fur, to run free on the small island, but the unsuccessful enterprise only lasted for three years.

Cattle rustlers appeared on some islands. For example, around the beginning of the twentieth century, mainland men would come to Lummi to catch animals, butcher them and flee with the meat. Some settlers who raised cattle on an island later turned them loose. In 1918, the *Bellingham Herald* reported that the two hundred or more cattle and horses running loose on Lummi Island caused the mailman to "run ahead of his horse with sticks and stones, trying to clear a passage through the herds" every day.[5] At one time, some Squaxin Island Indians kept a few cattle on their island, but eventually the herd became wild and the few people still living on the island wanted the now-destructive animals gone. The island-ers hired an Olympia cattleman, A. H. Chambers, to destroy the eighteen or twenty animals left. Chambers and six others spent a weekend hunting cattle on Squaxin Island in 1923 but only managed to kill three.

In the early twentieth century, subsistence farming declined but some island farmers continued to do well. The national farm organization known as the Grange has been prominent in encouraging island farmers. The Harstine Island Grange, organized in 1914, has worked to address social needs on the island as well as promoting agriculture. The South Camano Grange has been particularly busy in sponsoring community activities since it was founded in 1930. The Grange on Fox Island was perhaps the most vocal group agitating for a bridge to be built to their island. The organization's main purpose, of course, has been to promote agriculture, and farmers needed access to markets.

Over the years, island crops have changed, and fruit production became more and more important. From the early days of settlement, many pioneers planted orchards. In 1853, only two years after Isaac Ebey filed his land claim, he planted fruit trees—apple, cherry, peach, pear and plum. By the late nineteenth century, farms on Orcas Island featured various varieties of tree fruit, and soon the Orcas Island Fruit Company and the Orcas Island Canning and Buying Company began operations. In 1895, Orcas Islanders shipped some 160,000 boxes of apples from Eastsound, and customers near and far praised Orcas fruit.

The Babarovich family planted an orchard on Sinclair Island, north of Anacortes and Guemes Island. The family moved away in 1904, but the orchard bore fruit long after being deserted. Trees continued producing fruit on McNeil Island after the federal government took over the entire island in the 1930s for a prison, and early in the war years the prison farm set out new trees. On various islands, a visitor today can see an occasional abandoned orchard, tree limbs growing every which way, underbrush thick and high but fruit still visible, ready for someone to enjoy.

Residents grew plums, often called prune-plums, all over the islands, for the climate suited this. Prune-drying buildings appeared nearby because the fruit dried well, making shipping relatively inexpensive. A fruit-and-vegetable dryer opened on Whidbey Island in 1897, but its main product became dried potatoes to be shipped to Alaska. A prominent prune dryer at the Sylvan Fruit and Vegetable Works opened on Fox Island in the same year. It took six weeks to dry the prunes, which, once boxed and sold, went to markets as far away as New England. Farmers on Fidalgo Island planted plum trees, too, but the local firm organized to dry the fruit stopped operating before the trees matured enough to bear.

The height of the orchard industry in the islands came about 1910. Puget Sound island fruit found buyers far and wide, and George Myers' Orcas Island orchard was the best-known pear orchard in the nation. San Juan County had more than 75,000 apple trees in 1909. Even peaches did well. Island orchardists soon lost their markets, however. A shortage of vehicles during World War I badly affected the ability to ship fruit from the islands. Over the long run, large, irrigated orchards in Eastern Washington led to the demise of the island tree fruit industry.

Farmers learned that grapes could thrive. Western Washington farmers have successfully grown the fruit for wine since the nineteenth century. The climate has been marginal, but Vashon, Bainbridge, Whidbey, San Juan, Lopez, and Anderson islands have housed commercial vineyards. Puget Sound country is now the American Viticultural Area called Puget Sound.

A Puget Sound island claims the first winery established in the entire state. Confederate veteran Lambert Evans settled on tiny Stretch Island north of Harstine, bought land and planted a vineyard. One vine that he planted in 1872 still grows on the island. Adam Eckert came to the island from New York State in 1890, bought land from Evans and planted eastern grapevines, perhaps a Campbell Early grape or else a cross using Concord and Hartford varieties. The Island Belle grape he created proved a successful cross. This became the grape planted more than any other in Washington State, and during prohibition, people with grapevines in their gardens made Island Belle wine for home use, which remained legal. During that time, two grape juice plants operated on Stretch Island.

After the prohibition repeal in 1933, Charles Somers received Bonded Wine License #1 of Washington State and opened the St. Charles Winery on Stretch Island. Two other wineries soon opened on the island. Farmers planted more than eighty percent of Stretch Island to grapes, mostly Island Belles, until well into the 1950s. Somers' winery operated until 1965. Today, many Island Belle grapes from Stretch Island go to the Hoodsport Winery on the mainland, which bottles Island Belle blends.

Gerald and JoAnn Bentryn were pioneers of recent-day island winemaking. In 1977, they bought some land from the Suyematsu family on

Bainbridge Island for a vineyard. They planted German grape varieties on south-facing hillsides. They have sold the winery they started, but it still produces wine, and Suyematsu and Bentryn Family Farms has become involved in educational and outreach programs connected with agriculture.

More wineries have appeared on the islands, with four or more both on Bainbridge and Whidbey Islands. However, some of these wineries use only grapes from Eastern Washington, where the climate better suits wine-grape cultivation. On the Puget Sound islands, three kinds of European grapes, all producing white wines, proved most successful: Siegerrebe, Madeleine Sylvaner and Madeleine Angevine. As the climate appears to be warming, island growers are also trying other varieties, such as pinot gris and pinot noir.

Berries, too, flourish in Puget Sound country, and as late as 1960, Vashon Island produced half of the currants grown in Washington State. Farmers on the islands have grown many kinds of berries and even before the twentieth century began, shipped great numbers of berries to market, but it was in the first half of the century that berry cultivation became truly important on the islands, from Orcas south through Harstine. A local factor proved important for raising berry crops: good drainage.

Islanders developed various berry products. Peter Ericksen, who farmed on Vashon Island after he and his family arrived in 1907, produced a new berry which he created by crossing wild blackcaps—also known as black raspberries—with a cross Luther Burbank had made using logan-berries and wild blackberries. Ericksen called his creation the Olympic Berry. It proved successful and is still available.

The strawberry emerged as the most profitable berry grown on the islands. More tales can be told about strawberry production than about any other berry. For a time, Vashon and Fox Island farmers raced against each other to see who could deliver the earliest strawberries of the year to a certain Tacoma grocery store. One long-time Harstine Islander, Esther Goetsch, remembered working in her family strawberry patch and hearing her father say, "I don't have to hire berry pickers, I raise my own." The family had seven children.[6]

Asian immigrants deserve a lot of the credit for successful twentieth century berry farming on the islands, but the earliest who came, the Chinese, grew other things. They worked on various islands, but especially on Whidbey, where they became known as skillful farmers. Antagonism against the Chinese grew, and almost all of them left the farms. Thus, an opportunity opened for Japanese immigrants, who were as hard-working and productive as the Chinese and were also willing to work long hours for not much money.

Japanese families became prominent in the fruit-growing industry mostly on Bainbridge and Vashon Islands, though white farmers also continued in the business. The Asian families mainly cultivated strawberries, but some, such as that of Heisuke Matsuda on Vashon, tried many other kinds of berries, too, including loganberries and currants.

By law, these Asian immigrants could not buy land; therefore, they rented it or were allowed to use land when they worked for others. When men began to realize that they would not soon be returning to Japan to live, arranged marriages became common and after a time, land could be bought in the name of the American-born children—U. S. citizens—of the Japanese couples. When the children were still young, they began working in the family fields.

On Bainbridge Island, strawberry cultivation began shortly after the beginning of the twentieth century. The Suyematsu farm dates to 1928, when the family bought forty acres of land in the name of the oldest son, Akio. After a company logged the property—but never paid the Suyematsus for the wood—Yasuji Suyematsu and his sons blasted out the stumps. When the fields were ready to grow strawberries, the children made holes for the plants and the even younger children put a plant in each hole. While working in the fields as a child, daughter Eiko Suyematsu Shibayama soon got tired of eating strawberries and never again liked them, she said.[7]

Making a living by growing strawberries meant hard work. Mary Matsuda Gruenewald has described some of the toil as well as the periodic disappointment during the years she was growing up on a Vashon Island strawberry farm. She wrote, "during the months when it rained daily, we donned our boots and raingear, and trudged outdoors anyway. There were times when we had to take shovels and pickaxes and make trenches or dig ditches to redirect excess water. We had to keep a close eye on the ditches to make sure dirt didn't fall in and obstruct the flow of the water." She had good memories, too, of enjoying getting to know the pickers who came each summer and eating with them the morning snacks her father would bring out to the fields.[8]

The berry growers needed to hire pickers during the ripening season. Indians, many from Canada, came to pick, some staying in simple migrant cabins at the farms, some being collected daily at the ferry docks by growers' buses. After the 1924 prohibition of Japanese immigration, Filipinos, who could come to the United States legally, came to some of the berry fields, particularly on Bainbridge Island. Many Vashon and Bainbridge children, whatever their race, earned pocket money picking berries during the summers. Perhaps the high mark for Puget Sound island strawberries came in 1939, when the King and Queen of England visited Vancouver, British Columbia. Vancouver planners, looking for the best possible strawberries for the royal visitors, imported eight hundred crates of Bainbridge Island berries.

Both Bainbridge and Vashon had berry-processing plants. On Bainbridge the Winslow Berry Growers Association Cannery, dating from shortly after the beginning of the twentieth century, was a prosperous berry-processing concern. On Vashon Island, the B. D. Mukai family played an important role both in berry cultivation and marketing, and in the 1920s they opened the Mukai Cold Process Fruit Barreling Plant where the berries were packed with sugar and quickly sent to Seattle to be frozen. In 1938, due to growing prejudice against Japanese on the Pacific coast, Masa Mukai renamed the plant, and it became the Vashon Island Packing Company, or VIPCO. Forced to leave the island in 1942, the family returned after World War II to find their place badly run down. Strawberry cultivation continued for a time after the war, but finding the many pickers needed became more and more difficult. Government requirements for upgrades to migrant housing made it questionable whether growers could hire pickers for the season and still make a profit. Instead, the growers tried hiring day laborers and students, but they did not have the drive to work hard and be good pickers. Competition from California growers and improved air transportation added to growers' challenges. Masa Mukai quit raising berries but continued processing others' fruit in the VIPCO plant. Finally, VIPCO closed in 1969, and by the early 1970s, no more commercial strawberry farms remained on Vashon Island. Berry farmer Tok Otsuka turned to Christmas trees for a crop, and tree farms appear on various islands now. These days, a Vashon Island non-profit organization is refurbishing the Mukai property and the beautiful Japanese-style garden Kuni Mukai, B.D.'s wife, created.

The garden is unusual, because by tradition, it was only men who built Japanese gardens. It is open to the public all year.

Farmers on other islands grew strawberries, too. In December 1929, the *Anacortes American* trumpeted the success of the crop on Fidalgo and nearby islands, predicting that even more berries would soon be grown in the vicinity. In 1932, workers harvested and sold seventy-one tons of the fruit on Orcas Island.

Another influential agricultural business on Vashon Island was Wax Orchards. The August Wax family started the farm on sixty acres of flat land where they planted a cherry orchard but continued to raise chickens for a while. When the trees matured, each summer the Waxes hired migrant workers, most of whom had just finished picking strawberries, to harvest the cherries. The Waxes raised other types of fruit, too, and due to a 1970s hailstorm that bruised their apples and made them unsalable, the family began selling cider, jams and other products sweetened with natural fruit sugars. No longer is there an orchard on the land the Waxes bought years ago, though. In 2000, Tom Stewart bought most of the orchard land for his Misty Isle Farms, which raised Black Angus cattle.

Other crops prominent on islands for a while included peas. John M. "Pea" Henry acquired land and began growing peas on San Juan Island in the early 1920s. Workers fed the harvested vines into huge pea-vining machines, and a cannery opened in Friday Harbor to process the tiny vegetables. Up to fifty thousand cases of canned peas came from the island each year—but in 1939 the cannery floor collapsed, and some ten thousand cases landed in Puget Sound. Moreover, insects attacking the crop led to the decline of the pea industry.

An unusual plant raised in those days was ginseng. One could purchase it in the late 1920s at Anacortes Ginseng and Golden Seal Gardens. Goldenseal, like ginseng, is a vegetable product thought to promote good health. Growers also cultivated ginseng on Shaw Island for a time in the 1930s. A more unusual agricultural product that has become popular in recent years is lavender. When the herb is in bloom, fields on Camano, Whidbey, San Juan and elsewhere beckon tourists.

Chicken and egg farming were also extremely successful on the islands during the early twentieth century. Vashon Island farmers started the Washington Territory Poultry and Pet Stock Association in 1885, and five of local farmer Lewis Cass Beall's chickens won a national egg-laying contest in 1921. On Fox Island in the early years of the twentieth century, Hans and Minnie Botnen had up to three thousand hens as well as fruit trees and berry plants. Early in the depression years, Joe and Paul Long of Whidbey Island and their mother began raising chickens, at first working in strawberry fields for money to buy feed for their birds. By 1960, the Long brothers had more than forty thousand chickens. Although large chicken and egg businesses later left the islands, remnants remain, like one-time chicken houses remodeled into family residences.

It was not chickens but turkeys which brought recognition to Marrowstone Island. In the 1930s, farmers on the island raised more than three thousand of the big birds each year, and in 1937 more than twelve thousand. That was the year Marrowstone Island turkeys graced President Franklin D. Roosevelt's dinner table. As World War II approached, however, the turkey farmers had a problem. Ordnance practice began at Fort Flagler on the island's north end and the weapons' noise could disturb the turkeys' laying. After consultations, the base commander agreed not to begin firing drills until after the eggs hatched. Turkey raising was also an important part of the economy in Central Whidbey Island in the mid-twentieth century.

As well as fruit, vegetables, medicinal plants, eggs and animals, island farmers raised flowers, both bulbs and blooms. The Beall family of Vashon Island operated an outstanding greenhouse business, eventually having fifty-nine greenhouses on their twenty-three acres. Beall's raised many varieties of flowers between the wars, and due to heavy bombing on Britain during 1941, concerned English growers sent some seven thousand valuable orchids to the Beall greenhouses to safeguard them while English greenhouses grew vegetables in the war effort.

After the 1960s, the nation's economy changed, and raising orchids and roses commercially in Puget Sound country was no longer profitable. The Bealls shifted much of their operation to Colombia, South America, and finally, in 1989, the family sold their island plant. Mostly unused and deteriorating, greenhouses still stand along Beall Road on Vashon Island. Other islands have had prosperous greenhouses, too, and one of the first Bainbridge Island doctors, Cecil Kellam, constructed two greenhouse buildings near Pleasant Beach on the southern part of the island. On Fox Island, Lloyd's Greenhouse spread over two acres and grew mostly tomatoes.

Nurseries have appeared throughout the islands and remain active today. One that has special historical importance is Bainbridge Gardens. Early in the twentieth century, two brothers started raising produce, opened a grocery store and later a nursery. It grew to include greenhouses and a beautiful traditional Japanese garden that drew many visitors. The family had to leave during World War II and when they returned to Bainbridge Island found their place both uncared for and unproductive. Finally, thirty years later, Junkoh Harui, son of one of the founders, decided to revive the nursery and once again it welcomes customers and visitors to its grounds, which include a small memorial garden to Harui's parents.

Visiting the islands today, one can imagine their agricultural past while searching out today's farms and their products. San Juan Island's central lowland, visible from nearby hills, suggests its long-time agricultural emphasis, though by now, tourism has largely eclipsed farming on the island. Since the middle of the twentieth century, San Juan County has lost a third of its farms, and those that remain have about half the acreage of the early farms.

Island farming reflects trends such as agrotourism, through which visitors, presumably from urban locales, can visit working farms and participate in some of the tasks that go into producing food. As island farming has revived, it has become more specialized. Most island farms now are small, some in niche markets and some catering to local people with fresh eggs, milk, fruit, vegetables, and meat. Times have changed since San Juan Island resident Herb Price, planning to sell a large farm a decade after World War II, felt that his house, farm and timber should be considered more valuable than the waterfront he had, which "was nothing but a problem, fence posts wouldn't stay in the ground and it was next to impossible to keep the goats fenced in."[9] These days, location on the water, not timber nor agricultural potential, is what makes the property valuable.

Lopez Island, which is mostly flat, appears to have a stronger agricultural focus than other islands in the archipelago, and much land today remains in farm fields, both pasture and crops. Today, farmers on this island grow everything from wine grapes to kiwi fruit, even Kobe beef. Lopez Island hosted the first butchering trailer in the nation adhering to government standards. The truck and trailer go from farm to farm to kill and process livestock and package meat for use or sale. More than most of the other islands, Lopez's eyes seem to face inland. Many homes here are not located on the water but are out of view from the shore and some miles away. "Pastoral, placid and picturesque," a twenty-first century tourist brochure called the island.[10]

As the twentieth century neared an end, another agricultural crop found on the islands—and elsewhere—became newsworthy: marijuana, especially that grown on isolated Waldron Island. On August 9, 1997, thirty-five officers, federal and county, raided the island after receiving tips about marijuana cultivation and sales to children. Several of the law enforcement officers found a few growing operations, the largest containing some five hundred plants, and arrested seven people. The court convicted six people for manufacturing marijuana or providing a place for this, but only one went to prison and another got jail time. The situation produced continuing unease among islanders and a concern regarding strangers coming to the island. Better symbols of agriculture on the islands are two island museums. Anderson Island's Historical Museum occupies a pioneer farm site donated to the island's historical society by Alma Ruth Laing, granddaughter of Finnish immigrants John Oscar Johnson and his wife Alma Marie, who came to the island in the late nineteenth century. Featured are the furnished house built in 1912, barn—unusual in that it was framed with peeled poles, woodshed, chicken coops, egg room and other buildings. This is a living farm, too, for islanders can plant small gardens in a plot on the farm's land. The Johnson farm thus still supplies food and flowers to islanders today, and the family orchard still produces apples for harvest.

Commemorating the role of agriculture in the history of the islands is the San Juan Historical Museum, located on lands of the James King farm on the edge of Friday Harbor. On 445 acres, King raised cattle and sheep and kept an orchard of three hundred apple and pear trees. The family farmhouse, built in 1894, still stands and is furnished in period style. Other original buildings of the farm that are in the museum complex today are the carriage house, the milk house and a separate stone structure used as a root cellar.

Efforts to encourage agriculture on the islands abound these days, with county, state and federal organizations involved. In San Juan County, food security is a concern because of the islands' physical isolation from the rest of the state. Throughout the Puget Sound islands local farmers' markets offering locally grown products have become popular. Island organizations—churches and food banks, for example—raise garden produce to support their efforts to feed local people in need.

Agriculture remains alive and well on the Puget Sound islands, and so do the farming traditions of the pioneer era. Agriculture was an important economic activity on the islands as well as the mainland a century ago, but times changed and some of today's farming activities seem to be an adjunct to the tourist business. Boutique farming, one might call this. But islanders are becoming more concerned with food freshness and safety as well as emergency food supplies, and they are recognizing the advantages of buying and eating locally grown food products. In addition, more and more island farmers practice organic farming. Yes, farming is still important in the islands.

9 | Industries of Sea and Land

THE SETTLERS WHO HAVE COME TO THE PUGET SOUND ISLANDS over the last hundred and more years have not only built farms and communities, but have started industries. The islands today are certainly not known for industrial development, but these ventures have played a significant part in island evolution, from the fish processors and early shipbuilders of the late nineteenth century through Vashon Island's ski-producing K-2 Corporation of the late twentieth and telecommuters of the twenty-first century. As we have seen, it was logging that first opened the islands, but fishing accompanied logging and mining came soon after.

The sea naturally played a major part in the economy of the islands for the first white settlers, just as it did for Native Americans. For early loggers and settlers, fishing was an essential though part-time activity, the abundant sea life becoming an important portion of the pioneer diet. The earliest serious non-Native fishermen in northern Puget Sound waters copied Native American nets. The most productive fishing area around the islands probably was the Salmon Bank, a submerged ridge off the southwest coast of San Juan Island. Many Indians camped nearby along the coast in the old days, and the Hudson's Bay Company organized fishing there in the early nineteenth century. Settlers, meanwhile, fished everywhere in Puget Sound.

When travel by boat dominated the region, the islands were perfectly placed for industries connected with the sea. One of the earliest of these island industries was the processing of dogfish oil. This greased the skid roads which carried logs to the shore and lubricated mill machinery and lit lamps. A Fox Island plant that opened in 1871 could process some three thousand dogfish a day. Southern Vashon Island, the San Juan Islands and the Anacortes area, among other places, housed dogfish-processing facilities. In the early 1890s, though, petroleum products and various technical innovations removed the need for dogfish oil, and its production ended.

Development of a successful process to can fish led to a large commercial fishery. Once canneries could process large numbers of fish, fishermen began using fish traps, a method that resembled Native American weirs and brought in more fish. Traps placed where fish swam by caught almost all of them. Sometimes, too many fish awaited processing, and some would simply become waste. In 1898, eight traps sat by the Lummi Island shore, and early in the twentieth century, twenty-eight fish traps could be seen around the coast on Whidbey and Camano Islands. Indians, meanwhile, would canoe to the beach and set up their tents where they fished, often trying to intercept the fish before they came to the traps.

The fish traps' ability to bring in countless salmon was a leading cause of the severe decline in fish population, resulting in Washington State voters passing an initiative in 1934 to ban the traps. Some canneries had already closed, and the new legislation meant the end of business for others. Afterwards, reef netting—more efficient than in the nineteenth century— came back, but these days, only eleven reef net sites remain in the entire world. Eight of them are at Lummi Island. Other fishermen have used purse seines or gill nets. Thus, various ways to catch fish continue in use.

The Lummi Island Packing Company, a cannery, opened for business in 1896 on Legoe Bay along the west coast of Lummi Island. Later, renamed the Carlisle Packing Company, it continued operations until 1934. This large establishment even had its own post office. Two other canneries operated on Lummi Island throughout the first two decades of the twentieth century. Canneries opened on the San Juan Islands, too, including a large cannery at Deer Harbor on Orcas Island, two at Richardson on Lopez Island, one on Shaw Island and the Friday Harbor Canning Company. Anacortes has been the number one fishing port on the islands and canneries opened in the city in the 1890s. During the next few decades as many as eleven canneries congregated along Anacortes' north shore. The industry was centered around Puget Sound's northern waters.

The canneries needed workers. They hired men and women, Native Americans, Chinese, Japanese and whites. Anacortes soon was able to boast of being the "Salmon Canning Capital of the World." The canneries controlled the fish traps, which caught fish by the thousands. The salmon fishery peaked about 1910, though the front page of the *Anacortes American* proclaimed in August 1923, "Canneries Run Night and Day," because so many salmon came into town.[1] Fishing continued, though with smaller catches. In the mid-1950s, commercial fishermen would camp out on Lummi Island and take all the rooms in island resorts. As late as 1975, five canneries operated in Anacortes, but with fewer and fewer fish caught in nearby waters, they are now gone.

Commercial fishing has moved to Alaskan waters, and Puget Sound fishermen have plied their trade there despite the distance and the dangers. Until the late 1920s, the Anacortes fishing fleet heading for Alaska even included sailing ships. In the city now is a memorial to fourteen crewmen of the fishing boats *Altair* and *Americus*. These men died in February 1983 when the boats went down in the Bering Sea while on a crab-fishing trip. Both boats had been built in Anacortes and the fishermen's families lived there.

Aquaculture, or fish farming, has been introduced to Puget Sound waters in recent years. The most commonly raised fish have been Atlantic salmon, growing in large net pens along shorelines. On the Cypress Island coastline, a Canadian firm, Cooke Aquaculture, raised salmon in these cages, which have held more than fifteen million fish in some years. Other net pens lie off Hope Island near Deception Pass, and off the southwestern coast of Bainbridge Island. Aquaculture draws a lot of criticism, for the penned-up fish sometimes escape their pens. Opponents of the introduced fish worry that they might bring disease or crowd out the native fish. A virus among the fish reared off Bainbridge in 2012 meant that all of them were destroyed, but operation soon began again.

In August 2017, the net pen facility just off Cypress Island broke apart and some of the three hundred thousand fish it held escaped into the Sound. The Lummi Nation led efforts to catch these Atlantic salmon and the State Department of Fish and Wildlife urged people to catch as many as possible, adding that there would be no limits on these catches.

The Lummi, Cooke employees and others caught many fish—but not all. Soon State Senator Kevin Ranker of Orcas Island proposed legislation to ban new salmon net pen operations. This passed easily and the governor signed it. Meanwhile, leases allowed existing facilities to continue raising Atlantic salmon until 2022, and Cooke agreed to quit harvesting fish in Puget Sound by summer 2020.

In January 2020, the Washington State Department of Fish and Wildlife granted permission for Cooke to replace its salmon production with steelhead, using mostly infertile females. Opponents worry about these fish introducing disease to local steelhead, but final approval for this project came.

Shellfish-growing operations sit along several islands in the Sound. Oysters were once a very important part of Harstine Island's economy and these days a company owned by the Squaxin Island Tribe raises the mollusk off the Harstine shore. Recently the Squaxin Islanders have been working to reintroduce the Olympia oyster. Connoisseurs consider this tiny oyster, the only one native to Puget Sound, to be the tastiest of all oysters, but it became nearly extinct over the last century.

On Whidbey Island, members of the Jefferds family operate Penn Cove Shellfish. It is best known for the mussels the Jefferds grow there. The company runs the largest and the longest-established mussel farm in the entire United States and sells oysters and clams. At first, nearby Penn Cove residents were not happy about having mussel rafts in their waters, and noise from the processing operation continues to bother some people who live nearby, but now most see the mussels as a boon to Coupeville's economy.

In May 2012, mussel cultivation in Penn Cove received a serious, though temporary, setback. Arson destroyed an old fishing boat moored nearby. It sank, spilling a few thousand gallons of fuel. Jefferds immediately stopped harvesting. Officials laid a containment boom to capture the oil, and various state agencies, the Coast Guard, and volunteers worked on the clean-up. Washington State officials had earlier fined the vessel's owner and directed him to remove the boat, but he had never responded. A couple of weeks after the spill, the state towed the boat to a salvage yard far away. Following testing, mussel harvesting restarted nearly a month after the derelict vessel sank. Once again, mussels, freshly harvested and served in local restaurants, are a profitable—and tasty—tourist attraction.

A possible future problem looms, though: warming sea water, which could cut mussel production.

Other sea products have provided a livelihood for islanders. Shortly after the twentieth century began, the Cammon brothers of McNeil Island created a company to catch shrimp.

Early in that century, people at Port Stanley on Lopez Island harvested kelp to be used in fertilizer production. During World War I, Decatur Islanders operated a kiln to burn a mixture of kelp and driftwood, again to produce potassium. In various places, people have hunted for crab, and recently even Puget Sound geoduck and sea cucumber have found ready markets in Asia.

As fishing has declined with the decrease in fish numbers, pleasure boating has become more and more prominent, continuing a marine tradition in the islands. As early as 1956, the Port of Anacortes was the home port for about one thousand pleasure boats—along with one hundred commercial fishing vessels. Friday Harbor's port has five hundred slips for boat moorage and Roche Harbor has 377. In summer, both harbors are crowded with pleasure boats.

Life in the sea has generated many economic activities on the islands and not just for fishermen, fish processors and tourists. In 1904, the University of Washington began an ocean study program on San Juan Island. At first, the island facility emphasized harvesting specimens and training biology teachers, but the study center, located over the years at different sites near Friday Harbor, now stresses research and training research scientists.

Shipbuilding has also been important. Men have built vessels on the islands, sometimes simply on the beach. Most of the larger islands—Bainbridge, San Juan, Whidbey and Vashon-Maury—have been the home to prominent shipbuilders, and several of the island firms continue in business today.

Hall Brothers Shipbuilders moved to Bainbridge Island in 1879, locating at Port Blakely after local mill owner William Renton encouraged this. The mill and the shipbuilders complemented each other, for the mill supplied the timber to build ships and ships could move other timber to market. At first, Hall Brothers built only sailing ships, but by the 1880s launched steamers, too. This Port Blakely yard constructed seventy-seven ships. Most of the time some fifty to seventy men were at work there. Prosperity meant the need for expansion, and in 1903 Hall Brothers built a larger yard at water's edge in Eagle Harbor. In its new location, the firm brought jobs and thus people to this community, which would become Winslow, the commercial center of Bainbridge Island.

In 1916, ownership changed, and Hall Bros. became the Winslow Marine Railway and Shipbuilding Company. World War I brought increased contracts, but difficult years followed. Among the ships built at the yard in its later years was the ferry *Quillayute*, in 1927. It served Sound ferry routes, including the San Juan run, until 1951. By the end of the 1930s the Winslow firm was building steel ships. World War II brought huge orders, but that was the end of prosperous times for the company that had started as Hall Brothers. It closed in 1946. Others built boats there, though, until 1959. In 1962, the state bought part of the site for a Washington State Ferries repair facility. The one-time shipyard site now also houses a marina and a condominium building.

Albert Jensen & Sons, Inc. has been building boats on San Juan Island since 1910. Even before the twentieth century began, family members built boats, both sail- and steam-powered, on San Juan Island, and in 1910 they opened their shipyard near Friday Harbor. By 1940 the company had constructed more than one hundred boats, and during World War II the boatyard worked on military contracts. In more recent years, the Jensen firm, then run by third generation boatbuilder Nourdine Jensen, turned mostly to pleasure boat construction and then to repair and moorage. The company continues in business today, operated by Marine Services Group, which also runs three maritime-related businesses in Anacortes.

Nichols Brothers Boat Builders (NBBB), opened in Freeland, on Whidbey Island, in 1964. For many years, Nichols Brothers remained a totally family-run affair. The company built the passenger ferry *Tyee* for Washington State Ferries in 1985 and since the 1980s has built catamarans for transporting foot passengers between San Francisco Bay ports. Among the boats built in the 1990s were paddle wheelers for the Columbia River tourist trade. The company built the *Good Time II* and *Good Time III* for Seattle Harbor Tours and that company's successor, Argosy Cruises, still has these two vessels in its fleet.

Freeland residents have expressed concern about the boatyard's large footprint in this waterfront residential area. Local residents formed a non-profit organization, Friends of Holmes Harbor, in 2005 to protect the environment, largely because of concern about Nichols Brothers. Some people expressed support for Nichols Brothers, though, because of its historic role in the community and the jobs the company has supported. Now owned by an out-of-state firm, Nichols Brothers builds tugboats, ferries, and fireboats. In addition to the yard in Freeland, the firm has a smaller facility—an outfitting yard—in Langley, where sea trials can take place. NBBB continues to be the largest private employer on Whidbey island.

On Maury Island, the community of Dockton owes its history as well as its name to a maritime connection. The Puget Sound Dry Dock Company chose this site, well-protected in a Quartermaster Harbor cove, for its dry dock. Some eighty men, most brought in daily from Tacoma, set to work preparing the location, and in March 1892 the first ship was able to enter the dry dock for repair. The dry dock firm built a few houses and a boarding house for employees. The Yukon gold rush and the need for ships to sail to the Philippines during the Spanish-American War brought greater work to the dry dock, and the town grew. Pete Manson, who first worked at the dry dock in 1893, became dockmaster ten years later.

Pete Manson built Dockton's first pile driver in 1904 and with his brother John began the Manson Construction Company in 1905. The company grew and in 1911 moved to Seattle. Since then, Manson has become prominent in Puget Sound's maritime construction industry, among other things building or repairing various ferry docks. Meanwhile, after a strike threat and a brief shutdown in 1907, John T. Heffernan took control of Dockton's dry dock and moved it to Seattle in 1909.

In 1904 the Martinolich Shipbuilding Company began operations in Dockton and launched its first vessel, the steamer *Vashon*, in 1905. Many of the community's skilled workmen went to work for Martinolich, building fishing boats—purse seiners constructed so well they saw many years of use—as well as passenger vessels. During World War I, the company contracted to build three ships for the Norwegian government. The war ended, though, and the Norwegians stopped paying. Another firm later bought two of the ships when they were ready. Martinolich continued to build ships in his Maury Island yard until 1930, but when the Depression came, business declined badly, and the firm moved to Tacoma in 1935. Despite all this industrial activity in Dockton, only descriptive signs remain today to tell us of the maritime community's history.

Various small boatbuilding firms have existed on the islands. In 1903, William Reed started a shipyard on Decatur Island. Henry Cayou of Orcas

Island soon joined him and their small company built various sorts of boats, from tugs to tenders. Within a few years, some twenty men worked there. One vessel built on Decatur was the *Osage*, which delivered mail and goods to islands throughout the San Juans from 1930 to 1950. The Willits brothers built top-quality canoes on Day Island in the South Sound for more than forty years, starting in 1921. A newer firm that builds much larger vessels is Dakota Creek Industries, located since 1977 in Anacortes. Its work in recent years has included repair and modification of several of the vessels in the Washington State Ferries fleet, the *Sealth*, the *Issaquah* and the *Kittitas*.

Other products, not only boats, make the fishing industry possible. Among specialized island firms manufacturing products for the industry is NET Systems of Bainbridge, making fishing nets and related gear. In addition to specialized manufacturers, marine equipment sales and small boat building and repair play important roles in the islands' marine industry.

Industries not related to fishing and ships have also been important on the islands. Anacortes is by far the primary industrial city on any of them, and lumber and fishing industries dominated the city far into the twentieth century. In 1923, the *Anacortes American* reported products including "lumber for Kobe [Japan], shingles and lath and salmon for New York" and in "the late 1930s the city had eleven shingle mills, three codfish processing plants, five sawmills, one glass plant, nine canneries and three fish reduction plants," wrote Craig Smith in the *Seattle Post Intelligencer*.[2] Some mills closed after World War II, though others continued to produce plywood, but all are gone today. The Anacortes port continues to be busy, as the number of working vessels traversing Guemes Channel shows.

Two oil refineries opened on Fidalgo Island's March Point in the 1950s and are among the largest firms in the Anacortes area. However, serious accidents have taken place in both refineries. On November 25, 1998, during a restarting procedure after a power outage, a flash fire erupted in the Equilon Refinery, killing six men. Afterwards, the unit remained shut down for some time while receiving safety modifications. The state fined the company more than one million dollars and Equilon later paid $45 million to the families of the men who had died. On April 2, 2010, an explosion just after midnight at Anacortes' other refinery, Tesoro, awakened people across the bay in the city. Again, workers were restarting a unit, this time after routine maintenance. Seven men died. The State of

Washington later fined Tesoro more than two million dollars and ruled that the accident, like the Equilon tragedy, could have been prevented. The plant remained closed for six months and the state's penalties remained at issue for years. Both firms have had name changes, but they have kept industrial jobs in the region and continue to operate today.

Over the years, oil spills have fouled island beaches and nearby waters. In April 1971, some 260,000 gallons of diesel oil spilled into Anacortes Harbor and beyond because someone had left a valve open on a barge receiving oil from a March Point refinery. Ironically, it was Guemes Island beaches, not those of Anacortes, that got much of the oil. Another very small spill fouled Guemes Island's north shore in December 1976.

Various other islands, not only Fidalgo and Guemes, have experienced oil spills. For example, in December 1984, some fifteen hundred or more gallons spilled onto southeast Whidbey Island. In 1997 about one thousand gallons from the mainland Tesco Refinery near Bellingham spilled along Lummi Island and covered kelp off nearby Vendovi Island with oil. And about one in the morning of October 14, 2004, a tugboat captain reported an oil slick on south Puget Sound waters. It spread on to Vashon-Maury Islands beaches and along other shorelines. To deal with such incidents, the Washington State's Department of Ecology arranges drills to test and practice procedures for quick response and cleanup.

Industries have developed on the islands to take advantage of mineral resources. One of the earliest industries on many of the islands was brick manufacture, using island clay deposits. Whidbey Island brick production began as early as the 1850s. Brickworks on Fox Island started production in 1884 and at times, fifty people worked at the Fox Island Brick Manufacturing Company. The Great Seattle Fire of 1889 gave impetus to brickworks, especially on nearby Vashon, where fifty-two brickmakers operated by 1892. Meanwhile, the Fox Island company made pipe and tile as well as brick. The firm continued to find markets, and early in the twentieth century was making some 15,000 bricks weekly. Mainland brick became easier to transport, and after 1910, concrete was displacing brick. Brick manufacture on the islands declined and died.

During the late nineteenth century, the San Juan Islands appeared to have considerable potential for industry. Several lime kilns operated on Orcas Island and another small limestone operation began on tiny Crane Island, just off the southwest corner of Orcas, but quickly failed. In the late nineteenth and early twentieth centuries, a stone quarry and a herring processing plant operated on Waldron Island. In the early years of the twentieth century, Waldron Island sandstone became paving blocks used on some Seattle streets.

Lime production became a prominent and long-lasting industry on San Juan Island. Limestone has many uses: as a building stone and, crushed, in the manufacture of many products, from cement to glass. The rock is found at several sites in the archipelago. A lime kiln on the west coast of San Juan Island gave its name to Lime Kiln Point and, later, Lime Kiln Point State Park. Lime deposits both extensive and accessible were discovered only at Roche Harbor, though. Starting in the late 1880s, John S. McMillan built the site into a mining center, containing thirteen kilns, warehouses, tracks and trams, bunkhouses, and a store. In 1897 he added a factory to produce barrels for shipping the lime his kilns generated. To produce the lime, workers blasted the nearby rock, broke it up and transported it on a short railway track to the kilns along the beach. The kilns burned the small rocks into lime which could be loaded into ships right at Roche Harbor and taken to market.

McMillan's operation grew into a town—a company town, because McMillan controlled everything. One high point was the visit of McMillan's friend President Theodore Roosevelt in 1906. Several incidents over the years set back production: a destructive fire in 1923, the 1930s Depression and a 1938 work stoppage while workers attempted to unionize against management's wishes. War work kept the company busy in the 1940s. After World War II, as the limestone supply was running out and the machinery aging, Paul McMillan, the founder's son, sold the plant and town to Reuben J. Tarte. Soon after the 1956 sale, the power plant failed, and before long Tarte ceased industrial operation at Roche Harbor.

On Bainbridge Island, a very different industrial concern operated from 1904 until near the end of the 1980s but left severe environmental degradation. Late in the nineteenth century, a process to preserve wood with creosote became feasible. Puget Sound country was a prime source of large logs and it made sense to treat wood near its source. A plant using this process came in 1905 to the beach on the south side of the entrance to Eagle Harbor. A company town grew here, named, of course, Creosote. The factory in Creosote, reputed to be the largest such plant in the western United States, supplied lumber to many large-scale projects in the United States and beyond, from railroads to flood control systems. One of the first jobs there was to apply creosote to lumber that would help build the Panama Canal.

The Bainbridge Island plant operated through World War II and after. Ownership changed several times and the firm finally became the Wycoff Company.

By the 1980s, Americans were becoming more concerned about environmental pollution and Creosote became a target because creosote and the sludge from its manufacture were poisoning sea life in Eagle Harbor. The preservative is no longer used in residential construction because of health risks from exposure, and the Bainbridge plant closed in 1988. Wycoff worked at cleanup but felt forced to declare bankruptcy in 1993. Cost of thorough restoration appeared so high that a *Bainbridge Review* editorial even suggested leaving the site alone, asserting that "the cost . . . is too great to save the livers of a few English sole."[3] Instead, the newspaper suggested warning people not to eat seafood from Eagle Harbor, meanwhile spending the funds on programs that would more directly help people. Work at Creosote continues. Ferry passengers approaching the nearby Winslow dock see what looks like an empty beach at the one-time busy industrial site. It remains closed to the public but eventually, when recovery is complete, will open as a public park.

Some industrial plans for the islands have been abandoned. After World War II, environment concern and desire to preserve the natural state of the islands and islanders' way of life have aroused opposition to industrial development, particularly to large-scale projects. In July 1966, Northwest Aluminum Company officials announced plans to build a plant on Guemes Island. Aluminum production requires a lot of energy, and Washington State's hydroelectric power was relatively inexpensive. Boosters, including the state's two senators, Henry M. Jackson and Warren Magnuson, emphasized the thousand or more jobs the plant would bring and the economic boost it would mean for the Anacortes area. Skagit County promoters supported the plan. Aluminum company officials promised that nearby islands would be neither developed nor harmed.

Building such a factory would require rezoning up to seven hundred acres on Guemes island. Company officials announced that the plant would use only 140 acres of this land, while the rest would be planted and landscaped. Attendees at a Guemes Island Community Club meeting voted 101-2, however, to fight any necessary rezoning. Opponents of plant construction organized the "Save the San Juans Committee" and hired a Seattle lawyer, John Ehrlichman, later well-known as a prominent adviser to President Richard M. Nixon and a Watergate conspirator. Ehrlichman described Guemes as "extremely pastoral, passive, quiet, recreational and residential," and thus not the place for heavy industry.[4]

The Board of Skagit County Commissioners did rezone the Guemes site for industry. Opponents filed suit. Legal wrangling ensued, and after months of turmoil, the Northwest Aluminum Company announced on February 25, 1967 that it was dropping its plans to build on Guemes Island. Bitterness resulted, some who favored the industry blaming weekend and summer folks for stopping industrial development on Guemes Island while supporting it in their home communities. Meanwhile, the rezoning decision remained—until the Washington State Supreme Court ruled it illegal in April 1969.

Near the end of the 1960s, plans surfaced to build two nuclear power plants along the shore in Skagit County, on Kiket Island and on the peninsula known as Samish Island. Small Kiket, an island when the tide is high enough, is in the Swinomish Reservation. A late-nineteenth century causeway connects it to the mainland, and in 1929, a Seattle firm bought the island. Later, Seattle City Light and the Snohomish County Public Utilities District acquired the two Skagit County sites and planned the power plants. The power providers selected these locations partly because water for cooling was easily available. This water, warmer after being used, would be put through cooling towers and returned to Puget Sound.

Proponents of the plan suggested that the water would make nearby swimming beaches more attractive and possibly attract fish that liked a warmer sea. A leading member of the Swinomish tribe favored the project because of economic benefits it would bring to the tribal community. Opponents noted that should an accident occur at a Kiket Island nuclear plant, Anacortes residents' only practical evacuation route would take them closer to the plant. Technological challenges ultimately prevented use of the proposed cooling systems, and the project died. By 1980 both sites were looking for buyers. To proponents of industry, proximity to the sea and little or no population had made islands seem perfect locations for both aluminum and nuclear plants, but strong opposition from the public helped scuttle the plants.

Kiket Island now has a unique status. Purchased in 2010 with grant money, the site is now known as Kukutali Preserve and is jointly owned and administered by Washington State Parks and the Swinomish Tribal Community, with access for the public.

In the twenty-first century, Vashon-Maury Islanders found themselves in a similar battle. They wanted to prevent a large-scale gravel mining operation on Maury Island. For several decades moderate amounts of gravel had been transported from this site by barge from a dock built for this purpose. In 1998, the company wanted to expand the operation considerably. A group of Vashon-Maury Islanders formed an organization, POI—Preserve Our Islands—to fight the project. POI supporters feared harm to the island's water supply as well as to sea life. The company involved went through several name changes, but when the climax of the fight came in late 2010, Glacier Northwest was its name.

In late 2008 Glacier received Corps of Engineers permission to construct the large dock needed to ship more gravel and immediately began work. The company would have to suspend construction for several months starting in mid-January 2009 because spawning fish would need to be protected then. Glacier thus was working as many hours as possible before that date to get the new dock in place. Meanwhile, opponents rallied at the site to impede work, and also went to court.

Glacier stopped work in January as ordered, and in August United States District Court Judge Ricardo Martinez, a George W. Bush appointee, ruled that in issuing a permit to Glacier, the Army Corps of Engineers had not adequately considered the question of protection for endangered salmon and orca whales. A new study and a new permit were necessary before work could continue. As a result, in 2010, Glacier dropped its plans and King County soon purchased the site for a park.

In addition to industries on the islands, mainland work can adversely affect an island's environment. Probably the most important such case in Puget Sound history involves pollution from the American Smelting and Refining Corporation (ASARCO) copper smelter on the waterfront in Ruston, the small Tacoma suburb just across the water from the south end of Vashon Island. The smelter had operated since 1889, producing copper between 1902 and 1986. Arsenic, however, is one of the byproducts of the smelting process, and some of the arsenic gets released into the air, ultimately settling into the soil. Heading north due to prevailing winds, emissions from the smelter contaminated soil with heavy metals, mostly arsenic, on the southern parts of Vashon-Maury as well as some mainland sites. Testing at various sites showed dangerous arsenic levels in the soils. Lawsuits ensued against ASARCO, the smelter closed, and cleanup of affected land is still in progress.

Among the different industries over the years, some have not needed a waterfront location. Some companies developed on the islands because that is where their founders lived. Probably the most prominent of these firms is K2. Starting in 1961, Vashon Islander Bill Kirschner developed a snow ski made of fiberglass. By 1964, he and his brother Don began to sell skis—250 pairs—and in 1967 they created K2 to manufacture them.

The ski business grew quickly, especially after skiers began winning prestigious international races on K2 skis. The company made its skis in a factory built along Vashon Island's main highway. As the firm grew, it needed more capital, and acquired new partners. The product line expanded, with K2 making snowboards and inline skates as well as skis, and K2s made on Vashon became the best-selling ski in the United States. Bill Kirschner retired as chairman in 1982. After he sold the company, off-Island owners started making skis in California, moving jobs off Vashon Island, and after Kirschner died in 2006 the company cut all ties to Vashon. Put up for sale, Vashon's K2 plant sat unsold until 2018. The local buyers hope that renters can bring a variety of small businesses to the building. The property faces hazardous waste cleanup, however.

While K2 left Vashon at least partly because of transportation issues, companies which make small high-value products find ferries inconvenient but not prohibitive in cost. One example is Northwest Marine Technology, the only industrial firm currently established on Shaw Island. This company makes tiny tags that can be implanted in fish and easily read. Fisheries research is big business around the world, and NMT has sold more than one million of the tags. The company has several off-island branches, but continues research, development, sales, and some manufacture on the small island. The Shaw Island Subarea Plan adopted by San Juan County limits industrial firms to those compatible with "the existing character of Shaw Island." According to the plan, no "commercial recreational facilities" are allowed.[5] All this suggests that Shaw Island will keep its rural character and not see any new industrial development.

Bainbridge Island has opted for several modest and centrally located industrial parks. Well before the entire island incorporated, however, many islanders fought against the idea of allowing even light manufacturing. In recent years, communities on the islands, whether incorporated or not, have comprehensive plans, and this has meant limitations on industry. Only light industry is allowed on almost all the islands and only a limited amount of land is zoned for it. Occasionally, one will see a small industrial firm grandfathered in, perhaps housed in a barn sitting in an otherwise rural landscape, like Olympic Instruments on the west side of Vashon Island.

Given the transportation bottlenecks in access to islands, whether caused by a ferry or even a bridge, why do some industries locate on islands? In some cases, as with K2, a firm's founder lived on an island. Otherwise, the answer seems to be that the islands are inviting places where small-scale entrepreneurs want to live. A successful Bainbridge Island software developer, Scott McFarlane, said in 2014 that his company would relocate to Seattle in the future, for though the firm could get a start on the island, it would eventually have to move to the mainland. Sure enough, McFarlane announced in 2016 that the firm would relocate to a building under construction in downtown Seattle.

As we have seen, industry helped build communities on some of the islands, but, as on Bainbridge, most of those communities disappeared along with the industry that spawned them. Though many islanders once made their living, or at least a good portion of it, by fishing, few can say the same today. The industrial city that has survived—Anacortes—has had to find new industries to replace the ones that dwindled away. The industry that may spread on the islands in the future is information technology, whose practitioners can work in remote sites. These entrepreneurs can already be found on many of the islands. Today, more mainland companies are able to accommodate employees who work at least part-time from remote locations—like islands. Thus, industry will continue to have a role on the islands—but it will not be a major one.

10 | Communities

COMMUNITY IS THE FOCUS OF LIFE ON AN ISLAND. Tourists do not ordinarily come to the islands looking for communities, but these island centers are crucial for island residents. In the days when transportation was slow, communities offered necessities and—also important—camaraderie. As the years have gone by, many island communities have disappeared, but before automobiles came to dominate our culture a dockside community on an inhabited island was the heart of activity. For the early settlers, these gathering places meant the landing site and the general store. Some hamlets also soon garnered a school, church, post office and perhaps a tavern. Illustrating the role and number of these small coastal centers, in 1900 Orcas Island had nine post offices.

Here are stories of some of the places that arose, then died. The first community of any prominence on Lopez Island was Richardson, on the island's south shore. Yet this settlement's subsequent history illustrates one of the patterns seen on the islands. George Richardson founded the settlement in the 1870s and It developed as perhaps the primary fishing port in the San Juan Islands. It prospered, while catering to fishermen as well as to families who began farming nearby. Before the beginning of the twentieth century, several fish traps operated in the area. Soon commercial canning began in Richardson.

In 1901, a special supplement in the *San Juan Islander* reassured visitors that though coming toward Richardson a traveler saw "rugged and unpropitious shores," beyond these were "fertile and productive acres of land" and a wharf and assorted nearby buildings were welcoming.[1] The wharf had opened in 1889 and plenty of wood was available to fuel steamboats. The community's general store sold merchandise of all kinds. A hotel appeared. Residents banded together to build a community hall, which was ready for use in 1897. One drawback the community faced, however, was limited water. After two new salmon canneries opened at Richardson in 1913, barges supplied them with Blakely Island water. At that time, the salmon fishery was at its height, but within a few decades the decline of fish runs, and the outlawing of fish traps meant that the canneries closed. Eventually, the only commercial structures left in Richardson were the store, which had been rebuilt after a 1916 fire, and nearby fuel tanks. Fire destroyed the entire store building in 1990—one hundred years after the business had opened, but, luckily, the fire did not spread to the fuel tanks. Nowadays, there is no sign that a busy community once existed there.

Other prominent island communities have disappeared, too. On Bainbridge island, no buildings remain to suggest that Port Madison and Port Blakely were both busy commercial and industrial centers. Port Blakely had almost one thousand residents at the end of the 1880s. During the community's busy years, the town included a livery stable, church services, barber shop, candy and cigar shop, post office, hotel with a saloon, a company store on the dock, the school, fraternal lodges, a doctor's office, and a restaurant. Townspeople lived in houses, hotels, and dormitories. This mill town grew to have suburbs, including New Sweden and Japanese communities called Nagaya and Yama. West Blakely developed in the 1890s and soon had a grocery, community hall, church, and baseball field. Also near Port Blakely was a Native American village. These were vibrant communities, but the mills supported the towns, so the towns disappeared after the mills closed.

Camano Island's Utsalady shows a similar historical pattern. Once the town had a newspaper, hotel, school, a shipyard and even a park featuring deer. The name Utsalady endures on the north Camano shore, but just one historic structure remains, the Utsalady Ladies Aid Building erected in 1924. Across the road is Utsalady Bay and along the shore now are small lots and houses.

Other communities have survived, though with great changes. On San Juan Island, the lime industry was the basis for the company town built by John S. McMillan at Roche Harbor. This community grew to have about eight hundred people. Amenities included a church, post office and telephone system as well as the dock, a necessity in all these waterfront settlements. Unlike so many communities, though, Roche Harbor did not disappear when its industry closed. It became a resort.

One more thriving island industrial community, Maury Island's Dockton, was never as large as the company towns on Bainbridge and San Juan Island, but in support of its dry dock, boat building and other enterprises, it too was a busy center of life. A brickyard, a box factory which later morphed into a sawmill, a codfish packing plant and a salmon cannery also opened in Dockton. This was a self-contained community during its boom years in the 1890s. Once Vashon and Maury Islands had a better road connection, first by a bridge in 1918 and later a causeway, Dockton attracted residents, but by then the community's industrial heyday was over. The town's school and even its church are gone now. These days, a reminder of the busy years is Piano Row, a set of four solid but unostentatious houses built in 1892 for supervisors of the dry dock company—who were the only people in Dockton wealthy enough to afford pianos. Some descendants of the town's early fishermen still live in Dockton, and a county park sits on the beach in the community that once featured maritime industry.

Before automotive transport became common, residents traveled by boat and settlements sprung up in different areas along the islands' coastlines. Even on one island, many hamlets were not close to one another. For example, Lopez Islanders living in Port Stanley, Lopez Village and Richardson had limited contact with each other. Sometimes it could be easier to travel to the mainland than to other parts of one's island.

The early island communities that grew resembled small towns and villages throughout the United States in that they consisted of a cluster of commercial and industrial buildings surrounded by neighborhood streets where the townspeople lived. Once automobiles came to dominate island traffic, though, a new pattern emerged. Many settlers came to the islands for their beaches or their views or acreage, and even if these residents worked in town, they did not want to live in town. Land was available, for much of it was not farmed. These days, many communities on the islands remain commercial centers with relatively little nearby housing.

Even the island communities that thrive today did not see continual growth, and the nationwide Panic of 1893—as that depression was called—hit some of them especially hard. For example, business collapse brought commerce to a standstill in the South Whidbey Island town of Langley. Farm and forest products suddenly could find no market. As P. H. Knott put it, "All industries were paralyzed . . . one by one those pioneer settlers had to leave their homes and go elsewhere in search of work and money. The place was deserted."[2] Moreover, the town's dock collapsed in a spring 1894 storm. In Coupeville, meanwhile, the Island County Bank founded in 1892 had to close on December 1, 1893. A few years later, business looked up in both towns, partly because the Klondike Gold Rush of 1898 brought more and more people to Puget Sound. Some of the islands, and not only the smallest ones, did not develop villages or towns. Anderson, Fox, Harstine, Lummi and Shaw Islands do not have any, although scattered around these islands might be a grocery, school, and church. Perhaps these islands are not big enough or have never attracted enough residents to develop a population center. For a time, it seemed that Sylvan, the heart of early Fox Island development, would be the permanent center of that island's activity, but it did not happen. Now, the island's only store is inland, not far from the bridge, with a small post office nearby. Harstine and Fox Island residents can now easily supply their needs from the mainland because their islands have bridges, and Anderson Island has a centrally located store that stocks the necessities along with some items for leisure use, while Lummi and Shaw have small stores near their ferry docks.

Especially important in making a cluster of buildings a community were its school and church. Schools tended to define communities, and the school has often been a community's social center. Many small school districts existed on the islands before cars became common. Bainbridge Island, for example, had nine or ten of them. That the first school on the island was built in the north—at Port Madison in 1860—indicates that this was the first part of the island to see many residents. A school opened at Port Blakely in the 1870s. and others arose in Bainbridge settlements including Manzanita and Rolling Bay. In the twentieth century, efforts came to consolidate the Bainbridge schools, illustrating a trend common on the islands. The north end districts, Port Madison, Manzanita and Seabold, combined in 1910, but a decade later, when an effort at island-wide consolidation started, the north end briefly stayed out. Bainbridge Island had two high schools until 1928 when island-wide consolidation came. A bond issue passed, high school construction began, and the new Bainbridge High School opened, helping bring about a feeling of island-wide unity.

Two high schools opened on Vashon Island, in Burton in 1908 and at the town of Vashon in 1912, but since 1930, one high school has served the entire island. Now, in the twenty-first century, island schools find enrollment dwindling as too many young families cannot afford to live on an island. To counter this development, the Vashon Island School District welcomes off-island students. Most come from Seattle, and on weekday mornings commuters at Vashon's north end can watch youngsters stride off a ferry and board four full-sized school buses waiting to take them to Vashon schools, which enroll almost 250 off-islanders. About one-fourth of the island high school's students commute from the mainland. Meanwhile, the San Juan Islands' school districts also have a serious problem of declining enrollment, since local jobs for parents with young families are limited, while transportation expenses are high, and island students, like mainlanders, want to participate in interscholastic activities. Vashon Island's solution is obviously not practical for the San Juans, and since the state allocates funds to school districts mainly tied to student numbers, the districts in the archipelago have a continuing problem.

Even some lightly populated islands have elementary schools, where the students—perhaps fewer than ten—have often studied in one room. In the 1890s, a Waldron Islander named Ethan Allen became Superintendent of Schools for San Juan County. He needed to assess the county's schools, of course, and to do so traveled some ten thousand miles, he later estimated, in a boat he rowed between islands. Washington State has a law that requires "remote and necessary" schools when student numbers are very low and transportation to another school is out of the question. Five of these schools are on Puget Sound islands. The three San Juan islands with these K-8 schools are Decatur, Stuart and Waldron. Decatur has had between two and ten students in recent years. Stuart Island, like Decatur, has had just one teacher for a small elementary-age student body, but Stuart's school has been closed since 2013 for lack of students. Waldron has had a pair of part-time teachers for about fourteen students. Note that these tiny schools can use their surroundings and well-educated local residents to offer significant educational opportunities for their students. Lummi Island's Beach School has three classrooms and serves students through sixth grade. The school features an International Baccalaureate program, one of whose effects might be to bring a few mainland students to the island school. Anderson Island's remote and necessary school has two teachers and several support personnel serving about thirty students.

Some years ago, Dr. Jerry Pipes, San Juan superintendent of schools, suggested having a "little yellow school boat" for isolated schools. Though it was fun to suggest this, he obviously knew it would be too expensive.[3] Students on these islands and others, including Shaw, go elsewhere to attend high school, often to the mainland. Some youngsters commute daily, so their school buses are ferry boats. Other students live with relatives or friends, while some youngsters of all ages are home-schooled.

Various academies—private preparatory schools, sometimes colleges—operated on the islands in the early days. Alden Academy opened on Fidalgo Island in 1879 but closed in 1885 after its founder left. Its Congregational sponsors moved it to Coupeville, where the next year it became Puget Sound Academy. The Academy furnished a high school education and prospered until about ten years later when its building, a large two-story house, burned down. This was replaced, but as public high schools became available, the number of students dwindled, and Puget Sound Academy moved to the mainland. Another school, Whidbey Island Academy, continued in the Coupeville buildings deserted by Puget Sound Academy, but it closed in 1908. These days, various private schools operate on the islands, some only for younger students, but others offering high school diplomas. A successful one, the Spring Street International School in Friday Harbor, serves children from all over the world, in grades six through twelve.

Institutions of higher education on the islands included Vashon College, which opened in 1892 on ten acres near Burton, "at some beautiful point on Puget Sound, where students would have an environment not beset by temptations too strong for the resistance of youth," wrote A. C. Jones, its first head.[4] By the end of the century, the co-educational school had space for two hundred students to board. The curriculum included compulsory military training for all the boys. Younger students could attend a preparatory school, and at the college level, students received a liberal education and could prepare for a teaching career. Starting in 1906, though, two destructive fires spelled the end of Vashon College, a dormitory burning down then and the main building in 1910. The college closed in 1912.

Moran Academy opened its doors at Rolling Bay on Bainbridge Island in 1914 and offered a college education. As World War I raged in Europe, the school instituted a military program. The Depression meant fewer students, however, and the school closed in 1933. Five years later, another institution opened on the campus. The Puget Sound Naval Academy, designed as a military high school, began preparing boys for the United States Coast Guard and Naval Academies. The Bainbridge school continued until the early 1950s and in its final years had the use of a Navy surplus minesweeper, which the boys sailed on the Sound and beyond. In the twenty-first century, the campus houses a retirement home.

Now most high school graduates on the islands move on elsewhere, but Skagit Valley College classes are available on San Juan and Whidbey Islands, and the college has a marine technology center in Anacortes. Embry-Riddle Aeronautical University offers classes in Oak Harbor, thanks to the nearby Naval Air Station. Washington State University recently began offering remote college education, by video, in Coupeville.

Churches also appeared early in the islands. When settlers came, they brought their religious beliefs, holding services in homes or perhaps schools until they could afford a church building. Some also used visiting ministers to lead their services. Most of the earliest congregations were Methodist, Presbyterian, Baptist, Lutheran, or Roman Catholic. Some Norwegian Lutheran churches held services in the Norwegian language for many years.

A few nineteenth century religious edifices remain in use today. These include San Juan Island's Catholic Church. Its predecessor, built of logs in 1860, burned down, and the island's current St. Francis Church dates from 1884. Presbyterians completed the Valley Church on the same island in 1882 but later moved to a new building. The historic church, now restored, hosts special events, including weddings and memorial services. Center Church on Lopez Island, opened in 1889, served Presbyterians, Methodists, and Congregationalists over the years.

Emmanuel Episcopal Church on Orcas Island owes its existence to Englishman Sidney R. S. Gray, who had it built about 1885. Due to hard times, though, he left the island in 1893. For many years, subsequent vicars commuted among the San Juan Islands. Gray's immediate replacement, John William Dickson, lived on Shaw. To come to Eastsound, he rowed to Orcas Landing where the ferry dock now sits, towing a scow holding his horse. Upon landing, Dickson rode to both Eastsound and West Sound to hold services. At times during the early twentieth century, this Eastsound church had no vicar and ceased operation, but by mid-century it was once again becoming a busy and active place.

The islands have had many different churches and congregations over the years, including Jewish, Orthodox Christian and ones describing themselves as evangelical, non-denominational or independent. In the San Juan Islands, the Lutheran pastor commutes by air to offer Sunday services on San Juan, Lopez and Orcas Islands. These days, twelve different religious groups advertise in the *Vashon-Maury Island Beachcomber*, and even more do so in South Whidbey Island's weekly newspaper.

Over the years, religious idealists looking for a peaceful place to settle have come to the islands. Fundamentalists led by Rev. Thomas Gourley moved in 1911 from the Seattle area to Lopez Island, where the 175 members of his group established themselves on Hunter Bay in the southeastern part of the island. First living in tents, they built houses, a barn and, perhaps most urgent, a dock. Possibly more important to them, they erected a tabernacle. Some of the men worked in logging and other jobs. The group schooled their own children. But disagreements surfaced, money ran short and after five years the congregation compelled Rev. Gourley to leave. A few years later, the group disbanded, and members sold off the property.

A few members of another religious group, the national Peace Mission of Black evangelist Father Divine, came to tiny Vendovi Island between Lummi and Guemes Islands.

Father Divine's movement attracted adherents in the 1920s and 1930s, mostly from the eastern United States. The Peace Mission, notably, welcomed both blacks and whites at a time when segregated organizations were the norm in the United States. A few members led by Father Divine follower and fellow preacher Ross Humble lived on Vendovi Island and welcomed summer visitors. The serenity to be found in this natural setting, along with religious services, appealed to those who arrived. This haven lasted only for a few years, perhaps because it was so distant from the church's central activities in eastern cities.

Much more recently, a religious group left Illinois, coming to Vashon Island in 1977 because of controversy in their midwestern home. Sixty-five members of the Wesleyan Community Church migrated with church leader Louis Hillendahl. The group settled on sixty-eight acres in the middle of Vashon Island.[5] The church is no longer active, though some one-time members continued to live on the island.

A utopian community, the Free Land Association, established the community of Freeland in 1900 at the head of Holmes Harbor on Whidbey Island. This would be a cooperative rather than a religious colony. With a very small down payment, each family could buy five acres for its home and the hope was, pay for the rest with profits from the community store and any other businesses and industries that might be established. Community ownership, however, never went beyond the store and a small steamboat. Freeland slowly evolved into a community different from others only in that, for a time, most of its residents believed in socialism.

Over the years, people have continued to settle on the islands. Communities developed to serve them, and during the twentieth century most of the islands came to have just one dominant commercial center. Among the leading communities on the large San Juan Islands is Lopez Village, which became an island commercial center probably because of its relatively central location and because it is much closer to the dock serving automobile ferries than is Richardson. A store sat on the Lopez Village shore as early as the 1880s. Here, too, was a clam cannery early on and over later years various businesses sprung up in the vicinity, along with houses, churches, and a school. Since Lopez Village was not an important pioneer community, though, it never developed the compact structure of a traditional village. Like Lopez Village, Eastsound, the major community on Orcas Island, is centrally located on its island and contains the services islanders depend upon, but, also like Lopez Village, it is not near today's ferry landing. On neither island is the dock location expansive enough for a sizeable village.

The only incorporated community in the San Juan Islands, Friday Harbor, could claim in the early twentieth century to have many of the commercial establishments generally found in American small towns: six general stores, two barber shops, two smithies, two newspaper offices, a drugstore, bank and more. The town had a doctor, a dentist and three lawyers. It is also the county seat and, with over two thousand residents, the largest town in the archipelago.

On Bainbridge Island, Winslow became the center of island life. Merely a village shortly after the twentieth century began, the community grew to dominate commerce on the island. Bainbridge is the closest island to Washington State's largest city's downtown area, and thus Winslow's location at the ferry dock serving the route to Seattle attracts business. The community incorporated in 1947 after a close election, and in 1990 annexed the rest of the island after another fierce battle for votes. A crucial—and divisive—issue was whether the island should have strict laws to regulate and limit development or whether landowners should have wider latitude in making decisions about their property. Some labeled the people favoring limits as newcomers or elitists, while many old timers did not want the changes that limitations would bring. Again, the vote was close, incorporation passing by just 139 out of 6,379 votes cast, and within a year, some voters petitioned unsuccessfully to de-annex all the land outside the original town.

Soon the voters changed the new city's name from Winslow to Bainbridge Island. The island had more than sixteen thousand residents by then, so it became a city, no longer a town, and apartment and condominium buildings have since then added many people to the commercial center at Winslow. It remains a pleasant place, with supermarkets, a bookstore, and a library catering mainly to residents and many restaurants and specialty shops.

An incorporation drive also occurred on Camano Island, but residents voted in March 1991 to reject this, 2,569 to 334. Land use was again the issue. Both proponents and opponents wanted the island's rural nature protected. The voters may have feared that cityhood would bring higher taxes and, perhaps, developers obtaining control of government.

Some Vashon Islanders revived the idea of incorporating their island to take over much of the decision-making that lay with King County. In 1913, a bill had reached the state legislature to create a new Vashon County, but this obviously did not become law. Some islanders tried again to incorporate in the 1930s. Much later, on April 1, 1994, a change in state law made cityhood unrealistic for Vashon. Largely rural areas no longer could simply incorporate. Instead, a county would have to designate a region as an "Urban Growth Area" before it had that power. On Camano Island, in 2013 some residents again began looking at the possibility of incorporation—but incorporation, of course, does not solve a region's problems. Some Bainbridge Islanders have regretted voting for cityhood in 1990. Meanwhile, other islanders, including some Anderson Island folks, talk about feeling misunderstood by their county administrators.

Vashon Island's commercial hub is the town of Vashon. Burton was the center of activity until about the 1910s or 1920s, but over the years, some of the businesses there relocated to Vashon. A grocery and a few other commercial establishments remain in Burton, but most commercial enterprises on the island are now in the town of Vashon. In the early years of the twentieth century, when Vashon and Burton were not so different in size or importance, intense rivalry between them was strong enough that people talked of the imaginary Mason-Dixon Line between them. Vashon was oriented to the north and Seattle, while Burton's ties favored Tacoma.

Why did Burton lose pride of place to the centrally-located *inland* town of Vashon? Burton's location on the water is an advantage, but this community is not on the way to anywhere. Had a canal been dug across the land bridge between Vashon and Maury Islands in the early days as was suggested, however, Burton could have gained a lot of commerce.

As the crow flies, the town of Vashon is not far from the water. Vashon Landing, about a mile east, served the early community. From this boat landing came a steep uphill slog to the flat farmland encircling Vashon, but a horse and wagon could make the trip. Moreover, Vashon Landing was convenient from both Tacoma and Seattle. Today all that is left of Vashon Landing are some pilings in the water, though the beachfront once featured a lumber and brick works, a store, post office and, nearby, a cannery.

The town of Vashon did not truly gain significance until automobiles overtook the Mosquito Fleet in importance. The island's primary ferry dock is at the north end, closer to Vashon than to Burton, and with Seattle outstripping Tacoma in importance, Vashon benefited. Another advantage Vashon has is the amount of more-or-less flat land where it is situated, meaning that it was surrounded by farms. As island farming became less important to Washington State's economy, it was easy for the tiny crossroads community of Vashon to expand as entrepreneurs built more buildings along the main streets. Burton, on the other hand, is located in a more hilly area and is interrupted by water. In 1990, King County officials designated Burton as a historic district, for very few other towns still resembled their early twentieth century appearance so closely. But some local residents opposed this, fearing limitations on changes to their property. The county rescinded the designation and Burton remains itself, with no official recognition.

Camano Island's community is, in a way, the mainland city of Stanwood not far from the island. By the time a need came for a community to provide services, the island had a bridge to the mainland and nearby Stanwood could serve islanders. Camano students attend Stanwood High School, even though it is in a different county. Camano does have two small commercial centers nowadays, with restaurants, a small branch library, real estate offices, supermarket and more. The island finally got its own zip code, 98282, in 2000.

Whidbey is exceptional among Puget Sound Islands, as historically it had three leading communities. Oak Harbor to the north and Coupeville in the center both date from the 1850s, while Langley in the south was founded some thirty years later. Local residents incorporated all three towns in the early twentieth century.

Langley and the South Whidbey area attract commuters to the mainland as well as people building vacation retreats or retirement homes. This is a lovely small town beautifully situated on the water, more interesting than its odd description by Carey Quan Gelernter in a 1988 *Seattle Times* article as "a vision of tasteful yuppie quaint."[6] Heading north from Langley along the island's long, narrow stretch, one crosses Whidbey's Mason-Dixon line. Beyond, at the head of Penn Cove, is Coveland, the original county seat but nowadays little more than an area's name. Nearby is Coupeville, now celebrated as the historic center of the island, the county seat, and a tourist center, like Langley. Both communities have maintained an old-town atmosphere.

The presence of Naval Air Station Whidbey Island dominates Oak Harbor and the northern part of Whidbey Island. Oak Harbor is by far the largest city on Whidbey with a population in 2010 of 22,075, grown this large because of the navy base. Before World War II, Oak Harbor, Coupeville. and Langley were similar in size, each having between 250 and 350 residents, but during the 1940s, Oak Harbor's population tripled. It has continued to grow, as it supplies services to a sizable military community. Oak Harbor today is a commercial center featuring the kinds of businesses seen throughout America, from small gift shops and an independent bookstore to Walmart.

North of Whidbey Island is Anacortes. Though it lies on Fidalgo Island, this city exists in visitors' minds as the mainland departure point for islands: Guemes and the San Juans by ferry and Whidbey via the Deception

Pass bridge. Amos Bowman, who founded a city and named it for his wife Anna Curtis Bowman, arrived in 1876. He publicized the new city and its advantages, boosting Anacortes as the obvious western terminus for the transcontinental railroad then being planned to cross the northern states. Booklets and pamphlets appeared praising Anacortes as "The Great Railway Terminal of Puget Sound" and such. At least one company placed advertisements in the New York press touting Anacortes and its possibilities.[7] Anacortes' population grew from two hundred to two thousand. The failure of railroads to make the city a major terminus and the 1893 national economic collapse led to bank failures, though. Mills closed and many businesses shut their doors. After a few tough years, Anacortes slowly recovered, and other industries came. The city later had to reinvent itself with the decline of the extractive resources, timber and fish, that had been its economic backbone.

Though Anacortes has a smaller population than Oak Harbor, it feels more like a city because of its large and historic mercantile and industrial area. The approach to the city does traverse one of its least lovely parts, the very commercial Commercial Avenue, but one can drive to the small boat harbor to see the memorial there to those who have died at sea, or to Old Town or to the viewpoint at Cap Sante Park. And one of the loveliest parks in the islands lies in Anacortes: Washington Park on a peninsula at the western end of the island. Fidalgo is the most urban island in Puget Sound, but it has an island ambiance if one looks for it.

Island life has appealed to people because of its small-town flavor. For a time after World War II, Vashon, Bainbridge, Whidbey, San Juan, and Orcas claimed all or most of these: a grocery, a hardware store, an auto mechanic, fuel dealer, clothing shop, shoe store—often including shoe repair—a dime store, movie theater, bowling alley and a few restaurants. Residents could buy cars, household appliances or furniture on the islands. In those days, people could also scrounge for useful goods at the local dump, so that it almost seemed to become a social center. Doctors and dentists were on the islands, too, but for hospital care one needed to go to the mainland.

Nowadays, the auto dealerships, shoe stores and dress shops are mostly gone. Still found except on the smaller islands are libraries, doctors and dentists, pharmacies and on San Juan, Whidbey and Fidalgo Islands, hospitals. School systems often are the largest island employers, and shops catering to tourists have become more prominent in recent decades. The grocery store—these days a supermarket on the larger islands—might be the island's meeting place. Sometimes it is the post office and elsewhere it can be the recycling center. On Anderson Island, it is the historical museum.

Some very small islands are island-wide compact communities. In 1869, Pennsylvania farmer Anthony Williamson filed the first claim for Day Island on the edge of Tacoma. People appeared, camped, dug clams, and built simple homes. Developer Eugene Church bought the island in 1907, built a narrow road even today not wide enough for cars to pass, set out lots, put in a water system and an extremely short drawbridge to the mainland. People came and constructed summer cabins or permanent homes. Most of these early buildings are gone or extensively remodeled by now, but some tiny cottages on tiny lots sit on the island along with larger houses and apartment buildings. Nestled between homes is the privately-owned Day Island Yacht Harbor, the only island business today. Perhaps because Day Island is on the edge of a major urban area, it became fully developed early .

Developers planned communities on other small islands. One is Gedney, or Hat Island, about two-thirds of a square mile in area and midway between South Whidbey Island and the mainland city of Everett. The island's passenger boat takes forty-five minutes to reach the island. A development company bought the island in 1961, built simple roads, cleared, and graded land to create lots, advertised plans for a marina, golf course, swimming pool and airstrip and offered homesites for sale. Before the company failed in the late 1960s, people had bought many lots and built a few houses. Island property owners took over management of the island and in the years since then have created a volunteer fire department and improved the water system and marina. Islanders have grumbled about Snohomish County property taxes because of having to pay for road improvements even though their island, which has no public roads, sees no benefit. This island's residents exemplify a pattern seen on some other islands, too, with most owners presently spending only weekends and summer vacations there. A community survey in 2012 found that only about eight percent of Hat Islanders—about forty people—had their main residence on the island.[8]

Far south, near Harstine Island, is Treasure Island, less than one-sixth of a square mile in area. Officially, this is Reach Island. In 1905, Alfred

W. Zizz, who had changed his last name from Showengerdt, bought the island for nine hundred dollars. He lived there with his family until 1952, when he sold the island to Pope & Talbot. The company platted the island, dubbing it Treasure Island, building a bridge, and offering sixty-foot and wider lots for sale. Today, this is a pleasant residential community, managed by the Treasure Island Community Club. Raft Island, a few miles west of Gig Harbor, is also private. Just less than one-third of a square mile in area, it had 489 residents in 2000. It was developed in 1959 with a bridge and platted lots. In addition to residences, the island hosts All Saints Camp and Retreat Center, which houses various week-long camp sessions and makes its central building available to islanders for community gatherings. Herron Island sits in Case Inlet just east of Harstine Island. About half a square mile in area and with 152 residents in 2000, it is accessible only by ferry, and as on other private islands, the general public is not welcomed except by permission. An interesting feature of Herron Island is its welcome to deer, many of which graze here so that any resident who wants a garden needs a fence. A fenced community garden area sits in the middle of the island.

One can also find private islands in the San Juans. Crane Island, 220 acres between Orcas and Shaw, has fewer than ten full-time residents now, though electricity, telephone service and water are all available. Crane also has an airstrip, as do some other private San Juans without ferry service, including Center Island, a 178-acre bit of land near Decatur Island. Obstruction Island, between Orcas and Blakely Islands, is only about 218 aces in size. In the 1960s, an ownership group had the island divided into relatively large waterfront lots, while saving the interior as common land. Thus, just forty-eight lots exist. Structures—not always houses—have been built on about two-thirds of them. Obstruction Island does not have scheduled boat service, but it is not far across Puget Sound waters from its north end dock to an Orcas Island road.

Our island communities continue to evolve. One type that seems to be dying out is the group of people who live on boats. A few years ago, these people were at the center of debate on Bainbridge Island, where about twenty liveaboards sat moored in Eagle Harbor. People have lived on boats here for at least a century but concerns about sewage disposal and opposition from homeowners to the sometimes-unsightly vessels have led to controversy. Up to sixteen liveaboards are now allowed in

Eagle Harbor but owners must pay new, though affordable, fees. Other communities, such as Anacortes, Roche Harbor and Oak Harbor, also host liveaboards. Though they have been controversial, their presence helps guarantee harbor security.

Island living can create problems, perhaps most seriously, fire. When fire breaks out on an island, only local firefighters and equipment are quickly available, and a good water source to fight the flames may not be nearby. One could cite many examples of fires that have destroyed island homes and community businesses. In July 1920, a fire started by a spark in an Oak Harbor blacksmith shop wiped out half a dozen businesses in the heart of the town despite local folks fighting the blaze with a bucket brigade. This widespread destruction spurred creation of a simple fire department. After the fire, Oak Harbor's new commercial buildings arose a little to the west. Historic buildings seen in the city center today date only from 1920.

The small community at Orcas Landing suffered a destructive fire in early July 1949. Fire probably broke out under the store next to the dock. News only got to the fire department in Eastsound when a Shaw Islander telephoned to report seeing a fire across the channel, and it took half an hour for volunteer firemen to arrive. The conflagration destroyed two warehouses and the largest store on the island, and the fire leaped the ferry dock, but men kept nearby gasoline storage tanks, houses, and the Orcas Hotel safe. For two days the dock remained closed, foot passengers being shuttled to Shaw Island to catch the ferries. The hotel meanwhile catered to people stuck on Orcas with their cars. Later rebuilt, a well-stocked store operates at the dock today.

On Vashon island, a 1977 fire wiped out three main-street businesses in the town of Vashon on the night before Halloween. Inadequate water mains impeded the firefighters. Among the businesses destroyed was Vashon's only pharmacy. Though the fire obliterated many records, customers paid these bills anyway. Don Green moved out of his upholstery shop nearby so that a temporary drugstore could open there. This was just one of many offers of space, an indication of islanders' dedication to their community.

Fire demolished six main street businesses in Friday Harbor on May 9, 2002, and crews came from Lopez and Orcas Islands to help fight the blaze. Eleven years later, on August 17, 2013, another Friday Harbor fire destroyed a restaurant and several additional offices in its building. After

both fires, worry centered on relocating affected firms—people even offered tents—and how residents whose jobs were now gone could get along.
Employment opportunities on San Juan Island are scarce.

Fire equipment is important for isolated islands. Herron and Hat
Islands, which rely on boat service, both house fire engines to protect their
small populations. As part of its equipment, Anderson Island Fire and
Rescue bought a new fireboat in 2005, built to island firefighters' specifica-
tions to be fitted out as a rescue boat, too. This Anderson Island boat has
helped fight blazes on mainland shores as well as on the island.

Island life has changed immeasurably since the days of early settlement, when the many small communities on island shorelines were centers of commerce that served nearby residents. It is worth remembering
the many once-bustling neighborhoods on our islands which now are little
but names—Cedrona on Fox Island, Seabold on Bainbridge, Mabana on
Camano, San de Fuca on Whidbey, Dewey on Fidalgo Island, Argyle on
San Juan Island, Olga on Orcas and many others. Islanders know these
names, and one will hear, "Oh, I live at Maxwelton" (Whidbey) or "Rolling
Bay" (Bainbridge) or "Doe Bay" (Orcas). Therefore, these places remain
communities but what they feature are residences, with few extra amenities. Perhaps still remaining is a store or a church, such as the lovely
Congregational chapel at Sylvan on Fox Island. It was built in 1900 just
above the shore and survives today as a wedding chapel while a larger, more
centrally located, and newer church building serves the congregation.

Yet just as islanders identify their own part of an island—"I live at
Ballow" (Harstine Island)—their entire island is also their community.
People might not say, "I live on Fidalgo" or "Whidbey" but rather "south of
Anacortes" or "in South Whidbey." Folks living on Maury Island may not
claim to be Vashon Islanders. All residents also identify with their entire
island, though. Today, each piece of land in Puget Sound, except possibly
Whidbey, is an island-wide community. How different this is from the age
of the pioneers, when it was easiest to travel to a community across an
island by taking a boat—perhaps by way of the mainland.

11 | Mosquito Fleet Days

Boats are essential for people who live on islands. Native Americans in Puget Sound country were skilled both at building canoes and at guiding them through the waters. The first white settlers on the islands came by boat and they often chartered Native American canoes and paddlers, because these were available, and the paddlers were proficient. They knew how to handle local tides and currents, and the boats were safe. Then, as more and more people populated the islands and built the cities that sit on the mainland shores, the number of boats grew and grew. Skilled settlers built rowboats. Regular steamer routes and schedules appeared, and the boats which served the communities of the Sound became known as the Mosquito Fleet, because, went the claim, they swarmed all over the Sound like mosquitoes. The boats' day in the sun lasted until the automobile began dominating transportation. Then, ferries that could carry motor vehicles displaced the Mosquito Fleet.

Several books, mostly copiously illustrated, describe Mosquito Fleet vessels. This story, though, will also emphasize the places the boats served. The vessels, however, from the very first one, the *Beaver*, to the one remaining active today, the *Virginia V*, played a crucial role in island history. Island communities could not have existed without the Mosquito Fleet.

Most settlers on the islands in the early days used boats as a matter of course. When the trip was short, settlers would row across the water entertainment. Rowboats were everywhere. In fact, for ears that the McNeil Island prison operated, most inmates ... the island by rowboat. A guard experienced in boatbuilding structed a sailboat for prison use after a few years, and in 1911, a prison shipyard began operation.

Early settlers looked for land that would be accessible from the water. Cliffs or steep hillsides above the shore are common on the islands, meaning that a relatively flat plain with easy access to a suitable spot for a boat landing could require diligent searching. When vessels that did not have a shallow draft appeared, the search became more difficult, for where the land is flat as it meets the sea, the seabed is apt to be close to the surface.

Most of the named island communities are on or near the shore. These were established long ago and some have few if any residents now. A number of these sites, like Vashon Landing, are marked today only by pilings in the water where boats once docked. At other one-time landings, nothing indicates the once-frequent boat presence. Some communities used only a float, not a pier, and people would row out to the float to meet the boats that came. Sometimes boats stopped at a landing only when flagged by someone ashore. One important stop was Ebey's Landing on Whidbey Island. It was not well-protected, but it was just a short downhill walk from some of the best farmland in Puget Sound country and from there one could go directly to Victoria or Port Townsend.

The first Hudson's Bay Company vessel brought to the Sound, the sidewheeler *Beaver*, worked ferrying men and supplies to where they were needed. During those years, some boats on Puget Sound depended on sails, others on steam. Under sail, the *Beaver* crossed the Atlantic and rounded South America before arriving in the northwest in 1836. Fitted with engines after the voyage, she was the first boat on the Sound to run on steam, not wind power, and the abundant wood from nearby forests provided her fuel. The *Beaver* was not fast but was reliable, though she had a strong appetite for wood. She toiled in Puget Sound country for half a century. Among her varied duties was transporting Britons to San Juan Island during their Pig War confrontation with Americans. Seventeen years after the *Beaver* came to Puget Sound, the first American-owned boat, the *Fairy*, appeared, a sidewheeler like the *Beaver*. She was so small, though, that she arrived in Puget Sound atop a lumber schooner.

The sidewheeler *Eliza Anderson* was the boat that gleaned the leading reputation for service on the Sound in the early years of settlement. She plied the Sound waters for some thirty years. Built in Portland, when she appeared in 1858, her large size—140 feet in length—impressed people. She carried cattle and sheep as well as people, and the mail. Her best-known route was between Olympia and Victoria, with several stops including Port Madison on the way. Feeder routes took passengers and cargo from the various islands to the major ports to meet steamers like the "*Old Anderson*," to use the nickname she acquired.

One singular vessel in Puget Sound waters during the late nineteenth century was another sidewheeler, the *Politkofsky*, a steam-powered gunboat built in Sitka in 1866 for defense in Russian Alaska. She became American after the Russians sold Alaska to the United States in 1867, and George Meigs, Port Madison mill owner, bought her in 1869. His company ran the boat to transport people, cargo and to tow other vessels. This was a Mosquito Fleet vessel that had no regular schedule, nor were her stubby lines particularly beautiful. People living all around the Sound saw her as she ran here and there and they affectionately called her the *Polly*. She retired in the 1890s and spent her final days in Alaska where she lay at port as a barge during the Gold Rush.

Delivering goods and transporting people to and from the islands, steamboats played a major role in island economies, which woodcutting and fishing dominated in those early years. Docks on small islands could be significant for steamboats because of the cordwood stacked nearby. When the boats began to use diesel fuel, this market shrank, but by then the wood supply on the islands, which had diminished rapidly, was almost gone. Oil largely fueled the Mosquito Fleet by the mid-1920s, though tugs still took rafts of logs to sawmills.

Boats made deliveries to small islands. Often, residents relied on boats that carried groceries. For some time, the *Otter* stopped once a week at Johnson's Landing on the north end of Anderson Island so that people could do their shopping on the boat.[1] When Gus and Emma Carlson opened a store on the southern part of the island in 1914, their merchandise came by boat, and later the Carlsons began delivering goods to some of their customers the same way. Note that some vessels, not only canoes and rowboats, could run right up onto the shore. Sternwheelers could come in close and drop a ramp on the beach. As more and more docks appeared in the late nineteenth century, fewer islanders had to row out to a float or a boat to pick up their goods.

Along with the Mosquito Fleet, lighthouses played a crucial role in the development of commerce in Puget Sound country. As sea-borne trade grew, darkness, bad weather, smoke from fires, tides, pilot inexperience and error led to accidents, and to minimize these, Congress authorized the establishment of lighthouses in Washington State waters. Ten have operated on the islands, the first, on isolated mid-channel Smith Island, beginning service in 1858. Lighthouses appear on the outer rim of the San Juan Islands. The northernmost island of the chain, tiny Patos Island, has a light. Turn Point Lighthouse is on Stuart Island at the easternmost point of the archipelago. Lime Kiln and Cattle Point Lighthouses are on San Juan Island's western and southern shores and Burrows Island Light is on the island of that name just west of Fidalgo Island. Other lighthouses have guarded Admiralty Inlet: Marrowstone Point Lighthouse, on the extreme northeast tip of that island, Admiralty Head Lighthouse on a point just north of Whidbey Island's Coupeville ferry dock and Bush Point Lighthouse farther south on Whidbey. The final island lighthouse, much to the south, sits at Point Robinson, the easternmost point of Maury Island. Lighthouses appeared on the mainland, too.

The Coast Guard decommissioned Admiralty Head Light in 1922. With steamships having replaced sailing ships, this light no longer seemed necessary. Starting in the late 1950s, the others all began automatic operation, most recently Point Robinson in 1978. All these lighthouses can still be admired except for Smith Island's, a victim of erosion. That light was abandoned in 1957, with a new light and weather instruments installed on a fifty-foot steel tower, 250 feet away. The original lighthouse remained, housing equipment, but finally fell into the sea in 1998.

The keepers of these lighthouses were islanders, though perhaps temporarily. Ida Lee's family lived for several years on Stuart Island, where her father was the Turn Point Lighthouse keeper. The children attended a one-room school and family members had to be self-sufficient. Later they moved to Maury Island, where Ida's father was stationed at the Point Robinson Lighthouse from 1939 to 1944. She remembered the sidewalk there, because the keepers' children roller-skated on it. The family found Maury less isolated than Stuart, and a summer job for the children was picking berries in the Vashon Island fields. At that time, Karen Musselman's grandfather, Jens Pedersen, was also a Point Robinson lighthouse keeper. She remembers following him around but said that she would disappear if he started the generator, because "I knew they were going to eat me."[2]

Some lighthouses are museums now. Even the lovely Fresnel lens in the Point Robinson lighthouse is an anachronism today. It is beautiful and quite usable, still sitting on its long-time perch, but a LED mounted just outside the building has assumed its duty. The Fresnel lens remains the new light's backup.

Lights not in lighthouses have operated on the islands, and some continue in use today, for example at Sandy Point, east of Langley on South Whidbey Island, and on tiny Eagle Island between McNeil and Anderson Islands. Just as these lights on the Sound have been automated, so have the foghorns, which can now be activated by ships passing nearby. We must remember that the Mosquito Fleet did not have the benefits of signal lights and horns in the early days.

The Mosquito Fleet included many kinds of boats—old, new, long, short, fast and slow. Some boats had special functions, for example, carrying the mail. Coupeville had mail service before 1870, when the *Mary Woodruff* stopped there on her weekly trips between Seattle and Bellingham. Gaining a contract from the post office could keep a boat operator in business. Some boats, built for speed, transported only passengers. Yet others would take almost anything and regularly moved people, mail, and cargo. Grocery boats with more or less regular schedules helped make island life practical. What is important about the boats is whatever their length, form of propulsion, rate of speed, capacity and all the rest, they could do the job.

Once steam replaced sails, schedules for regular service were possible, but boats could not always keep to these schedules. The Orcas Hotel at that island's ferry landing owes its start to Mosquito Fleet boats that never arrived. William E. Sutherland had the hotel built and by 1905 passengers stranded at the dock could wait in comfort.

Boat service would vary, of course, dependent upon tides and weather and sometimes even on a captain's fancy. When rival companies served the same route, captains might stage impromptu races. Two separate companies put the *Vashon* and the *Burton* on the Tacoma-Quartermaster Harbor run. The two vessels proved equal in speed. Many races ensued—attracting passengers but also leading to minor collisions and a price war. In 1907, a new boat, the *Magnolia*, replaced the *Burton*, and the war continued, culminating in a battle fought with clams. The *Magnolia* was picking up a cargo of sacks of clams at Dockton when the *Vashon* arrived and challenged her. *Vashon* crewmen ripped the sacks open, and the two crews pelted each other with clams until all the clams were back in Quartermaster Harbor. Various other Mosquito Fleet boats that shared routes sometimes raced each other, for example the *Fairhaven* and the *Skagit Chief* serving Whidbey Island.

Mosquito Fleet boats stopped at many places on the islands and a boat's arrival was an important part of a community's day. Farmers with goods to ship to market would have to plan their work with the boat schedule in mind, for stops were brief, though fairly regular. People would walk to the dock to catch a boat, to welcome friends, or just say hello to a boatman. Others would amble that way because the boat's arrival was the high point of a tiny hamlet's day. Friends and neighbors would gather at the dock if only to say hello to each other and to the boat's crew.

In the late 1800s and early 1900s the larger, better-populated islands had docks at many of the communities along the water, while smaller islands might or might not have had actual docks. In the South Sound, several docks served Anderson Island, including one at Johnson's Landing on the north end and another at Vega, on Oro Bay. Nearby McNeil Island, home to many early settlers, had one along Pitts Passage on its west and others at Still Harbor on the east and Bee on the south shore, serving the prison area.

Harstine Island residents depended on floats, not docks, and some boats would stop if signaled. Even the mail was delivered to a float. Fox Islanders cheered when Sylvan, the leading community on their island, got a float with a runway—we would call it a walkway—in 1901 and people no longer had to row to a float to catch a steamer. A few years later came a dock with a store built upon it.

Among the more-than-thirty stops on Vashon were Vashon Landing, Manzanita, Burton, Portage, Dockton and Magnolia Beach. Some boats that stopped at Colvos Passage docks went to Tacoma while others headed for Seattle. Thanks to boat service, a number of prosperous Tacoma families built summer homes on Maury and southern Vashon, while Seattle folks generally built farther north.

Nels Christensen, a homesteader at Lisabeula on Vashon's west side, began the West Pass Transportation Company and had a succession of boats named Virginia built in or near Lisabeula. During the 1920s, the *Virginia V* had a regular route between Seattle and Tacoma via Colvos—or West—Passage, serving places both on Vashon's west side and the Kitsap County mainland. The boat still carries the name "Lisabeula" on its name-plate to indicate the vessel's original home port.

Bainbridge Island also had thirty or more landing sites, from Agate Pass at its far north to South Beach along the southern shore near the route of the Seattle-Bremerton ferry. At the end of the nineteenth century, Ports Blakely and Madison on the east side of Bainbridge were busy while Eagle Harbor, today's center of commerce, saw traffic only growing slowly. The tiny Eagle Harbor community of Winslow, then called Madrone, wanted regular boat service to Seattle, so local residents met this need by build-ing their own steamer. Women raised money by holding dances and oth-er events, and experienced builders in the area constructed the vessel in 1901. The boat, named *Eagle* after Eagle Harbor, traveled to various ports on the Sound but only briefly served her community because a 1903 fire of unknown origin destroyed her at her Bainbridge pier. By 1909, though, "Eagle Harbor is known all over the world among shipping men as the safest harbor on the Coast, and there are no less than fifty steamers and sailing vessels at anchor repairing, loading or waiting for a charter," wrote Albert E. Parker.[3]

On Whidbey Island, Mosquito Fleet stops included Freeland, Greenbank, Coupeville, San de Fuca, Oak Harbor, Ebey's Landing, Keystone, Clinton, Langley, and probably other communities, too. In Langley the original dock, built in the early 1890s at the middle of town, proved too prone to storm damage, so town founder Jacob Anthes con-structed a new one around the shoreline bend to the southeast, in a more protected spot. The U-shaped dock had space for warehouses both on the shore and at its outer section where passengers boarded. This unusu-al structure eventually became unsafe. Its replacement, shaped more like a backwards question mark, now encloses moorage slips for about thirty to forty boats.

Whidbey routes evolved, and not all the communities mentioned above had regular service throughout the Mosquito Fleet era. Some places, like Monroe's Landing on the north side of Penn Cove, saw occasional steam-ers rather than scheduled stops. At the other extreme, boats from Seattle came to Coupeville every day, at least during the summer. Different boats serving Whidbey Island headed for Bremerton, Tacoma, Seattle, Everett, Victoria, Vancouver and the San Juan Islands. An important route included Utsalady on Camano Island, thus connecting Island County's two large islands. Utsalady, as Camano Island's earliest white settlement, had boat service early on. Other communities building docks on Camano which attracted regular service were Camano City in 1908 and Mabana in 1913. Mosquito Fleet service to Camano City ended, though, when the dock fell apart in 1923, while boats continued to stop at Mabana until 1936.

On Fidalgo Island, stops appeared at Munk's Landing on March Point and on the south shore community now known as Dewey, near Deception Pass. But the center of commerce developed at Anacortes, which became a major Mosquito Fleet stop because express steamers and ocean-going ships called in there. By the 1870s, steamboats even stopped at Guemes Island, too, so rowing a boat was no longer the only way a resident could get to Anacortes across the narrow channel.

Mosquito Fleet boats served the San Juan Islands, with many stops on the larger islands. On Orcas, among the places where boats stopped were the site of the current ferry terminal at Orcas Landing plus West Sound, Deer Harbor, Eastsound, Doe Bay, Olga, and Newhall—later known as Rosario—with Eastsound the most heavily patronized.

The main stops on Lopez Island were Lopez Village along the west coast, Port Stanley in the northeast, and Richardson on the south shore. On San Juan Island, Roche Harbor and Friday Harbor had the main landings, but Argyle, not far south of Friday Harbor, was also an important stop in the early days. Vessels of the Puget Sound Navigation Company, organized in 1898, sailed to the San Juan Islands and several mainland ports. The firm began a rise to prominence early in the twentieth century, buying up small, independent lines. This is significant, because the company, better known as Black Ball, later turned to car-carrying ferries and in the 1930s and 1940s dominated Puget Sound ferry service.

Some steamers had regular stops at floats or docks on the smaller islands in the San Juans, including Thatcher on Blakely Island and Urban on Sinclair Island. These landings and Decatur, Stuart and Waldron Islands had postal service by boat. Most of the Mosquito Fleet boats that came to the San Juans also called at Port Townsend, Bellingham, or Anacortes. Only in 1883, more than a decade after the first white settler came to Lummi Island, did the first commercial boat serve that island. A steamboat added a stop on the island to its trips between Seattle and New Westminster, B.C. Emma Tom Smith told of how her mother used to travel from the Lummi Reservation on the mainland to Bellingham. She would canoe across to Lummi Island and then catch a Mosquito Fleet boat to the mainland city.[4]

Often, a general store opened for business at a boat landing, as this was a prime location for receiving merchandise as well as a logical place for local residents to purchase a needed item on their way home. Sometimes a post office would be open there, too, perhaps in the store. In a few places, a general store remains at the site of an island landing to this day, as on Guemes Island, near its current ferry dock. At the Orcas Island ferry dock and one-time Mosquito Fleet landing, a post office and store as well as the hotel have long been in business.

Here are a few Mosquito Fleet schedules. From 1908 to 1917 the *Rosalie* operated overnight trips between Seattle and Bellingham. In 1912, on the northbound voyage, her departure from Seattle came at midnight. The first stop, at Port Townsend, was scheduled for four a.m. The boat then continued, touching in at Smith Island, Richardson, Argyle, Lopez, Friday Harbor, Roche Harbor, Deer Harbor, West Sound, Orcas, Eastsound, Rosario, Olga and Anacortes, in that order, arriving in Bellingham at 3:30 p.m. Puget Sound Freight Lines also operated a steamer, the *Mohawk*, on the Sound. A 1929 schedule shows Monday-Saturday service with one daily round trip between ports in the San Juans and Bellingham, sailing on to Seattle on three of those days. In addition, the company offered summer Sunday round-trip excursions from Bellingham. Excursion boats became popular throughout the Sound in the early twentieth century, and among the many special Sunday trips was a 1903 "Grand Excursion" from Tacoma to Shelton by way of "McNeils Island."

Not all the marine transportation was legitimate. Smuggling people and goods from Canada to the United States via the islands by fast boat happened all too often. Early on, when smugglers were bringing in Chinese men, a boat wrecked on the Camano Island shore in 1896 contained more than one hundred pounds of opium apparently meant for these workers. Liquor was cheaper in Canada than in the United States, so some boatmen sneaked it across the border, often to sell to Indians. Smugglers even brought wool across the border in the nineteenth century, for in the United States it fetched a higher price than in Canada. Thus, bales of wool somehow came to the San Juan Islands, and island sheep gained a questionable reputation as the best wool-producers in America. Later, when prohibition became the law of the land in 1920, more liquor, still legal in Canada, entered the U.S. on speedy rumrunners. More recently, cocaine and other illicit drugs have been smuggled through the San Juans.

All boaters, whether lawful or not, needed to learn their routes well, since they might find a sudden fog enveloping their vessel. Accidents did occur, especially in fog or darkness when boats collided, when something went wrong and fire broke out, or when a storm suddenly blew in. Over the years, innumerable vessels, from fishing boats to pleasure craft, have grounded or overturned. Often, but not always, crew and passengers have survived. Island boaters have rescued many boat passengers, and for many years the United States Coast Guard has not been too far away.

For islanders, accidents, and loss of life on the water were all too possible, perhaps comparable in some ways to today's automobile accidents. Probably the best-remembered accidents involving the boats that served the Puget Sound islands were the sinking of the *Dix* in 1906, the *Tolo* in 1917 and the *Calista* in 1922. The *Dix*, a somewhat top-heavy vessel built in 1904 and just over one hundred feet long, usually operated on the run between downtown Seattle and Alki Point in West Seattle. This journey did not include the more open waters of the Sound. The *Dix* was replacing a boat on another route on Nov. 18, 1906, however, heading from Seattle to Bainbridge Island's Port Blakely. Once the boat left the city pier, the captain turned the wheel over to the mate, as tradition dictated, to go among the passengers to collect their fare.

It was evening and the sky was dark. Soon the *Dix* approached the much larger steamboat, *Jeanie*. The mate unexpectedly turned the *Dix* in the wrong direction and the two vessels collided, the *Dix* sinking almost immediately. No one knows exactly how many people died in the sunken vessel: at least thirty-nine, probably about forty-five, for some may not have bought tickets. Thirty more people survived. It became apparent after the accident that the Dix's inexperienced mate was not licensed to run such a vessel. He died in the crash and received blame for the disaster, but the captain, who had overall responsibility, found his career destroyed. For the Port Blakely community, home of most of the victims, this was a devastating tragedy.

Captain H. B. Lovejoy's company built the *Tolo*, originally an eighty-eight-foot-long steamboat named *Camano*, in Coupeville for the

Coupeville to Everett route, which included stops at intermediate ports on Whidbey and Camano Islands. Remodeling in 1910 lengthened the boat to 108.9 feet. In 1915, the Kitsap County Transportation Company bought her and renamed her. The *Tolo* was en route from Seattle to Bainbridge Island on October 5, 1917, when in the dark and fog off the southernmost point of the island the *Tolo* and a tugboat collided. As soon as possible, the *Tolo*'s captain saw some of the passengers into his vessel's lifeboat. The tugboat and a nearby steamer, the *Kennedy*—responding to a distress call from the tug—rescued others. Of the fifty-three passengers and eight crew, four people died.

Whidbey Island's *Calista* was making her regular run from Oak Harbor to Seattle on July 27, 1922. The Martinolich Shipyard on Maury Island had built this 140-foot steamer, which could carry 250 passengers. Built for a Whidbey Island firm and named for a Whidbey pioneer, the *Calista* spent her life transporting Whidbey Islanders. On the fateful day, she made her usual stops on Whidbey and Camano Islands and carried on towards Seattle with passengers, sacks of mail and some freight. Near the city, the sea was calm but the fog thick. Just off West Point north of Elliott Bay, the fog suddenly lifted to show a large Japanese liner, the *Hawaii Maru*, about to collide with the *Calista*. Hearing the inevitable impact, a nearby tug headed for the crash site. The *Calista* crew helped get people into lifeboats, overloading them, but they held the burden. Japanese sailors also immediately turned to the rescue effort. It took twenty-eight minutes for the *Calista* to sink, and because of this, all sixty-three people on board survived, as did as a couple of crates of chickens, but the mail ended up in Puget Sound.

Freight vessels have occasionally foundered, too. For example, the *T.W. Lake*, transporting lime from Roche Harbor to Anacortes, sank in December 1923, during a powerful gale—and all the boat's eighteen crewmen perished.

More and more pleasure boaters come to the islands but not everyone who takes to boating knows what to do in dangerous water or weather conditions. Also, wakes from fast vessels can swamp small craft. Even Islanders have run into trouble on the water. Vashon Islanders who were young in 1943 still remember the April day when a storm caused power loss and school cancellations. Five high school boys decided to take a boat out into Colvos Passage. The strong wind and great waves capsized the boat and only one of the boys made it to shore. Eighteen years later, an entire Stuart Island family perished on the day after Christmas when their small boat caught fire and disappeared somewhere in the waters between Friday Harbor and Stuart Island. This accident led to renewed concern among many families in the San Juans about safety on the sea.

Even after the Mosquito Fleet years, accidents occur on Puget Sound. Islanders have rescued mariners in trouble and have seen vessels large and small grounded on island shores, though fewer in recent years thanks to improvements in navigational aids. Various commercial vessels from Seattle or Tacoma traveling to the Strait of Juan de Fuca have grounded on San Juan or nearby islands. In the South Sound, the nuclear-powered submarine USS *Sam Houston* landed on a Fox Island beach on April 29, 1988. Ten years later, September 5, 1998, a spectacular grounding occurred on Anderson Island when a Russian cargo ship, the *Monchegorsk*, took the wrong channel and beached itself in Amsterdam Bay just off an island resident's yard. This happened even though an experienced Puget Sound pilot was on the bridge at the time.

Many private boats have grounded over the years. Canoes and rowboats do not offer any threat when they run into a reef or shore, but today's power boats are different. A vessel carrying perhaps 450 gallons of fuel hit a Lopez Island reef in March 2011. Luckily, quick action first by the owner and then a State Department of Ecology response team prevented a fuel spill. An October grounding that same year caused more concern. The barge *St. Elias*, whose load included some thousand pounds of military munitions, ran aground a few miles southwest of Anacortes while being towed to the U.S. Naval facility on Indian Island. Luckily, this did not affect the ordnance carried on the vessel, and the *St. Elias* was soon again underway. Ironically, this grounding took place just a month after the Indian Island base had participated in an exercise to practice responding to oil spills.

Divers have visited underwater grave sites of some ships lost at sea. In Puget Sound fog, the square-rigged sailing ship *America* foundered on rocks along San Juan Island's west coast on August 30, 1914. Under tow at the time and loaded with coal to be delivered to Seattle, she still lies where she sank. Among the items salvaged was the *America*'s figurehead, which now graces Orcas Island's Moran mansion at Rosario. Other vessels, like the *Dix*, will remain undisturbed. No one ever salvaged anything from the boat's deep grave, but in May 2011, divers found what they are sure is the *Dix* on the seabed, some five hundred feet deep off West Seattle. They left her alone.

Boats anchored in the Sound but abandoned are different. They can leak oil and if in shallow water other boats can hit them. Unfortunately, removing derelict vessels is expensive. The fishing boat that burned and sank in Penn Cove in 2013 is one example. Another that year was the tug *Chickamauga*, a wooden-hulled vessel built nearly a century ago, which sank in Eagle Harbor in October. Funded by a fee on pleasure boats, Washington State now works to remove what is left of sunken boats. The state has also begun bringing criminal charges against negligent owners. Removal does not only affect boats. The Washington State Department of Natural Resources has been extracting debris such as anchors and pilings from unused docks, like the pilings one can see off the shore of southwest Bainbridge Island. Creosoted structures, in particular, can harm sea creatures. Some islanders resist removal of the pilings, though, because over the years, sea life has encrusted them and birds roost atop them.

Boating and shipping remain important to the islands, and several island communities have created local port districts, through which elected commissioners can regulate port matters. The earliest island port district was established on South Camano Island in the 1920s. The only Puget Sound island port that serves ocean-going ships is the Port of Anacortes, established in 1926. Other port districts came after World War II. An impetus for creation of the Port of Friday Harbor in 1950 was the desire to construct a small boat harbor for tourists in addition to the fishing boat moorages that had long existed there. On Whidbey Island, the Langley Port District dates from 1961. It, too, originated to provide protected moorage. As the Port of South Whidbey, it now has jurisdiction over various boat and beach facilities on that part of the island. Coupeville's district dates from 1966 and has restored the town's historic dock. Bainbridge Islanders voted in 2011 on whether to create a port district, but they soundly defeated the proposal, three-fourths of the voters saying no. They may simply have opposed creating a new district with taxing power. Not just port districts but marinas serve private boaters, and some state and county parks also provide mooring facilities.

Just as it is impossible to identify a specific date for the beginning of the Mosquito Fleet era, there has been no definite end. Around 1912, a barge under tow began carrying a few automobiles—or horses and wagons—per trip on the first car ferry service across Deception Pass. As the use of automobiles proliferated and islanders came to want to use them on the islands, roads saw improvement and entrepreneurs began to adapt boats so that cars could drive on and off them. The desire for passenger vessels, both at prominent docks and outlying ones, dwindled, finally being almost completely overtaken by ferries that also moved automobiles. In one way, though, the Mosquito Fleet survived, because thanks to redesigning, its vessels continued to operate, now able to carry vehicles as well as foot passengers.

Most historians agree that the last Mosquito Fleet service provided on a regular schedule ended in 1939.[5] By then, well-established automobile ferries served the Sound. However, labor troubles in the depression years stopped those boats several times—while Mosquito Fleet boats still seaworthy could step in temporarily. World War II also provided an impetus for Mosquito Fleet vessels to provide service for commuting war workers. In 1942, George Rickard's *Yankee Boy*, a forty-two-foot cruiser, began service between Vashon Island's Quartermaster Harbor and Tacoma, supplementing the car ferry running between Tahlequah and Point Defiance.

Almost all Mosquito Fleet boats are long gone, but the *Virginia V*, built in 1922, still operates. Her regular run up and down Colvos Passage survived until 1939, later than any other scheduled Mosquito Fleet route. The *Virginia V* has been carefully restored and is designated as a National Historic Landmark. One can ride her now and then on excursions. Historical societies on Bainbridge and Vashon Islands regularly schedule round-the-island trips on the *Virginia*.

The Hat Island boat service also exemplifies the Mosquito Fleet. This small island, between Everett and South Whidbey Island, has more than 250 houses upon it but no automobile ferry service, only a boat for people on foot. Meanwhile, a barge transports cargo to the island, even automobiles. In 1978 some islanders petitioned Snohomish County to take over the passenger service. The vessel only sailed on weekends, but perhaps the county could provide weekday service, too. However, county officials saw the problems nearby counties had with providing ferry service and thus declined to become involved.

While Mosquito Fleet passenger service on Puget Sound faded, commercial boats have continued to move freight. One of these vessels no longer in service is the *Nordland*, built in 1929. Her first job was as the ferry between the Olympic Peninsula mainland and Indian Island, where she ran until the opening of the bridge over the canal in 1952. A new owner, Bob Schoen, took the *Nordland* to the San Juans. Owners changed over the years, but the boat kept running on a charter basis, transporting goods and people to various islands without scheduled ferry service until her retirement in 2007. Using other vessels, her firm, San Juan Ferry & Barge, continues to transport everything from livestock to well-drilling equipment and even small houses. These days, this is one of several companies freighting people and goods around the San Juans, while Outer Island Excursions takes passengers from Anacortes and Orcas Island to some of the smaller islands. Thus, non-boaters can travel to islands in the archipelago that are not served by Washington State Ferries.

In 1906 the *Seattle Mail and Herald* proclaimed, "It is difficult to understand why the people are so ready to build roads and bridges to promote travel and commerce, and are slow to see the advantages and importance of building and operating ferries for the same purpose."[6] This sentiment applies today, a century later. Some have suggested that the Mosquito Fleet was reborn when Washington State Ferries inaugurated passenger-only service in 1990 between Seattle and Bremerton and downtown Seattle and Vashon Island. Three boats used on these runs were built on the islands: the *Tyee*, on Whidbey by Nichols Brothers and the *Snohomish* and *Chinook*, in Anacortes at the Dakota Creek shipyard.

Earlier, the state had considered buying hydrofoils built by Boeing to transport foot passengers to downtown Seattle. When State Department of Transportation officials explained this plan at a Vashon Island meeting in 1977, islanders indicated strong opposition, because they feared that the new service would bring too much island development. When Washington State Ferries began passenger-only service with conventional vessels thirteen years later, Vashon Islanders expressed little anxiety. In 2003, when the state proposed ending this service, islanders objected. In July 2008, King County took over this run and the state sold its surplus passenger boats. It took several years, but two of them finally sold for less than they had cost and headed to Tanzania to provide service between the mainland and its island of Zanzibar. On July 18, 2012, the overloaded *Skagit*, renamed the *Karama Star Gate*, sank during high winds after leaving Dar es Salaam for the island. Apparently, more than one hundred people died, though at least another hundred survived.

More than a century ago, the Mosquito Fleet made it possible for people to live on the Puget Sound islands. Communities arose near island docks, but times change and in the twentieth century motor vehicles began coming to the islands. Yet in recent years some islanders again find passenger boats a quicker and more convenient way to reach their city jobs. Yes, the Mosquito Fleet is rising again.

12 | Rails and Roads

WHEN ONE THINKS ABOUT ISLAND TRANSPORTATION, ferries and bridges automatically come to mind. Once boats began to serve the islands regularly and frequently, needs for transportation *upon* the islands grew. Native Americans and then the European-Americans used trails. These became wider and people used horse-drawn vehicles. A few short railroads appeared, and in the twentieth century, roads for motor vehicles took over, playing a leading role in creating island-wide identities.

By the middle of the nineteenth century, railroads were being constructed across the United States and even played a small role in island history. Before the Civil War, Territorial Governor Isaac Stevens pointed out that a railroad coming from farther east might traverse Fidalgo Island and continue across Deception Pass, then south on Whidbey Island as far as Keystone, which offered the closest water connection to Port Townsend. Ships could meet the railroad either at Anacortes or Keystone. Railroad Engineer Daniel C. Linsley inspected possible northern routes in 1870 and reported that it would be possible to build a bridge across Deception Pass. "It is only a question of time until Port Townsend and Anacortes will be connected by a large railroad ferry," boasted the *Anacortes Progress* in 1890.[1] The railroad furor led to the platting of two towns, Chicago and Brooklyn, in the narrow strip between the western coastline of Whidbey Island and Crockett Lake, for this is where the rail cars would supposedly board ferries to cross the Sound. Supporters even built a causeway across the lake to reach Chicago, and pilings still indicate the site.

By 1890, hoping to extend rail travel from the mainland, investors had rails laid towards Anacortes, and on August 5, the Seattle & Northern Railway made the first rail trip between the mainland and the city's station. Several months later, tracks connected this line with an existing Northern Pacific north-south line, and on November 25, 1890, with much fanfare, Northern Pacific sent a train from Tacoma direct to Anacortes, terminating at the dock site where the Guemes Island ferry lands today. Thus, starting in 1890, the city had rail service connecting to the main lines between Seattle and Vancouver, B.C. This offered passenger travel for many years and was the only railroad ever provided on any of the islands other than short lengths of tracks to industrial sites. In 1891 came an attempt to extend the Anacortes line farther west to Burrows Bay on the west side of the island, but the work remained unfinished. Now, rails no longer reach downtown Anacortes. With the rails gone, the causeway which took the tracks across Fidalgo Bay to city center became the Tommy Thompson Trail, a scenic sea-level walkway. Railroad tracks from the mainland only go as far as March Point, where refinery shipments arrive by rail.

Anacortes once had another rail line, but its train made only one abortive trip. Promoters planned an electric line to connect Anacortes with Fidalgo City, the neighborhood in the southern part of the island that is now called Dewey. Perhaps building this line merely meant the investors could receive land grants, for on what was to be the inaugural journey, March 29, 1891, the trolley car apparently did not have enough power to get up the first hill on the route—about a mile from the Anacortes station—and the enterprise collapsed. Meanwhile, local rails built along Guemes Channel to Burrows Bay served canneries and a mill from the 1890s until well into the twentieth century.

Entrepreneurs also touted rail projects for Vashon and Bainbridge Islands. In 1908, promoters announced a plan for a streetcar line—an electric railroad—from Vashon's north end to Burton and on to the south end of the island. The firm constructing the railroad would also build a power plant and eventually furnish electricity to island homes. Fast boats would run from the island rail terminals to Seattle and Tacoma, and the entire trip between the two cities via Vashon Island would take only fifty-five minutes, claimed the promoters, who also declared that this would be the

fastest way to travel from one city to the other. When the group propos-
ing the Vashon line held a meeting on the island in looking for islanders'
support, the "largest and most enthusiastic group of citizens ever assem-
bled in the history of the island" attended, according to the *Vashon Island
News*.[2] But the railway plan never came to fruition. On Bainbridge Island,
similarly, a real estate man named W. S. Jackson led an effort to establish
a streetcar system linking that island's communities, but this was another
project that failed. Roads, not rails, became the transportation routes and
they developed in a similar way on all the islands.

Travel by wagon was no faster than travel by boat, and water transportation remained central to island life. The early roads, in fact, generally
went from farms to docks and therefore were farm-to-market roads. As
the islands developed, more and more of their farms did not have easy access to a dock, and some roads owe their development to property owners
arranging for a good approach to their acreage.

Whidbey might be the first of the islands to get what could be called a
road. To connect farms in the Ebey's Prairie area, farmers laid out several
short roads that county commissioners approved. By the 1860s, officials
were authorizing roads about thirty-five or more feet wide and assign-
ing property owners to help locate road sites. In addition to farmers'
wagons, by 1866, Whidbey Islanders used buggies on central Whidbey
roads. Some of the pioneer routes on Whidbey Island evolved into today's roads in the Coupeville area. These include Madrona Way along
the beach and Sherman Road heading to the cemetery. One Coupeville
road cut right through a Native American cemetery, remembered Lower
Skagit tribe member Susie Kettle. Jacob Anthes, who founded Langley,
wrote about establishing trails and wagon roads from Langley heading
inland but he also noted that South Whidbey folks felt that county officials in Coupeville resisted development of roads—and schools—in the
island's south end.[3] Until well into the 1920s, road construction plans,
and funding did seem to go mostly to the north half of the island where
more people lived and worked.

Boosters in 1911 were looking forward to the splendid trunk highway
"running the length of Whidbey Island" they hoped would soon be built.
As there were twenty cars in Oak Harbor at the time, islanders felt this
road was surely needed. By 1916, a main road came. Tourist brochures in
the 1920s mentioned the excellent roads on Whidbey Island. The south

end ferry, which a Black Ball Ferry Lines brochure called a "floating bridge," docked at Columbia Beach, and from there it was thirty-one miles to Coupeville and "there is no crowding; the roads are ample, smooth and inviting."[4] Island County—that is, Whidbey and Camano Islands—had 325 miles of paved road in 1935. Finally, in 1967, the current limited access route opened.

Camano Island's first road joined Utsalady Bay and Livingston Bay in 1867 but apparently saw few wheeled vehicles, so perhaps it was but a glorified trail. By the early twentieth century, many roads were being constructed on the island. In 1906, one extended across the island as far as Camano City on the island's west coast. The first car appeared on Camano Island in 1908, and a Camano resident first bought one in 1911. By 1917 a road even extended to Mabana, far to the island's south.

As early as 1866, Kitsap County commissioners ordered that any road in the county terminating at the water should meet a boat landing, indicating that these men understood the need to coordinate water and land transportation. However, Bainbridge Island's first road, which came before Washington attained statehood in 1889, was an inland route joining Port Blakely and Port Madison. Eagle Harbor settlers had to walk to Port Blakely to get their mail until 1890, but once the logging road suitable for horse travel joined the two communities, better postal delivery became possible. Rural free delivery in the United States began around the beginning of the twentieth century, and the first rural mail route on Bainbridge started in 1905, the carrier traveling on horseback.

Until 1912 men on the Bainbridge Island either paid a four-dollar tax or worked two days per year on the roads. In 1910 Winslow Way, now the main commercial street in Winslow, was "barely a road . . . a dusty, crooked track, filled with potholes when it rained," according to Carl Pratt.[5] Between today's ferry dock and the shops on Winslow Way the street crosses a sizable ravine, full of undergrowth and not obvious unless one looks for it, but it was a barrier to early transportation.

By 1921 Bainbridge Island had 140 miles of road, and in 1927 Bainbridge Islanders registered some 1,300 cars. Federal money for Washington State roads came in 1931, with some allocated for a highway connecting Agate Pass and Port Blakely, where the ferry from Seattle then docked. However, there was only enough money to construct a little less than two miles of road, and state funds could not be used because the island then had no designated state highways. This road was intended to become a state high-way crossing a bridge via Agate Pass.

Bainbridge Island's Agate Pass Bridge opened on October 7, 1950, but critics castigated state politicians for not having arranged for better ap-proach roads. The *Bainbridge Review* called them "death-trap thorough-fares." The traffic came, and to protest, some islanders took down road signs. Four years after the bridge opened, a modern highway became the road link between the bridge and the Winslow ferry dock. More and more vehicles sped across the island. For the local Chamber of Commerce, Walt Woodward urged that the new road be limited-access, in order to preclude "a cheapening commercial growth of beer taverns, juke joints, hamburger stands, second-hand car lots and junk yards."[6] Barely a bit of this type of development came, notably one McDonald's fast food outlet. Despite the lack of roadside amenities, by the twenty-first century, congestion, some-times gridlock, has come.

Lila Hannah, born in 1865, grew up on southwestern San Juan Island. She wrote, "Going to the store [in San Juan Village] was by farm wagon in good weather, for in winter there were washouts and bridges went out, roads were poor, and settlers were hopelessly stranded until they could get together and make repairs." Her family lived about eight miles from the store, and her mother would fret about whether their flour would last until they were able to get to town.[7] Road improvements came slowly in the San Juan Islands, where much paving did not come until after World War II.

One scenic road in the San Juan Islands opened surprisingly early. In 1894, hoping to draw tourists, Orcas Islanders built a road suitable for two horses pulling a buggy to the top of 2,409-foot Mt. Constitution. In 1912 the first automobile reached the summit. On nearby Fidalgo Island, the road to the highest point, Mt. Erie, did not come until after World War II. Luckily, W. S. Halpin, the owner of the mountaintop land, had decided not to sell it for development but waited until it could be bought for public access. The local Kiwanis Club purchased it in 1948, and by the early 1950s motorists were enjoying the view from the summit.

In 1877, Lopez Islander C. A. Swift reported that "we have opened over twenty-five miles of road, nearly all of which is passable for loaded wag-ons."[8] And on Lummi Island, until 1906 the only road went from the site of today's ferry dock to Legoe Bay straight across the island. Lengthened that year, it continued around Village Point on the island's west side all the way to Point Migley.

Because the islands were surveyed before much white settlement, many property lines run north-south or east-west, and roads follow this grid when practical. As one travels these roads, the glacial origins of the islands—except the San Juans—becomes clear. Going east or west, one is cutting across the ridges left after the glaciers scoured the land, and the hills can be steep. Try Koura Road or New Brooklyn Road on Bainbridge Island or Bank Road on Vashon Island, but in an automobile, not on a bicycle. Few island roads include long straight sections, almost always because of the terrain. When work was done on Marrowstone Island's East Marrowstone Road, it gained a jog because a resident prevailed upon the work crew to spare a maple tree housing his grandson's tree house.

Starting about 1912, Vashon Islanders and Tacoma businessmen worked for establishment of regular ferry service from the south end of the island to the mainland city. Holding up the project was lack of a road from the proposed island dock site to existing roads.

Islanders raised $6,585 for grading such a road, and King County commissioners authorized construction. Tacomans thought King County officials might have purposely delayed the road project because they did not want to encourage Vashon Island commerce with Tacoma rather than Seattle.

Henry J. Kaiser, later a prominent industrialist known for shipbuilding and auto manufacture, won his first government contract in 1920, calling for laying down eight miles of concrete road on Vashon Island. This stretch of road from the north end ferry dock to the town of Vashon was the first paved road on the island.

Only in the mid-1920s did Dockton, on Maury Island, receive a road connection that was an improvement over the steep track that "none but experienced mountaineers ever attempted to negotiate," wrote Oliver Van Olinda. Helen Puz recalled that when her sister was born on Maury Island in November 1921, the doctor had to get out axe and saw to clear fallen trees from the road before he could drive to Helen's family home to deliver the child. In 1925, the "good road with easy grades" opened, and youngsters living in Dockton could easily get to their high school in Burton by road. Before then, a launch picked them up and carried them across Quartermaster Harbor.[9]

In the early 1930s, the section of the island's current main highway between the intersection at the middle of the island—known as Center—and the south end ferry dock opened. Because this was a county relief measure, unemployed islanders got the road construction jobs. Planning the location for a road along the west side of Vashon Island was a different matter. "Evidently the fact that the [survey] lines run through one man's barnyard, and another man's gooseberry field makes no difference. Apparently, this is as it should be, for the road is a 'farm-to-market' road, and naturally it should live up to its name." So wrote the *Vashon Island News-Record*.[10]

On all islands, it was a big event when the first automobile appeared. The earliest car on Whidbey Island, a Holsman from about 1902, looked much like a buggy—and had no reverse. The first car on San Juan Island probably came in 1905 when Al Coffelt brought a 1903 Orient Buckboard to the island. With motor traffic, speed limits soon came. In Oak Harbor it was twelve miles per hour in the early days of cars.

Fidalgo Island, the gateway to the San Juans, received taxi service in 1907, a horse pulling the cab. The first cars had already come to the island by that time, but it was not until the 1920s that Anacortes had a paved highway. Marrowstone Island's first car, a Gleason, came over by scow in 1910. The first cars came to Bainbridge Island on barges from the Kitsap mainland in 1912, and Dr. Frank Shepard's Model T probably was the island's very first car.

Ruby Walls remembered when cars being brought to Vashon Island traveled as freight on a steamboat. At the island, they were unloaded with ropes and set down on the beach. L. C. Beall received credit for bringing the first car to Vashon, a twelve-horsepower Franklin, in May 1907. By 1915, Vashon Islanders had more than forty cars, but horses and buggies also lasted for some years after cars appeared. As autos came, so did pressure for more and better roads.

On Anderson Island, once Pierce County began providing car ferry service in 1922, cars started coming, but rarely were there places on the island where they could pass. Islanders remembered that though the roads handled the new machines well during summertime, after the autumn rains started not only could a car easily get stuck, but render impassable the narrow road where it stalled. Slowly, Anderson Island roads became paved—but not until the 1960s.

A spurt of road building and paving had come in the 1930s, after Franklin D. Roosevelt created organizations including the PWA, WPA and CCC to help fight the Depression. These agencies, with help from local counties, put people to work improving roads and carrying out other projects. As improvements came, automobiles proliferated, and Mosquito Fleet boats disappeared. By 1941, Vashon-Maury Island had 175 miles of roadways, eight miles of concrete and forty miles oiled.

Today's state highways are the through routes on Bainbridge, Whidbey, and Fidalgo Islands. A very short stretch of state highway sits on Camano Island. Built to different standards, these roads carry more and faster traffic, which is especially noticeable on Bainbridge and Whidbey Islands. Lost is the island ambience. The only traffic lights on Bainbridge Island are along the state highway. In fact, the only traffic lights on any of the islands are on the state highways and in the cities of Anacortes and Oak Harbor. Unlike state highways and so many mainland roads, most island roads encourage moderate, not fast speeds—even for motorists rushing to a ferry dock. We can rejoice at how often roads pass through landscapes that are a joy to look at, whether for the first or the millionth time.

Some roads were never built. For example, an effort began in the late twentieth century to build a bypass around the town of Vashon so that the island's main highway could avoid a stoplight. Merchant opposition apparently doomed the effort.

More and more cars appeared on the islands. One August Sunday in 1927, over eighteen hundred cars crossed the bridge to Camano Island—that was a lot, but contrast this to a *daily* average of over twelve thousand cars in 1992. With the car came automobile accidents. The first person killed on a Bainbridge Island road was seventeen-year-old Patricia O'Connell who was walking along the road at Manitou Beach when a car struck her in June 1930. Witnesses claimed that the girl had suddenly stopped in front of the vehicle to pick up something on the road. Thus, the driver received no blame. On Vashon Island in 1937, eight-year-old Grace Okubo died after a drunken driver hit her. This happened at an intersection along the main highway, and the tragedy generated a campaign by islanders for better traffic control. As a result, the county installed blinking four-way stop lights at the town of Vashon, at Center and in Burton.

In a way, public bus service replaced the islands' Mosquito Fleet stops. A bus route between Utsalady on Camano Island and Stanwood on the mainland began in 1915. Five times a day the bus made the fifty-minute trip, then returned. In 1931 a new bus service began, serving many spots on Camano before crossing to Stanwood. In November 1920, Whidbey Island "auto stage" service began making one daily trip between Oak Harbor and Anacortes, meeting the train to the mainland. Other buses headed south from Oak Harbor to Whidbey's south end dock where people could catch boats heading for Everett. Today, buses serve all of Whidbey Island, from Clinton to Deception Pass and beyond—and riding the bus on Whidbey and Camano Islands is free, paid for by local property taxes.

The first Vashon bus, truly pulled by horse power, took passengers uphill from Vashon Landing to the town of Vashon, not a long trip but tiring because of the steep grade. Later, north-south gas-powered bus service started on Vashon Island, but for a long time, separate lines ran to the north and south ends of the island. Many islanders affectionately remember "Harlan's bus." From 1954 to 1980, Harlan Rosford owned and operated a bus that made three round trips six days a week from Burton to the north end ferry, onto the boat and then to downtown Seattle. Harlan would pick up things like film, medicine and anything else that was not too large. He and his passengers, whether regulars or not, became a friendly community. His operation eventually became part of King County's Metro Transit.

On Orcas Island, the Orcas-Moran State Park Stage Line advertised three daily trips for the summer of 1928, serving the Orcas Landing ferry dock, West Sound, Deer Harbor and Eastsound as well as the park. Such a service would be a boon today to residents and visitors alike. During World War II, Bainbridge Island commuters had some bus service. Kitsap Transit began county-wide operation in 1983. Buses at the dock in Winslow meet the boats from Seattle and travel to many communities on the island and beyond, mainly during commuting hours. One can also prearrange a bus trip to any island location. Some transit routes on various islands have proved unsustainable. For a time in the 1990s, Pierce Transit served Fox Island, but patronage remained low, and the county discontinued the route. Vashon Island's west side briefly had a few runs, but there, too, the ridership was inadequate.

School buses operated on some of the islands in the 1920s, perhaps ear-lier. On all the islands, roads played a role in school consolidation. Once makeshift school buses could reach all an island's communities, central-ly located schools would follow. When consolidation began bringing all Bainbridge Island students to Winslow High School in 1927, the district for a time brought some students to the school by boat.

While buses carried people, trucks moved freight. Delivery trucks handled various products in Anacortes as early as the first decade of the twentieth century. Trucking outfits serving most of the islands were well-established by the 1930s. Two local men started a trucking service on Marrowstone Island early that decade, carrying passengers as well as goods to Port Townsend in their vehicle, a Model A truck chassis upon which they constructed a body for both passengers and freight.

Today, cars and trucks share island roads with bicycles. The islands' rural nature seems perfect for this, except for the hills. Lopez Island's tourist publicity points out that because it is the least hilly of the San Juans, it is the best one for cycling. On the other hand, Bainbridge Island's annual late February bicycle race, Chilly Hilly, has attracted riders for more than forty years. Its title is apt, for the route rises from near sea lev-el to three hundred feet at one point. Recently, Vashon Islanders started a similar yearly bike ride, the Passport to Pain, a seventy-eight-mile course also up and down island hills.

Motorcycles, too, ply the island roads. Some commuters find them a relatively inexpensive way to guarantee a spot on a crowded ferry. Vashon Island is the site of a motorcycle rally each year on a late summer Sunday. The sponsors, Vintage Motorcycle Enthusiasts, have donated funds to Vashon's food bank, and to keep possible troublemakers away, organizers do not widely publicize the event and its scheduled date. Better known is the Oyster Run, a motorcycle rally in Anacortes. Started in the 1980s, when it first came to the city it did not receive much of a welcome. Most of the businesses, in fact, closed when the bikers arrived. Over the years, city and riders alike have embraced the Run, which occurs each year in late September or early October. Whidbey Island also sees many bikers who take the ferry to Clinton and ride the length of the island on their way to Anacortes. Despite the positive features of these rallies, though, some islanders complain about motorcycle noise and the ferry space that masses of them fill.

A highway feature common to every island that has car ferry service is the line of traffic waiting for the ferry or coming off the boat. On Bainbridge Island, a traffic light just off the dock separates the vehicles exiting the ferry, but on Vashon Island, a ferry bringing commuters home from Seattle will generate a line of traffic that extends all the way to the town of Vashon for about five miles, where a four-way stop causes temporary congestion.

People who travel on a ferry by foot want parking spaces on or near the dock. The small islands have little problem providing such parking, but on the larger islands and at mainland docks, the story is different. A large pay lot sits next to the Anacortes terminus of the ferry runs serving the San Juan Islands. Bainbridge Island features a parking lot right next to the dock. Vashon Island has free lots both at north and south ends, but both require uphill trudging. The north-end lot's overflow extends onto road shoulders even higher up the hill. Parking near mainland docks is also a problem. Where should a foot passenger heading for Guemes Island park in Anacortes, for instance, or where in Steilacoom can someone heading to Anderson Island leave his car? Where can someone heading for Bainbridge Island park in downtown Seattle?

Mainland communities and islands alike must cope with automobiles overtaxing ferry dock holding areas and lining up on nearby streets, impacting non-ferry traffic. On sunny summer Friday afternoons, the line at Mukilteo for the boat to South Whidbey Island can extend for blocks. The same happens at Fauntleroy, the West Seattle terminus of the Vashon Island route. Some Fauntleroy residents have long campaigned to move this ferry dock out of their neighborhood, where it is the only Washington State Ferries facility in a residential area, they point out. Dock improvements proposed in 1980 were only partially implemented because of neighborhood opposition. For example, a second ramp for loading automobiles on to the boats was not built.

Just as parking near ferry docks is difficult and in various places expensive, parking in island communities has become frustrating. In the 1940s, the King County Commissioners limited the time one could park in the town of Vashon to two hours. In an island's main community today, most available parking places can be in parking lots, and sometimes, even on weekdays, it is hard to find a place to leave a car. Bainbridge Islanders face this problem in Winslow.

For people who live on the islands today, roads are necessary. They bring people uphill from the dock. Times have changed since island communities all stood on the shore and people traveled between them by boat. Roads bring commerce, visitors, and the amenities of modern life. Buses drive along island roads to take island children to school. Roads have created the ability to travel easily throughout an island, which has had a major role in developing an island identity for residents so that, as we have seen, an island—even a large one—becomes a community.

Do the islands need any more roads? Fred John Splitstone published a little book, *Orcas: Gem of the San Juans,* in 1954, and in his conclusion, talking of the future of the island, he wrote, "In time a road will be built around the North Shore, opening up about seven miles of property well located for summer homes." Splitstone envisioned these cottages all the way from the north of Orcas island to Point Lawrence, the easternmost point.[11] No such road has been built, though. Instead, most of this land remains unimproved, for which we can be thankful.

13 | Leisure

INEVITABLY, THE PUGET SOUND ISLANDS BECAME DESTINATIONS for leisure, and for well more than a century tourism has played a more prominent role than in many nearby mainland communities. For example, William Ristow wrote in August 1986, "During a typical August, upwards of 60,000 people visit the San Juans."[1] Such a tourist influx definitely affects the life of those who live on the islands. It is an important aspect of island economy; residents gain employment in tourism-related work. In addition, islanders also enjoy leisure activities they have created for themselves.

In the late nineteenth century, commercial interests began touting the islands for their holiday potential. Mosquito Fleet vessels made island beach resorts easily accessible, and island population started swelling in the summer months, just as it does now. With the advent of the automobile, more and more vacationers came, and they still come, straining the ferries that serve the islands while bringing coveted tourist dollars.

Over the years, far too many resorts have existed on the islands to name them all. Among the early ones was a tent camp and dance pavilion which opened in 1887 at Glendale, far south on Whidbey Island. Other Whidbey resorts included Still's Park near Coupeville. The inn there, built by 1900, is now called the Captain Whidbey Inn, and it continues to welcome visitors. On Orcas Island, the Norton Inn, which

evolved into today's Deer Harbor Inn, opened in 1891. This beach resort on the southwest arm of the island originally featured canvas tents
erected on wooden floors. The complex had tennis courts and a saltwater
swimming pool as well as a dining room where vacationers praised the
food. Two other inns opened on Orcas in the 1890s: East Sound House,
which evolved into today's Outlook Inn, and West Sound House. On the
southern part of Lopez Island, some eastern Washingtonians began a
summer settlement called Islandale in the first decade of the twentieth
century. This attracted prosperous families who wanted to escape the
summer heat east of the Cascade Mountains, and soon one could read of
a "Yakima colony" or an "Ellensburg colony" at Islandale, but the development did not succeed as its investors had hoped.

Small islands attracted tourists, too. Groups came by boat to Cypress
Island, mainly to Secret Harbor where many rhododendrons grew wild.
An excursion boat could carry eighty people or more to the island. Often,
some of the visitors would camp in the Secret Harbor area for the entire
time the showy flowers bloomed. On Allan Island, less than three hundred acres in area and just west of Fidalgo, a Coast Topographical and
Geodetic Survey camp welcomed visitors who picnicked and had a chance
to examine the scientific instruments and researchers' findings. The island,
now dominated from above by its airstrip, is privately owned, recently by
former Microsoft entrepreneur Paul Allen, who sold it in December 2013.

In the late nineteenth century, Bainbridge island featured small shoreline
resorts as well as the two prosperous mill towns. In about 1900, Malcolm
McDonald began creating the Pleasant Beach Resort on the island's west
shore. He originally pictured this as a place where the people of Port Blakely
could go to relax. He built hotel, pavilion, swimming pool and bathhouse,
and the pavilion became the original location for the Kitsap County fair.
Picture the dances, complete with five-piece band, held all summer. Pleasant
Beach even included a bowling alley, a ballpark and bicycle trails, and sometimes one could watch a prize fight. At one time a board sidewalk extended
between Port Blakely and the resort a little over a mile away.

Summer homes began to appear on Bainbridge in those years.
Restoration Point at the island's southeastern tip was convenient for
Seattle businessmen, and a group of them bought land there in 1891,
then developed it. The Country Club of Seattle continues to hold and
use this retreat, which now includes a nine-hole golf course, but the

club grounds remain private, and it seems sad that the public does not have access to historic Restoration Point, where Captain Vancouver, who named it, came ashore.

Among the attractions that brought visitors to the islands around the turn of the century were the Chautauquas. These gatherings lasted up to a month and emphasized culture as well as pleasure. They featured musical, dramatic, political, and religious presentations in communities across the United States. Named for the Chautauqua Assembly, a camp experience at Lake Chautauqua in western New York State, these retreats brought pleasure and knowledge to people often far from city or university at a time before radio, movies or television could provide such stimulation.

The earliest Chautauqua in Puget Sound country took place on the east coast of Vashon Island in 1885. Three years later the Puget Sound Chautauqua began holding an annual program a few miles farther south on this shore. Though the community there is now known as Ellisport, it began as Chautauqua. The campus, which was the first town platted on Vashon Island, came to include a dock, hotel, many cottages, tents, and a pavilion with seats for perhaps twelve hundred people—all this plus about two miles of beach, including a specified spot for swimming. Chautauqua Post Office opened at the site in 1888. Several companies brought visitors by steamer from Seattle and Tacoma while a Chautauqua was in progress. It would present many kinds of programs on subjects as diverse as temperance and natural history and, in the evenings, entertainment. Several more summer meetings took place here. The Seattle Symphony provided music in 1893. Chautauquas also met here in 1895 and 1900.

A different organization produced a Chautauqua at Maxwelton on Whidbey Island's southwestern shore, first during two weeks in July 1910. The site featured an outdoor amphitheater with bleachers that according to that year's brochure could seat four thousand people. On one of the days, women's suffrage was the main topic. Even famous evangelist Billy Sunday spoke. Not everything worked perfectly. The Chautauqua Ladies' Orchestra of Chicago missed their first scheduled performance because their train was delayed in Oregon.

Bainbridge Island had a Chautauqua site, too, for several years, at Manitou Park on the island's east side. Because the site was closer to Seattle and easier to reach than Maxwelton, the 1911 Puget Sound Chautauqua took place here. Hoping to cater to summer visitors, entrepreneur W. E.

Parker had built a hotel at the site about 1909, and that became the venue, with events planned for thirty days. The property became the home of the boys' school, Moran Academy, in 1914.

Later in the decade, Anacortes held a week-long Chautauqua for a few seasons. By the 1920s, though, the movement was declining in popularity. Excessive snow led to the collapse of the Whidbey amphitheater in 1916 and the Vashon pavilion, declared unsafe in 1919, had to be demolished. Little but memories remained of the Chautauqua movement on the Puget Sound islands, but in 1994 when the Vashon Island School District built a new elementary school a mile or two from the once-vibrant Chautauqua complex, an islander chose the name Chautauqua for the new school, to commemorate that bit of island history.

By the beginning of the twentieth century, local and county fairs were beginning to appear. Island County's first fair was a harvest festival in 1895 sponsored by the County Horticultural Society. Since 1920, the fair has taken place on South Whidbey and today's fairgrounds are on the edge of Langley, where the WPA built an impressive fair building in 1937. It is still in use today, housing an auditorium and offices.

Both counties composed totally of islands have held annual county fairs for many years. San Juan County's fairgrounds are on the edge of Friday Harbor. At the inaugural fair in 1906, farmers exhibited everything from tobacco to chestnuts, along with more usual crops. The fruits on display included pears, quinces, figs, plums and prunes, apricots, grapes, and of course various apple varieties. The fair did not become an annual event for some years, but in 2006 it held a centennial celebration.

Bainbridge Island first held a fair in 1921 at Island Center Hall. Due to the fair's popularity, the fair association built new fairgrounds in 1928 on Strawberry Hill and the celebration took place there annually until World War II. The island's Filipino farmers took over responsibility for the community hall in 1943, and it is now included in the National Register of Historic Places. These days Bainbridge Island hosts several festivals, a Fourth of July extravaganza plus celebrations presented by the Japanese and Filipino communities.

Most island celebrations now are called festivals rather than fairs, and these celebrations no longer have agriculture at their center. People who grew up on an island but moved away often return for this annual event. Vashon Island's festival continues to be named in most years for strawberries, even though very few strawberries are grown there today. On Bainbridge Island, the Filipino-American community puts on the Strawberry Festival, which provides a connection to the role that these people played in the island's strawberry industry in earlier times.

Beginning in 1936, Anacortes held a grand summer festival called the Marineers' Pageant. Suspended during World War II, it took place again in 1947 and a few years thereafter. The final celebration, July 25-28, 1957, included "The Greatest Watershow in the West!" Featured were the festival queen and the obligatory parade down the city's main street, Commercial Avenue, as well as a talent show, children's events, jalopy races and a water show with both boat races and "water entertainers," who "ski, jump and fly from the tail of a kite," according to the pageant's brochure.[2]

People have not needed resorts or festivals to enjoy island beaches. Many families or groups of friends once rowed across from the mainland to a deserted beach for a summer picnic. By the beginning of the twentieth century, some families were establishing summer camps on island shores. At first, campers might simply use empty land without anyone's permission, but very early in the century, people were buying beach lots with vacations in mind. In 1902 some prospective vacationers hired a launch to take them along Whidbey's southern waters, and when they found the lot they wanted, they bought it on the spot. For families such as these, accommodations might evolve from simple tents to tents on purpose-built platforms and finally cabins. These summer homes on the beach did not need road access. Some of the cabins are still used, and some require a long walk if one wants to approach by road. Among the many places on Whidbey Island that saw such vacation communities develop were Penn Cove, Maple Cove, and the beach just north of Clinton.

Perhaps because it was the easiest island to reach from the mainland, Camano Island became an early tourist destination. At the turn of the twentieth century, tent camps began appearing, mainly in the northern part of the island. Many travelers to Camano arrived by water, but in the 1920s, auto parks appeared, not too different from today's campgrounds. Cabin camps and resorts followed, though by mid-century many had closed.

Early in the twentieth century, the Eckert family of Stretch Island in the South Sound hosted boatloads of vacationers and put on various social activities. Eckert Fruit Company facilities could be cleared for dancing and dinners. Nearby Harstine Island's Community Hall, opened in 1914, has held social functions since then, islanders celebrating the hall's one hundredth anniversary in 2014. Fox Island, too, attracted vacationers, especially because it was so near a large population center: Tacoma. Hoping to attract some of these people, the Wines family operated Sylvan Lodge on the north shore, not far east of today's bridge. Nearby appeared Camp Miajima, a YWCA camp whose centerpiece, a Japanese-style teahouse, had been built for the 1909 Alaska-Yukon-Pacific Exposition in Seattle. After the exposition closed, the Tacoma YMCA brought the dismantled teahouse to Fox Island and re-erected it at the camp. Unfortunately, the building has long been gone.

Seattle newspapers carried advertisements for island excursions lasting from a day to a week. The San Juans seemed ideal for a week-long cruise, but a Sunday day trip could show off this archipelago, too. One excursion offered in the early 1920s left downtown Seattle at 8 a.m. and stopped at both Friday Harbor and East Sound while cruising through the San Juans before docking back in Seattle at 10:30 that evening.

Armchair travelers could dream about driving around the islands. In 1919, a national writer, Helen Starr, compared the "Little known San Juan Islands" to the islands in the St. Lawrence River, saying the San Juans were far more scenic. One could "with his car board one of the small boats which regularly travel to the San Juan group." She added, "There is still another short and beautiful island trip which the pioneering motorist can take from his Seattle hotel any afternoon and return in time for tea. A fine paved road running through lovely woods reaches a ferry at Des Moines, and a short stretch of sound water is crossed to heavily wooded Vashon Island. There are summer resorts, tiny towns and an affluence of enchanting scenery."[3] The enthusiastic writer did seem to underestimate the time required for the Vashon visit.

Lummi Island featured several resorts in the first half of the twentieth century. Being close to the international border, they attracted Canadians to the island. One of the resorts, The Willows Inn, continues to welcome visitors in the twenty-first century and is a widely known for the excellence of its gourmet meals featuring local products.

The most prominent resort on San Juan Island today is Roche Harbor, built around wealthy entrepreneur John McMillin's estate. After the Tarte family bought the limestone operation in 1956, they soon ceased production and began work to turn the town into a resort. The next year, they opened a restaurant and soon the hotel, which had been built in 1887 to welcome the lime company's customers. Besides the hotel, the resort now features a store, a large parking area, cottages, and houses as well as two remaining lime kilns, the earliest ones constructed. A beautiful garden enhances the scenic setting, while a customs station for boaters from Canada sits alongside the boat moorages. Other resorts on the San Juan Islands have also attracted visitors. The archipelago's 1959 telephone book listed twenty-two resorts, seventeen of them on Orcas.

Some resorts have emphasized fishing and hunting. Among the Camano Island resorts that advertised fishing were Maple Grove Resort, Camp Grande and Madrona Beach Resort. The Marrowstone Point Fishing Resort was popular in the 1930s. Fishing also attracted people to Hat Island, but fishing resorts faced difficulties as the number of fish in Puget Sound declined. Times have changed and these days one can travel by seaplane to a good fishing spot, such as tiny, uninhabited Cutts Island, near Raft Island in the South Sound.

Three-mile-long Spieden Island just north of San Juan Island featured hunting for a few years. It was complete with lodge, boathouse, and airstrip when developers bought it in early 1970. They brought in about 250 exotic animals—different kinds of deer, sheep and goats plus game birds—and dubbed the place Safari Island. Residents of nearby islands looked askance at this effort to attract wealthy hunters, and CBS television aired a short but very critical documentary report about the island. This commentary, of course, led to public controversy and criticism, and the game farm lasted for only a few years. The owners sold out, probably because the adverse publicity damaged the enterprise. New owners briefly hosted educational programs and once again the island became Spieden Island. It is still privately owned, now apparently held as an open-space tax shelter. Some of the unusual animals remain on the island, and in recent years concern has shown that they suffer from hunger due to overpopulation, the island being severely overgrazed.

For a time, San Juan Island offered a different hunting experience. In the 1960s, while rabbits overran the island, tourists came to participate in organized nighttime hunts. The hunters, armed with long-handled nets, boarded "bunny buggies," that is, cut-down cars. When a local spotter's strong light found rabbits, the hunters would leap from the vehicle and try to scoop animals into nets. An unusual sport, indeed.

Visitors continue to come to the islands to view, but not kill, animals—specifically, whales. They are sometimes visible from ferries, mainly in the San Juans but also as far south as Vashon Island. Both Friday Harbor and Langley feature whale museums. Charter and sightseeing firms on Whidbey, Fidalgo and the San Juan Islands offer whale-watching cruises, but with the whale population endangered, boats and drones cannot closely approach them.

Not only have the islands offered family camping spots, resorts, fishing, hunting, and sightseeing, they have hosted summer youth camps. From 1921 to 1923, Skagit County Boy Scouts went to Cypress Island where they sheltered in tents for a summer session up to a month long. The camp then moved to other islands, including Guemes, but in 1927, the Skagit Council bought property on Cypress and began building a permanent camp which held successful summer sessions in 1928 and 1929. The council then merged with that of Whatcom County, though, and no longer used the Cypress Island property.

One long-time island youth camp is Camp Fire's Camp Sealth on Vashon Island. The camp originated on Blake Island, whose owner, William Pitt Trimble, offered to let Seattle Camp Fire Girls hold a camp on the island in 1920, and 650 girls attended. One story holds that Chief Seattle—or Sealth—had been born on Blake Island, so the campers named their site Camp Sealth. The Trimble family did not extend further invitations to the campers, and in 1921, with help from the Seattle community, Camp Fire purchased their current site, four hundred acres of Vashon Island west side beach which had previously been the Luceta Beach Resort. The Camp Sealth website has noted with pride that this was "the first permanent resident camp for girls in Washington State."[4] Since 1975 the camp has welcomed boys as well as girls, also serves special needs campers and offers various distinctive programs. Campers can arrive by boat, and for about half a century, they came on the *Virginia V.* Also on Vashon Island is Camp Burton, originally a Baptist camp. Here various organizations hold week-long camping sessions. Campers have included many different groups, from young cancer survivors to mentally disabled adults.

Eighteen-acre Tanglewood Island nestles against the northern shore of Fox Island, a bit southeast of the bridge to the island. In the 1930s, Dr. Alfred Schultz bought the island, then known as Grave Island because Native Americans had placed their dead in trees there. Shortly after the end of World War II, Dr. Schultz opened a boys' camp on the small island. The island became Tanglewood Island, a name more appropriate to a boys' camp than Grave Island. On the tip of the island, a round tower—a fake lighthouse forty-five feet high—welcomed campers. Nearby lay a mostly round pavilion and a saltwater pool. On summer Sunday mornings, a parade of boys in camp tee shirts rowed across the water to attend nearby Sylvan Church on Fox Island. The camp experience featured canoe craft. In 1961 eight boys and four adults paddled Willits canoes all the way to Juneau, Alaska. They camped on their way, fished, gathered food from the sea and replenished their small grocery supply when they came upon a community. This has rightly been celebrated as a highlight of the camp's history. Camp sessions continued for twenty years and the island is still privately owned. Early in the twenty-first century the lighthouse lost its top section and in 2014, island landowners demolished much of the pavilion—without county permission.

Camp Orkila, on the northwestern Orcas Island shore, has offered camping to youngsters since 1906. Before Orcas Island had regular ferry service, boys took excursion vessels to Eastsound, then hiked two-and-one-half miles to this YMCA camp. Starting in 1967, Camp Orkila has welcomed girls. In 1947 the YMCA bought 106-acre Satellite Island, just off the shore of Stuart Island and about ten miles from the main camp on Orcas, and campers can go to Satellite Island on overnight trips. Camp Orkila is an example of a private enterprise that benefits its home island in several ways. For instance, in 2016 the M/V *Whitefish*, a Camp Orkila boat, aided in the rescue of kayakers in trouble on the Sound.

Another long-lived camp in the San Juan Islands, Camp Nor'wester, opened to boys on San Juan Island in 1935 and in 1946 moved to a site it occupied for more than half a century, the Sperry Peninsula on southeast Lopez Island. Since 1940, Nor'wester has included units for girls. Its site was leased, not owned, though, and in the 1990s its owner offered the valuable property for sale. When Paul Allen purchased the peninsula, people thought he would surely allow the camp to continue. He wanted the site for a private retreat, though, with no place for Camp Nor'wester. Although Allen offered his help in finding a new location for the camp, many people expressed anger at his decision, feeling that converting the 387-acre site into a part-time retreat for one family was thoughtless and selfish. To some environmentalists, though, Allen's plans appeared to respect the land and prevent its intensive development. Camp Nor'wester did find a new site, 135 acres of remote Johns Island, a narrow 225-acre island nestled near Stuart Island at the northwestern edge of the San Juan archipelago.

In addition to resorts and summer camps, the islands feature public parks. Islanders have expressed ambivalence about developing parks on the islands, however, for parks bring visitors, and with the visitors come road improvements, parking lots, campers, motels—in other words, development that many islanders do not want.

As we have seen, the San Juan Islands contain a national historical park and a national monument. State parks, too, offer glimpses of island history and leisure activities as well as helping sustain natural landscapes. Cama Beach State Park stands out because of its creation. LeRoy Stradley of Seattle bought Camano Island beach property in the early 1930s to build an affordable resort. it opened in 1934 with forty cabins, recreation hall and store. Visitors cooked on wood stoves in the cabins and went to a separate building for bathroom facilities. The store stocked groceries. Favorite activities included boating, swimming, fishing, and clamming. Campers could also enjoy tennis, badminton, and horseshoes. Evening entertainment in the Recreation Lodge featured movies, children's games, square dancing and other activities. Fires destroyed several cabins in the 1950s and in 1977 the Recreation Hall burned down, a major loss, but the resort stayed open until 1989, fifty-five years after its opening.

This story is not so different from that of other pleasure grounds, but its subsequent history makes it special. Stradley granddaughters Karen Risk Hamalainen and Sandra Risk Worthington inherited the property and wanted it to have a future. They sold it to Washington State at a bargain price, some millions of dollars less than developers would have paid for it. Now it is Cama Beach State Park, where visitors may stay in the historic cabins. Not only does the site provide a wonderful beach vacation, it brings twentieth century history alive to the visitor. Spencer Spit State Park on Lopez Island has a similar history, for their owners also sold their land to the state. This waterfront area had been the Spencer family home, and this family also wanted to let the public enjoy the place. A park since 1967, this too is a wonderful place to visit, especially when the tide is out, and one can venture far along the beach's sandspit.

Other parks also had interesting beginnings. Deception Pass State Park came into being in 1922. The site had been unused military land, some of it on Fidalgo Island and some on Whidbey. After World War I, the Island County Farm Bureau, hoping to lure tourists to Whidbey Island, urged that the never-developed forested tract become a park. President Warren G. Harding signed the deed granting the land to the State of Washington and the official transfer came on July 20, 1922. Local people built a few park structures, but the area truly became a park after the CCC came in the 1930s. Men from near and far participated in the program to improve the park. They cleared the forest where necessary and often, by hand, built the park's beautiful kitchen shelters and other buildings, trails, campgrounds, roads and signs. The Deception Pass Bridge opened in 1935 and made the Whidbey section of the park more accessible. Thanks to the bridge's beauty, it is a Washington State icon, and it has helped make the park the most popular of the entire Washington State Park system. These days a small museum in a one-time park bathhouse in the Fidalgo Island portion of the park commemorates the work of the CCC. In 1988, former CCC workers themselves restored the building and created this museum.

Were Moran State Park easier to reach, it might rival Deception Pass in popularity. This 5,175-acre Orcas Island park includes the highest point in any of the islands, Mt. Constitution. The park dates from 1921 and owes its creation and development to Seattle entrepreneur Robert Moran. In 1904, doctors urged Moran to retire, and he bought property on Orcas Island to build a mansion at Rosario, completing it in 1909. Moran bought up land in the vicinity, and in 1913 he offered some two thousand acres of his Orcas holdings, including the mountaintop, to Washington State for a park. State law precluded acceptance, but after legislative action, officials were able to receive the property, and on July 16, 1921 Moran State Park became the first park in the now-extensive state system. Moran sold the family home at Rosario in 1938, and in the 1960s it became the center of a resort.

The CCC helped develop Moran State Park as well as Deception Pass State Park. Young men spent nearly five years on Orcas Island. The most impressive legacy of the CCC is the Observation Tower at Mount Constitution's peak. The fifty-foot tower became a well loved landmark. The State Parks and Recreation Commission's plan in 1972 to remove it led to a tremendous outcry, and a scheme for repair and restoration resulted instead. Meanwhile, a television tower atop the mountain was up for a lease renewal, and a demand for its removal arose among the public. Many people felt that this private antenna did not belong on state park land, especially not on this scenic spot. Other transmitting equipment also sat atop the peak. Historic photographs show various antennas arising from the CCC tower, but today they are gone. Today, visitors can barely see several distant antennas, and only someone specifically looking for them will notice them. Federal government programs during the Depression created and improved other parks, too. The Works Progress Administration built Maury Island's Dockton Park, which opened in 1936. The WPA also built the cabin at Bainbridge Island's Yeomalt for the Boy Scout camp there.

Three island state parks—Fort Flagler on Marrowstone Island and Forts Ebey and Casey on Whidbey Island—were military installations, as their names suggest, but their facilities now are used for conferences and camping as well as sightseeing and learning about history. An additional former military area is now a Bainbridge Island city park: Fort Ward. It became a state park in 1960, but budgetary troubles led the state to turn over both this park and Fay Bainbridge State Park to the island's park district in 2011. Fay Bainbridge, far north on the island, looks out over the water to the east with Seattle in the distance. The park's unusual name honors the Fay family, owners of the land who sold it to the state in 1944.

When the state lost its lease for a park on Squaxin Island in 1994, it bought tiny Hope Island just west of Squaxin. In the early days of settlement Hope Island had a few residents, and on the island today visitors can still see grapevines producing Island Belle grapes and old apple trees still bearing fruit. This little island, just over one hundred acres in size and open only to boaters, is especially popular with kayakers today but boating families have wonderful memories of the Squaxin Island Park and lament its closure.[5]

Blake Island is a different kind of state park. At one time, a bootleggers' haven, the island belonged to the wealthy Trimble family for many years. They created a pleasant home there, but after Mrs. Trimble died in 1929 the family left. The island remained deserted most of the time thereafter, and in 1948 two South Kitsap High School boys took their boat there. They entered the abandoned Trimble mansion and built a fire in a fireplace. Some time after they left the island the house burned down, possibly because of the boys' fire. The two kept their escapade secret for many years afterward.

In 1958 a development firm proposed locating a hotel, resort, and private homes on Blake Island. The site would also include an Indian village, a nine-hole golf course, shops, a public park, and hydroplane service from the mainland, but public opinion strongly favored a state park, and Washington State was able to acquire the land. Soon, Seattle caterer Bill Hewitt, who could see Blake Island from his Vashon Island home, suggested building an Indian longhouse on Blake Island. Hewitt created Tillicum Village in 1962, the year of the Seattle World's Fair.

Anyone visiting the islands today should check out city and county parks. Throughout Whidbey and Bainbridge Islands are little-known parks, and in the San Juans, small Shaw Island has a county park on its south shore. This park, like various others, sits on land once held for military use. In the 1920s, San Juan County purchased it with funds collected by Shaw Islanders who had long used the site for picnics. It contains eleven campsites.

In Anacortes a unique city park, Causland Park, occupies a full block in the middle of a residential area. The Seattle & Northern Railway sold the land to the city in 1903 for a park. In 1919, remodeling made it a war memorial, honoring the region's World War I veterans and named in honor of Lt. Harry Causland of Guemes Island, who received the Distinguished Service Cross for the heroic action in France that cost him his life. Not only is this park symbolically important, its design reflects the period of its creation.

The Port of Everett's Jetty Island is also an unusual island park. This mile-long narrow artificial piece of land originated as a breakwater to improve a shipping channel and to shelter Everett's harbor. Built of riprap, rock, and sand from dredging operations to keep the Snohomish River navigable, Jetty Island has more recently been replenished with river silt by the Army Corps of Engineers. Now the island is both a wildlife refuge and a sunbathing and picnic spot. Since 1985, Everett has provided free daily three-minute passenger boat rides to the island during the summers.

Since World War II, the islands have become a mecca for pleasure boaters. Even before the war, Puget Sound was a popular boating destination. Movie actor Spencer Tracy rated a small *Seattle Times* article at the end of his week-long boating vacation among the San Juans in 1937.[6] For boaters, some of the small San Juan Isles include marine parks. Many are accessible only from the water, and some of the islands, including those northernmost San Juans—Patos, Sucia and Matia—consist today almost entirely of park land or otherwise protected acreage, and some of this exists thanks to Puget Sound boaters who raised funds to buy much of the land and then gave it to the state.

Marinas specifically for boat storage and moorage exist on various islands, though opposition has sometimes impeded their development. Private facilities to lure tourists have been much more controversial than public park development. On Orcas Island, a proposed marina at Deer Harbor stirred local protests in the 1970s. Residents claimed the existing marina in the harbor was adequate and cited environmental damage the construction would cause, but the basic concern was development. Not all local people objected to the plan, and the San Juan County Commissioners—though not the commissioner from Orcas Island—supported it. It took nine years for Cayou Quay Marina to open for business after having obtained its original building permit. Noting in the early 1960s that Vashon was the only large island in Puget Sound without an up-to-date resort, several mainland businessmen proposed building one next to Vashon's north end ferry dock. They planned a restaurant and marina with a harbor for boats. Despite having obtained county permission, the entrepreneurs never built the facilities.

Near the end of the twentieth century, local kayak enthusiasts worked with state parks officials to establish the Cascadia Marine Trail, a route through Washington's inland waters with more than fifty camping spots designated for paddlers only. These are located on mainland and island sites from Anderson Island all the way north through the San Juans. Island sites are found on Hope Island (Mason County), Vashon and Maury, Blake, Bainbridge, Indian, Marrowstone, Camano, Whidbey, Fidalgo and Lummi as well as on Anderson and various San Juan Islands.

An issue common to all islands is public access to the shoreline, whether to launch a boat, enjoy a walk along a beach, picnic, or simply gaze at the view of water, islands, and mountains. Lack of beach access is not a new concern. In the late 1940s, Camano Island had no public beaches. Many residents wanted to change this, and the South Camano Grange spearheaded a local campaign to obtain a park for the community. The state agreed to transfer land it held, but part of the plan was for local people to create the park. On July 27, 1949, at least five hundred people brought building supplies and willing hands as well as bulldozers to clear and level land. By the end of the day, Camano Island State Park existed, complete with road, trails, and picnic tables—even restrooms. The community effort stands as perhaps Camano Islanders' proudest accomplishment. Other spots on the island also offer beach access today, including Cama Beach and Iverson Spit. Fox Island also did not have good beach access, but in recent years the DeMolay Sandspit Nature Preserve on the northern tip of the island has been open to the public. It offers a wonderful sandspit to explore.

Periodically , a national newspaper such as the *New York Times* or the *Christian Science Monitor* has carried a feature article about the Puget Sound islands, with emphasis often on the San Juans. One wonders how many visitors—or permanent residents—have come because of laudatory comments like this one in the *Monitor*, describing the islands of Puget Sound and those in nearby Canadian waters: "On all of these 'lovely islands' the weather is warmer than on the mainland, spring comes earlier, rains fall more gently, berries grow larger, winters are milder, and there are fewer fogs." Both the *New York Times* and the *National Geographic Traveler* ranked the San Juan Islands among the very best travel destinations in 2011,[7] even though accommodations for visitors are relatively modest, consisting mostly of bed-and-breakfast establishments.

Leisure includes entertainment islanders have created for themselves. From early times, islanders have met for picnics and dances and have presented plays and music for each other. For years high school sporting events drew many island spectators, and recently, additional leisure activities and entertainment have proliferated. No longer is the summer fair an island's sole annual festival. In the fall, residents and visitors come together to make cider on islands from Anderson on north. One might attend a Christmas festival in Coupeville featuring tree lighting, while the Bainbridge Island annual Mochi Tsuki Festival at the New Year carries on a longtime Japanese tradition: pounding rice to create the dough called *mochi*, which is then shaped, sometimes around a sweet filling. Many islands have drama groups and chorales, while Vashon has an opera company and Bainbridge and Whidbey have symphony orchestras. Bainbridge Island and Friday Harbor boast new art museums. These days, venues on various islands offer performances from classical music to jazz and rock by local and mainland musicians.

A perception of leisure is what the islands now mean to non-residents. The islands are scenic vacation spots, where one comes to relax. Perhaps the need to take a ferry or cross a bridge to get to an island reinforces the feeling that an island is a place to get away from the pressures of daily life. Those early northwesterners who built simple cabins on island shorelines could not have dreamed that so many people would follow their path. Over the years the islands have housed resorts and camps, parks, and entertainment. These days, whether it is life in a cabin or a waterfront estate or a weekend visit to an island bed-and-breakfast inn, the islands signify leisure and the good life.

14 | Defense and War

PUGET SOUND IS THE MOST EXTENSIVE SYSTEM OF INLETS, harbors, and islands on the nation's west coast between San Francisco and Alaska, and, therefore, a lot of military interest has been centered on the Sound. Two decades after the 1841 Wilkes visit, the question of military defense played an important role in bringing the United States and Great Britain to the brink of war in the San Juan Islands. Puget Sound country has never faced attack from a foreign country, but because of the area's strategic significance, military preparations have played an important role in island history. At the end of the nineteenth century and again when world tension arose leading to World Wars I and II plus the Cold War, defensive plans and practices have impacted the islands.

Shortly after the Civil War ended, President Andrew Johnson designated certain areas around Puget Sound as military reservations, especially in locations like Deception Pass and Admiralty Inlet. This would reserve these sites for possible future fortification. Many never saw military use and eventually members of the public bought the land. The island sites included seven areas set aside on the San Juans: one on the long southwestern shore of Shaw Island, two on north Lopez Island and another on this island's southwestern coast, facing San Juan Island's Cattle Point. On San Juan Island they were on the shore just north of Friday Harbor and at Cattle Point. The government also set aside land on Canoe Island between Shaw and Lopez. The military reservations also included land on the northwesternmost point of Whidbey Island and at Double Bluff on Whidbey's southwest shore, Hope and Skagit Islands east of Deception Pass, the Marrowstone Island site that became Fort Flagler and the south end of Vashon Island. In Dalco Passage between Tacoma and Vashon, according to local lore, ships' crewmen practiced shooting cannons at military land on the island; cannon balls have turned up in banks of soil.

Despite federal ownership of these sites, officials postponed defensive preparations for many years. Island military construction only began after the 1891 establishment of Bremerton's Puget Sound Naval Station, known familiarly as the Navy Yard. Three coastal artillery forts, popularly known as the Triangle of Fire, came into being in the 1890s to protect the new Naval Station. These were Fort Casey, next to the Admiralty Head Lighthouse on the west side of Whidbey Island, Fort Flagler on north Marrowstone island, and Fort Worden, just north of Port Townsend. These locations facing Admiralty Inlet could monitor marine traffic into Puget Sound.

Once the Spanish American War began in 1898, construction on the Triangle of Fire sped up to deter any possible Spanish incursion. At the forts, the need to protect large guns from destruction by the enemy complicated construction, requiring disappearing gun carriages that could raise and lower the guns behind earthen barriers. The forts first received guns whose barrels had a six-inch inside diameter. Accompanying them came mortars, which could lob shells a short distance. Later came ten-inch guns. In 1901, tests of Fort Casey's guns attracted islanders to watch the activity, but also shattered some windows in Port Townsend. One complication at Fort Casey was the need to move the lighthouse site, and thus the present lighthouse dates only from 1903.

Acreage on Bainbridge Island's west shore became U.S. Coast Artillery property about 1900. Fort Ward, built here, would also protect the Navy Yard. Construction of gun batteries, or groups of guns, began and in a few years, support structures and equipment were in place, including quarters for troops.

A fort almost unknown today existed on another Puget Sound island. Starting in 1909, The Army Corps of Engineers constructed Fort Whitman on Goat Island, 129 acres of land rising 255 feet above Skagit Bay. This tiny island is about halfway between the northeast coast of Whidbey Island and the southern tip of the Swinomish Reservation on Fidalgo Island. Fort

Whitman would protect Deception Pass, which was mined during both world wars. Military builders constructed a rock dike from Goat Island east to the end of a mainland peninsula. A wharf and tramway soon reached the weapons site. By 1911 the Army had a battery with disappearing guns and observation post there. Personnel manned Goat Island during World War I, but afterward the fort merely stored military supplies.

By World War I, Fort Casey had thirty-five mounted guns and Fort Flagler had twenty-six. During the war, troops underwent training at the forts but many of the guns were removed to be used elsewhere. Food crops grew and livestock grazed on Fort Casey's grounds, helping to cope with wartime food shortages. Some of Fort Ward's guns ended up on warships, while the fort remained manned, ready for use, with torpedoes and gunners in position.

Fighting never came near Puget Sound. Armament design had progressed to the point that coastal defenses could no longer offer adequate protection against attacks which now could come from the air as well as from the sea. In 1920 Fort Casey acquired a hanger to hold balloons, which could carry men aloft to spot fires and perhaps be otherwise useful. Tests showed that the Whidbey site was unsuitable, however, due to erratic winds. In the 1920s, Washington State National Guard troops and ROTC members trained there. In the 1930s, men tore down some of the forts' buildings, for they had deteriorated and were no longer useful. The coastal defenses on Puget Sound had become obsolete.

World War I touched the region in another way. Industrial production increased, one new facility being a new shipyard that opened on the south shore of Guemes Island. Timber and machinery arrived and on August 28, 1917, the new yard laid its first ship's keel. Slow delivery of materials hampered subsequent ship construction and only near the end of November did such work begin. The war ended before the two completed ships were launched in 1919. As for the shipyard, work ceased and the 1921 buyer of the property tore down the buildings.

World War II fighting began in Europe in 1939. Because of rising world tension, modernization efforts began at all three Triangle of Fire forts. By the summer of 1941, Fort Casey housed more than four hundred men and Fort Flagler three hundred. After the United States declared war on December 8, 1941, the Army reconditioned the remaining guns at the forts, where troop training was the main activity.

During the war, Fort Whitman was briefly reinforced. Forty-eight men stationed there in temporary housing oversaw a new battery. Citizens of nearby LaConner helped the men feel at home, most significantly by getting heaters and wood stoves for them. After the first year or two of World War II, Puget Sound no longer seemed to be in danger of invasion, and by 1944 Fort Whitman became inactive. The federal government removed the buildings in 1945 and in 1947 transferred Goat Island to the Washington State Game Department.

The government deactivated the larger forts in 1953, and they became part of the state park system. Seattle Pacific College—now University—acquired part of Fort Casey and operates the Camp Casey Conference Center there. This portion of the one-time fort includes the barracks, officers' quarters, auditorium, and other structures. Meanwhile, Coupeville bought the Fort Casey water system and continues to use it.

Seattle Public Schools briefly planned to buy part of Fort Flagler for outdoor learning programs, but the idea led to controversy, foiling the plans. The fort became a state park and musical and other groups have used its facilities. A small military museum sits on the grounds and popular campgrounds exist at both Forts Casey and Flagler.

For many years after deactivation, Forts Casey and Flagler had no guns of the type installed there before 1910. Their remaining guns had long since become scrap metal for reuse during World War II. However, displaying examples of these guns could help visitors grasp fort history. Two Navy men once stationed on Whidbey Island discovered similar guns slowly rusting away in the jungle at Fort Wint in the Philippines. When the Japanese invaded these islands in 1942, U.S. forces had disabled the weapons rather than melting them down.

In the early 1960s, efforts began to bring these guns to Washington State. Thanks to Whidbey Island supporters and U.S. Senator Henry M. Jackson, the guns did not go to the Smithsonian Institution, which wanted them, but to Whidbey Island. Washington State Parks worked to get the Philippine government's cooperation and then asked the U.S. Navy to declare the weapons surplus. Raising money to move and install the guns, then dismantling and shipping them followed, and Bremerton Navy Yard workers restored the weapons. During transfer of the weapons to Whidbey Island, one trailer could not get off the Keystone ferry slip due to the weight of its load and had to sit there until the tide rose. Finally, Fort

Casey and Fort Flagler each received two three-inch guns, and in 1968 two ten-inch guns complete with carriages came to Fort Casey from Fort Wint. One now sits in its lowered position, protected from sight behind its earthen barrier while the gun next to it is raised, ready to fire.

During World War II, Bremerton's naval facility was a priority. The approach by ship to the Navy Yard necessarily takes one past some of the islands. Shortly before the United States declared war, the Navy placed huge nets, held by spiked cables, across a few Puget Sound channels to prevent submarines from using these passages. One net lay near the location of today's Agate Pass bridge. Another crossed from the south end of Bainbridge to the vicinity of Port Orchard. This one bisected the route of the ferries that traveled between Seattle and Bremerton and required opening the net to let each boat through. Tugboats stationed in the passage thus contained mechanisms to open and close the net, but a net once snagged the ferry *Chippewa*. More netting to catch torpedoes stretched from Port Townsend across Indian Island to Fort Flagler. Placing nets across the six-hundred-foot deep channel between Fort Flagler and Whidbey Island was not possible, instead, hydrophones set on the seabed could detect sound and thus warn of possible intruders. President Roosevelt designated much of Puget Sound a "defensive sea area," closing the waters to all vessels which did not have advance permission to sail.

Because of World War II, the United States government established new military facilities on Bainbridge Island at Battle Point, and the Navy reopened Fort Ward, which the Army had mothballed in 1928. Even before Pearl Harbor, the Navy began training recruits in a secret facility at Fort Ward in communications work. First came a listening post and a school for radio operators and then a code school to train people to send and receive the Japanese version of Morse code. The trainees included Waves—the women in the Navy during World War II. They transcribed intercepted Japanese military transmissions which they heard through their headphones as meaningless dots and dashes. In addition to the communications infrastructure, new guns appeared nearby. The Navy radio facility operated there even after World War II ended, training people in Russian code during the Cold War. In the mid-1950s, an Army battery moved in, as Nike missiles would soon come to Bainbridge Island. The Army left Fort Ward in 1958.

Five miles farther north on Bainbridge Island and directly east of Battle Point is the site of an 860-foot high transmitter tower installed when World War II began. Messages from here went across the Pacific in Morse code. The Navy acquired the Battle Point site because a transmitter closer to the Fort Ward receiver would have led to radio interference. In 1970, the government gave the grounds to Bainbridge Island for a park, but for safety reasons specified that the tower had to be dismantled. Also, as part of the Bainbridge effort during World War II, the Boy Scout Camp at Yeomalt on the island's east side became Camp Hopkins, an anti-aircraft unit which was the center for several places on the island where the Coast Artillery was spotting and tracking aircraft and operating searchlights and anti-aircraft guns.

Among the Bainbridge Island firms which found new life in war production was Winslow Marine Railway and Shipbuilding, which had started life as Hall Brothers. During the war, the work force grew from about one hundred to more than two thousand employees, and the shipyard produced seventeen mine sweepers, twelve tugs for harbor work and other vessels.

The largest Second World War installation by far on the Puget Sound islands was the Navy base built on Whidbey Island. The government first bought land near Oak Harbor from the family of pioneer settler Samuel Maylor. On Dec. 8, 1941, surveying began. The day coincided with the American declaration of war by chance, as the Navy had been planning for almost a year to build a base somewhere in the Puget Sound region to refuel and care for flying boats, or seaplanes. In addition, a naval base could help protect the Sound. The Whidbey site seemed ideal, for weather there was better than in much of the rest of the area, and the site also featured a good water-based landing area near dock facilities. The Navy laid out an airfield and on September 21, 1942, commissioned Naval Air Station Whidbey Island. Soon Navy flyers began training there in different kinds of aircraft.

In the community, rents skyrocketed, and trailers proliferated. New businesses opened, and traffic became difficult. The Navy bought some seventy farms. Families moved, many to houses in town, but some folks left the island. The dispossessed families and the entire community mourned the loss of prosperous, well-maintained farmsteads. Yet at the same time, North Whidbey people felt that they were supporting the nation by welcoming the Navy and its men.

Unlike other military installations on the islands, the Whidbey Island Naval Air Station continues in operation today. Once the war ended, many thought that the Whidbey facility would be decommissioned. With the Cold War developing and newer airplanes requiring relatively long landing fields, the spacious base on Whidbey Island appeared necessary. It became the only naval field west of Chicago and north of San Francisco available for operation regardless of weather conditions.

The Naval Air Station has dominated northern Whidbey Island for more than half a century and is responsible for most of the population of the island. These days, more than ten thousand people, military and civilian, work there. In addition to confiscation of land, the base's impacts have included noise and traffic both from construction and operation. Also, during World War II and later, several planes from the Naval Air Station have crashed into Puget Sound or on Whidbey Island, yet, more happily, Navy fliers have participated in many rescues in Western Washington.

Life at another military base on Whidbey Island, Fort Ebey, began in 1942. The army developed this site to protect the entrance to Admiralty Inlet, intercepting the enemy before he neared the other coastal artillery stations at Forts Flagler, Worden, and Casey. A few miles north of Fort Casey, small Fort Ebey featured observation stations as well as gun emplacements to ward off possible Japanese incursions. Also, during the war the government placed guns at other Whidbey sites: Deception Pass, Ebey's Landing and Dugualla Bay.

The U.S. government acquired Indian Island, that narrow piece of land between Marrowstone Island and Port Townsend, in 1940. After condemning the property of the island's ninety-four landowners, the Navy established U.S. Naval Magazine Indian Island and the U.S. Naval Net Depot. During the war, armament transshipped there grew to over thirteen hundred tons of ammunition in a single month. Weaponry produced in U.S. factories would be sent to Indian Island to be stored in magazines and then transferred to ships. After the war, the anti-submarine nets which were no longer in use sat in storage there. Most of Indian Island remains a military reservation today and continues to store and transship munitions.

During World War II, Marrowstone Island was also involved in the nation's defense, with guns installed at several places on the island as part of the Anti-Motor-Torpedo-Boat Program. As during World War I, Fort Flagler became a troop training center. When World War II neared an end, the Navy needed to store surplus vessels, and one of the places they chose was Scow Bay between Indian and Marrowstone Islands. Though Marrowstone residents protested, the Navy dredged the harbor and brought in several hundred mothballed vessels which stayed there until 1948. Meanwhile, more than one hundred landing craft remained for a time in storage on the Fort Flagler beach where a public campground now sits. During the Korean War, Fort Flagler featured training, including target practice and maneuvers.

On Fidalgo Island, the government designated all the salmon packed in Anacortes in 1942 for the troops and for shipment to the allies, and during the war the Sagstad Shipyard built vessels for the Army on Swinomish Reservation land. One-third of the men working there were tribe members.

On San Juan Island, in August 1942 the Coast Guard took over the University of Washington Friday Harbor Laboratories. They became barracks rooms and Coast Guardsmen, not marine scientists, received training at the former laboratory. In February 1946, the government returned the laboratory site to the university and fisheries education and research could resume. Radar operated at Friday Harbor for early warning and defense from 1942 until 1944. The Jensen shipyard in town built tugs and scows for defense use. San Juan islanders who went to the beach and looked at what washed up there found an unexpected bonus during the war when ocean-going vessels apparently threw unused food containers overboard before landing at Puget Sound ports. Henry Hoffman of Shaw Island picked up a five-gallon can of dried potatoes, unopened, that his family proceeded to eat for the next few months. The family also found many packs of cigarettes wrapped in canvas. The cigarettes were soggy and unusable, but Hoffman's father was delighted with the canvas, because he could find none for sale during wartime.[1]

While the nation was at war, the Puget Sound islands had observers watching the sky. Residents including students and retirees staffed the posts twenty-four hours a day. The observers were to note both airplane noise and sightings, using charts illustrating the shapes of different planes to help in identification. Observation sites in the San Juan Islands included a Coast Guard post at Stuart Island's Turn Point, very close to the international border. Another was in a tugboat's pilothouse at Roche Harbor, while on Orcas Island, soldiers were stationed as observers atop Mt. Constitution as early as 1941, and the Orcas Home Guard formed an observation unit. On Orcas Island, in 1942, the Coast Guard began to use the former CCC camp, Camp Moran, to train recruits. After the war, the Washington State Patrol ran a training camp at the site. Camp Moran is now an environmental learning center, available to the public for a rental fee.

Vashon Island, relatively far south in the Sound and beyond water approaches to Bremerton and Seattle, had far less military involvement during World War II than did the islands to the north. As on all the islands, north and south, civilians on Vashon assisted the war effort. Led by local retiree Paul Billingsley, residents manned the new Aircraft Warning Service posts located at Cove, Maury Island and south of the town of Vashon. If enemy planes appeared, flares would be shot into the air from eight locations. Unusual preparations included the stashing of "rocket bombs"—firecrackers—at eight secret spots. Red flares on Vashon Island would signify nearby enemy aircraft and green the all-clear. Flares instead of sirens would signal warnings, Billingsley said, because of the difficulty of making sirens heard everywhere on the island. Islanders set up an auxiliary police force, most members carrying rifles ordinarily used in hunting. An empty school building could become an emergency hospital with eight beds, and islanders drew up plans for immediate transportation home from school for every child should this be required.

As the war continued, military observers took over from the volunteers on Vashon, establishing Battery C, or Charlie Battery. The troops enjoyed being stationed on the island and islanders who were children during the war remember the military trucks that pulled their sleds up snowy roads in wintertime so the children could slide downhill. Islanders welcomed the military men, for many local people were away from home in the armed forces. With the nation at war, Vashon voters created a fire district, giving the island its first official fire department supported by tax revenues. Earlier attempts at creating a fire district had failed at the polls. District personnel would be volunteers, as before, but equipment and organization would improve. The war apparently led voters to support a fire district, for they voted 429 to 4 to create it.

Twice during the war, military planes, P-38s stationed near Tacoma, went down in Colvos Passage, the waterway to the west of Vashon Island. People rowed out from Vashon and rescued both pilots. One of the planes crashed into deep water near the middle of the passage and still lies there, but the other, closer to Vashon, was soon raised. What caused the incidents? People speculated about sabotage, but the government hushed up news about them. Newspapers did not report the crashes.

Even small Blake Island, that quiet piece of land between Bainbridge and Vashon Islands, had a role in the nation's defense, for the Army located a coastal artillery facility there. Wartime rumor, never confirmed, held that the Army also stored munitions on the island, as it was both isolated and close to several military installations.

War disrupted life on all the islands. A desperately needed school in the recently consolidated school district on Orcas Island was about to be built with finances secured from the state and from a local bond issue. The war came along and suddenly building materials and construction workers were unavailable. On Bainbridge Island, church bells no longer rang, their tolling to be heard only in case of an air raid. Among wartime shortages were the glass balls from Japan used by Puget Sound fishermen as net floats. Their replacement was easily obtainable, though: beer bottles.

With plans for reduction in ferry service between Fox Island and Tacoma in 1943, islanders argued against this, pointing out that seventy war workers commuted to their jobs from the island. Federal officials asked Pierce County Commissioners to have the Fox Island ferry make one run a day to McNeil Island, delivering fresh fruit which inmates would process for army use. As their part of the war effort, McNeil Island prisoners grew and harvested fruit and vegetables, then canned or dried them for military troops. Other items produced at the prison included cargo nets for the Navy and wooden vessels for the Army to be used for supplying remote military facilities in Alaska.

Were there any positive effects on the islands due to the war? Certainly, islanders benefited from lower ferry rates instituted thanks to increased ridership. Also, military men on the islands helped during emergencies. In January 1943, when a winter storm brought high winds, downed power lines and trees, and dropped eighteen to twenty inches of snow, troops came to the rescue, delivering food and other needed supplies and transporting doctors and patients. In March 1943, with many local men off to war, it was Coast Guardsmen who fought a fire in Friday Harbor that destroyed a block of businesses. In December 1945, after the war had ended, the Navy rescued Marrowstone Island's ferry, the *Nordland*, which was carrying a full load, including students, at the time.

Extra-strong winds were too much for the boat, and a Navy tug kept it from slamming onto the beach.

World War II had a shameful impact on the islands, one that resonates to this day. Because of war hysteria conquering common sense and causing fear, some islanders lost their basic human rights. The result of the hysteria and fear was the incarceration of people of Japanese ancestry, known as Nikkei, in concentration—or relocation—camps. The United States government worried about possible Japanese invasion of the west coast and felt unsure of Nikkei patriotism. In the spring of 1942, officials ordered that all Nikkei who lived on or near the west coast be removed inland, mostly to camps the government would set up for them. In the west coast states, almost 120,000 people had to leave their homes.

Bainbridge and Vashon were the two Puget Sound islands with sizable Nikkei populations. It was the older Japanese, the ones who had immigrated from Japan and are called Issei, who seemed to be most threatened, for they had not been allowed to become citizens. Both Issei and Nisei, who are the first generation of children born in the United States and thus American citizens, found the early restrictions on them especially hard, because for a time they were forbidden to take the ferries. Nikkei feared the future, so they hid or destroyed their Japanese treasures and stopped sending their children to Japanese language schools.

On February 4, 1942, thirty or more police from the county, state and federal governments made a surprise raid of Nikkei homes on Bainbridge Island. The officers took weapons and dynamite that farmers used in land clearance. The men detained fifteen Nikkei, seemingly the most prominent on the island, though quickly releasing a few of them. In a similar operation on Vashon Island, almost sixty FBI agents appeared three days later, responding to concerns that the island's Japanese had armaments, but little turned up. Mary Matsuda Gruenewald, then a Vashon Island teenager, remembered her heart pounding as the FBI men searched the Matsuda home. They took a 22-caliber rifle and a radio.[2]

Bainbridge Island was the first community in the entire United States to lose all its residents of Japanese ancestry. The island's location accounted for this "honor." Bainbridge housed military facilities and commanded the approaches to the Bremerton Navy Yard. Nearby to the west was a naval torpedo station. In Seattle, just across the Sound to the east, were the Sand Point Naval Air Station and the Boeing Airplane Company.

Shipyards both on Bainbridge Island and in nearby communities were immersed in military production.

Two hundred twenty-seven Bainbridge Island people went to Manzanar, a government-built barracks in the eastern California desert. They received just six days to prepare for their March 30, 1942, departure, to arrange that their property be cared for—which did not always happen—or sold, and to decide what to include in the small amount of luggage they had permission to take. Meanwhile, a few Western Washington Nikkei were able to leave "voluntarily," if they could find an inland community where they could live.[3] Thirteen of fifty-two students—one quarter of the Bainbridge High School graduating class of 1942—missed their commencement ceremony on the island because they were incarcerated at Manzanar. Later, officials moved most of the Bainbridge contingent to Camp Minidoka in Idaho. Troops took Vashon Island's 126 Nikkei away on May 16, and perhaps three hundred people saw them off at the ferry dock. The Vashon group went first to an assembly center north of Fresno, California, and then to Tule Lake in the dry, eastern part of the state. Later, most were dispersed to different camps.

Relocation and incarceration were truly disastrous for the Nikkei. This government policy also greatly affected the communities whose residents were now gone. On both islands, Nikkei had volunteered for various activities to help the war effort, but this had not prevented removal from their Puget Sound area homes. On both islands, strawberry crops needed harvesting despite the departure of farmers, packers, and many of the seasonal workers. Only forty percent of the 1942 crop on Bainbridge was saved. Meanwhile, even after having to live in government-run camps, many Nisei volunteered to serve in the U.S. Armed Forces once this was made possible in 1943. Other Nisei faced the draft.

On Bainbridge Island, Walt and Milly Woodward, publishers and editors of the island's weekly newspaper, the *Bainbridge Review*, made a point of supporting the Nikkei. Walt Woodward hired Paul Ohtaki, a young Bainbridge Nisei who had worked for the newspaper, to be the Manzanar correspondent and the *Review* regularly carried short columns reporting the activities of the Bainbridge contingent at camp. Among the events covered was the ceremony held there for the Bainbridge students' graduation.

During the postwar decades, many people and organizations honored the Woodwards for their stand, but during the war this Bainbridge couple was exceptional. At first, the Vashon newspaper also supported the Nikkei. Even just after Pearl Harbor, *Vashon Island News-Record* editor Agnes Smock urged respect for the local Japanese. In reporting their departure a few months later, her paper noted, that "Army officers and federal men who assisted in the evacuation remarked that the Japanese from Vashon Island were by far the finest class they had contacted." A 1943 editorial written by a new newspaper owner and editor proclaimed, "Leave the Japs where they are . . . We don't want them back on the Pacific Coast nor on this island." In early 1945, three young Vashon Island men burned down three empty houses on the island that were owned by Japanese families because of "drink and dislike of the Japs," reported the *Seattle Post-Intelligencer.*[4]

Meanwhile, perhaps about two hundred Bainbridge Islanders went to a gathering in November 1944 to discuss ways to prevent local Nikkei from returning. The *Bainbridge Review* criticized the meeting's objective and urged people not to be "guided . . . by hysteria and blind, war-in-flamed viewpoints." Afterwards, anti-Japanese fervor largely died down on Bainbridge. More than half of the island's Nikkei but probably not quite one-third of those from Vashon returned to their island homes after the war. The Saichi Takemoto family, the first to return to Bainbridge, found their farm fields uncultivated, their house entered and many of their goods gone, but the Tats Moritani family returned to a strawberry farm well-tended by local Quaker volunteers.[5] However, the Bainbridge Grange would not admit Japanese or Filipino farmers, although this policy did not last. On both islands, the Nikkei who returned found more support than antagonism even at first, and as the years went by realized that they were recognized simply as community members. Finally, it is important to note that despite the anti-Japanese hysteria in this country when the war began, no evidence of Nikkei subversion ever appeared.

Bainbridge Island now features a memorial to honor the island's Nikkei and to send the message "Let It Not Happen Again." War hysteria must not lead to future injustice. The Bainbridge Island Japanese American Exclusion Memorial is located at the approach to the old Eagledale ferry dock from which the Nikkei were taken away. Vashon Island honors its Japanese-American community with a historical display at the Mukai Farm and Garden.

After the Second World War ended, military influence did not disappear from the islands. At Fort Flagler, maneuvers and training including

target practice took place for a time during the Korean War, while training continued at Fort Casey until 1950. Meanwhile, the Naval Air Station
on Whidbey Island had become "a war baby grown into a giant," wrote
Stuart Whitehouse shortly after the war ended.[6] Oak Harbor has become
economically dependent on the Naval Air Station whose workers live and
shop in the area, making it possible for businesses to open and prosper.

If the United States government ever deactivated Naval Air Station
Whidbey Island, Oak Harbor would feel a massive impact. In 1991 Secretary
of Defense Dick Cheney announced that the Whidbey Island base was on
the Navy's closure list. Had this happened, more than sixty percent of the
Oak Harbor School District's students would have left, while some eight
thousand jobs—military and civilian—would have disappeared. Supporters
explained why the base should stay open, and soon the Whidbey base was
no longer on the closure list. Whenever anyone talks of base closure, as in
2008 when Senator John McCain introduced a bill in the U.S. Senate that
would close some facilities, North Whidbey Islanders worry.

The emergence of the Cold War led to continuing military activity on
the islands. During the 1950s and 1960s, the Army Corps of Engineers
built about a dozen missile batteries in a protective ring around Seattle
to respond to any enemy aircraft approaching from the Pacific Ocean.
Battery A of the 433rd Anti-Aircraft Artillery Missile Battalion operated
on Vashon Island from 1956 to 1974. At a central Vashon site, each Nike
missile lay in an underground magazine. Various buildings housed support and administrative services and nearby the Army arranged for construction of a small housing park for military families. The base included
generators capable of providing power for the entire island, though they
were never so used. On Bainbridge Island, a Nike Control site, with radar
and searchlights, sat at Eagledale, missiles at Strawberry Hill and headquarters for these installations at Yeomalt. The Bainbridge sites ceased operation in 1960, but the Vashon battery, which originally housed Nike Ajax
missiles, received Nike Hercules missiles that year.

The Nike sites never fired a missile and all ceased operation by 1974.
After the Bainbridge site closed, that island's park district obtained its
twenty-five acres. Strawberry Hill Park replaced the Nike base and has
found some of the military facilities useful. The missile assembly building
is now a mini-gym. The government also made the forty-some acre Vashon
site available to its community. Some of the former military buildings now

house the island's largest medical center and, until it moved to a larger space in 2015, a thrift shop to help support island health facilities.

Dramatic Cold War military maneuvers called Exercise Sea Wall took over life on San Juan Island in September 1961. While island schools and Friday Harbor shops closed, Army, Navy and Air Force units all participated in this large-scale military exercise. Buses and temporary bleachers made it possible for local residents to watch the action. Three days of activities included amphibious landings and simulated ground battles between the "Aggressors" and the U.S. troops. Even guerrilla actions, air attacks and a fake nuclear bomb appeared. Of course, the Aggressors lost, and finally came the surrender ceremony.

In the late 1960s, the United States Defense Department planned to establish a new anti-ballistic-missile defense system at more than a dozen locations throughout the nation. This would replace the obsolete Nike missiles on Vashon, Bainbridge and elsewhere. In Puget Sound country, new installations would be at two sites, one south of Port Gamble on the Kitsap County mainland and the other on Bainbridge Island, two miles north of Fletcher Bay.

Whereas North Kitsap County residents welcomed the idea of a military facility bringing jobs, Bainbridge Islanders protested loudly. People talked about the impact on schools, property values, water supply and sewage facilities as well as fearing that the area would become an enemy target. Opposition petitions gained many island signatures. An army spokesman at a meeting on the island tried to encourage islanders by noting how much the army had done for Huntsville, Alabama, increasing its 15,000 population ten times over.[7] He must not have realized that this was absolutely the wrong thing to say on a Puget Sound island. In February 1969, the Pentagon suspended planning and construction while the project underwent a thorough review, and Bainbridge Island never saw the proposed ABM facility.

As the Cold War continued, a Reagan administration plan released in the early 1980s specified communities in the United States which should be prepared to receive refugees should a nuclear attack occur. One of the areas chosen, the San Juan Islands, should welcome some sixteen thousand Whidbey Islanders, according to the plan, for the Naval Air Station might be a target. San Juan islanders of course pointed out the proposal's obvious flaws. What boats could quickly move so many people? Where on the islands could so many people find food, shelter, medical supplies, and facilities? The plan suggested that perhaps six thousand refugees, but no more, could hide in small boats for two or three days, until the worst of the radioactive fallout was over. What would the others do? Were the reason for the plan not so serious, laughter was the obvious response.

Nowadays, Whidbey's Naval Air Station is at the center of two controversies. Many residents on the northern islands as well as in the Port Townsend area continue to be frustrated by noisy practice flights, especially at a field a mile or so southeast of Coupeville, with dimensions marked so that pilots can practice touch-and-go landings as though this were an aircraft carrier. Summertime night landing practices can be especially irritating, because with darkness coming very late, they can last beyond midnight. Some nearby residents say they need earplugs to sleep. Local citizens have even traveled to Washington, D.C. to lobby against the noisy planes. By 2015 Whidbey Island housed eighty-two especially noisy Growler aircraft and in 2019 added thirty-six more, also increasing the number of flights near Coupeville. Many Whidbey residents understandably continue to object. If these noisy practice flights are not allowed, however, there is a chance that the Navy could leave Whidbey Island altogether, devastating the island economy.

Another problem has surfaced on northern Whidbey Island. Some landowners near the NAS have found their wells contaminated by foam used in NAS fire-fighting exercises. The EPA has held that over a lifetime these chemicals in drinking water can lead to serious health problems, and tests show that the chemicals have polluted Whidbey well water. The Navy has supplied bottled water to affected households, and in January 2018 the Navy announced a plan to filter Coupeville's water supply. Contamination has also been found near Oak Harbor, however, and in stormwater runoff that impacts farm fields where animals graze.

From the beginning of the twentieth century, military facilities have occupied land on the islands. Most have been temporary, but World War II and subsequent military activities have had a permanent effect on the islands. The northern part of Whidbey Island has been changed immeasurably. War also wrongly displaced numerous people from Bainbridge and Vashon Islands and too many of the Nikkei did not return. Their incarceration led to unnecessary suffering and the memory of a sad time on the two islands. To this day, older people still remember when the nation was caught up in war fervor and the nation did an unforgivable wrong to many islanders.

15 | Ferries: Black Ball and More

FERRY BOATS HAVE MADE IT POSSIBLE FOR MANY, perhaps most, islanders to be islanders. These vessels have helped drive island history, influencing island residents to live where ferry service exists and where reaching the ferry dock is convenient. The ferries are a fact of life. They existed even before cars came on the transportation scene, because a ferry is, simply, a boat that takes goods or people across a body of water. In general usage in Puget Sound country, however, ferries have come to mean the boats that carry automotive vehicles as well as people.

The evolution from Mosquito Fleet to ferry systems was slow and far from uniform, the major change being, simply, that people drove cars on and off the boats. Before remodeled boats started carrying motor vehicles, a few cars made it to the islands as cargo, but the state of island roads in those days did not encourage automobile use. The lightly populated islands such as Waldron and Decatur Islands in the San Juans have been served by Mosquito Fleet boats but have never received auto ferry service—and the people who live there are happy not to have it. Stuart Island, for one, has avoided the "curse of ferry service," allowing it to retain a "pristine, rural quality," noted *Seattle Times* writer Gretchen Huizinga.[1]

Another significant change in boat service exemplifies the ferry business. Boats mostly began to travel across the water from one dock to another rather than calling in at many piers along a shoreline and then crossing a channel to a major port, as did so many Mosquito Fleet vessels. Only in the San Juan Islands does a vestige of the old system continue, with Washington State Ferries serving the four most populous islands. Another transition is the conversion from private to public operation of the ferries, which has taken over almost all the service in Puget Sound country.

Ferry service on Puget Sound has evolved over the years. Very early came Camano Island's cable ferry, a barge which carried horse-drawn vehicles. Oher ferries were converted Mosquito Fleet vessels. The *Chippewa*, an early self-propelled ferryboat, was built in Ohio in 1900 and brought to Puget Sound in 1906. She worked for the Navy during World War I and in 1926 became a car ferry, with her hull widened so that she could carry more vehicles. At different times she served Bainbridge and the San Juans. A 1932 remodel saw her converted from steam to diesel power, but she was a single-ender, meaning she had to turn around on each trip. Not until 1964 did the *Chippewa* retire.

Some islands once had ferries but now sport bridges connecting them to the mainland. Travelers crossed Deception Pass by ferry. Service using a barge under tow started in 1912, when horses and wagons, not cars, formed the load, but a car crossed on the barge as early as 1914. Starting in 1919, Mrs. Berte Olson, the first female ferry captain of a Puget Sound auto ferry, owned and operated the ferry service with her husband. Several years later, the Olsons built strong docks and replaced the tug and barge operation with a boat, the *Deception Pass*, which could carry up to twelve cars.

Bainbridge Island had no bridge to the mainland until 1950. In 1912, the first ferry service for automobiles used a barge to cross from Point White to the Kitsap County mainland, but beginning in 1924, the ferries instead crossed from Fletcher Bay farther north on the island to Brownsville. The island also had service between Bainbridge and Seattle starting in 1923, when a boat operated by the Kitsap Transportation Company began running on a schedule from Port Blakely. Ironically, this was just about the time when the Port Blakely Mill shut down for good. Most of the influential people who would use a car ferry lived nearby, though. In 1937, Eagle Harbor took over as the Bainbridge destination. For a few years, vessels stopped both at Eagledale and Winslow, backing across the harbor. The Eagledale service stopped in 1949 after high tide damaged the dock and repairs seemed too costly. Now, Winslow houses

the only Bainbridge terminal, though in 1949 some residents worked—
unsuccessfully—to have the Winslow stop relocated to Port Blakely.

A ferry operated by Mason County ran to Harstine Island starting in
1922. The scow on the route, the *Island Belle*, could only carry about three
cars and she made just three round trips daily. A larger vessel, a barge
called the *Harstine*, came in 1929 and the *Harstine II*, an eight-car vessel,
served the route from 1945 until replaced by a bridge in 1969.

Fox Island, west of Tacoma, had ferry service to the foot of Sixth
Avenue in the city for many years. As early as 1914, cars came to the island
on the upper deck of the steamboat *Transit*. She could haul up to six of that
era's cars, but service depended upon favorable wind and tide. The Skansie
Brothers Shipbuilding Company in nearby Gig Harbor built the *Fox Island*
early in the 1920s. This vessel took over the run, carrying about eighteen
Model A-size vehicles. Later, the Skansie brothers ran the Washington
Navigation Company, which assumed the Fox Island ferry run and operated it until 1940. For a time, the run was triangular, serving Tacoma, Fox
Island and Point Fosdick, which is on the mainland across The Narrows
from Tacoma. Pierce County took over the Tacoma-Fox Island route in
1940, leasing it to a private operator who replaced the *Fox Island* with another Skansie-built vessel, the *City of Steilacoom*.

In 1944, the county assumed operation of the Fox Island run when
Captain Floyd M. Hunt, who had been running the service, decided to
abandon it. The *City of Steilacoom* made six or eight daily forty-minute
trips from dock to dock, the final one of the day leaving Tacoma at seven in
the evening. Near the end of its years of service, round trips had increased
to eleven. Things occasionally go awry for every ferry system; in 1953, the
Tacoma News Tribune reported that Pierce County Ferry Supervisor Gus
Partridge got an eleven p.m. phone call one night from a woman reporting,
"I think there's something wrong with your ferry. It's drifting down by the
Narrows bridge."[2] But soon, ferry service to Fox Island ceased, as a bridge
to the island opened in 1954. The island's old dock and pilings stood until
2013, year by year becoming more dilapidated. As part of a program to
remove creosoted structures from Puget Sound, the remains of the dock
and its associated 160 piles no longer sit at the edge of the island.

The story of Indian and Marrowstone Islands is exceptional. Early
Norwegian settlers "improved" the connection between them with fill, so
a person could easily walk or drive a horse and wagon from one to the

other, but in 2020, a small bridge was built to replace the fill. The two long, slender islands also had a natural connection to the mainland. As traffic on the Strait of Juan de Fuca and Puget Sound increased during Mosquito Fleet days, though, mariners urged that a canal be dredged between Indian Island and the mainland. The reason: the passage around the north end of Marrowstone featured treacherous winds, rough seas, and hazardous rocks, so much so that in winter, sternwheel steamers did not traverse the route. Native Americans even beached their canoes to carry them across the ridge where the canal now sits rather than risk the water passage around Marrowstone Head. The communities of Irondale and Port Hadlock south of Port Townsend were growing, and entrepreneurs eyed their industrial potential, which a canal would boost.

With ominous signs of approaching war in Europe, early in the twentieth century American defense planners noted that opening a canal would create a new water route from the Sound to Port Townsend and thus make it easier to defend that city from attack. Perhaps because few people lived on the two islands when the canal was dug, their opposition could easily be disregarded. After congressional agreement to fund construction, dredging began removing a ridge of gravel about 450 feet wide. The channel, known ever since as Portage Canal, opened to traffic in 1915. It is seventy-five feet wide with a depth of fifteen feet at low tide.

Islanders wanted a ferry, of course. A private barge operation to Port Townsend offered service by 1920, and a car ferry began crossing to the mainland near Port Hadlock in 1925. As the number of cars on the two islands grew, residents clamored for a bridge, but learned in 1927 that it would require military permission. However, ship traffic, not automobile passage, was the government's main concern. Because of these difficulties, islanders instead concentrated on getting better ferry service, which came in 1929. As the vessel, the M.V. *Nordland*, carried only about six cars, islanders found the service more and more inadequate, though it became free in the mid-1930s. Not until 1952 did a bridge open.

Other ferry routes on Puget Sound continue in use. San Juan ferry service started in 1922 as a summertime experiment. Two boats, the *Harvester King*—a scow built to harvest kelp—and the sternwheeler *Gleaner*, plied the route. The *Harvester King* could carry about a dozen cars and the *Gleaner*, twenty-five. Every day one of them started at Anacortes and the other at Sidney, Vancouver Island, and crossed the

Sound with stops at Orcas Island and Roche Harbor, each vessel making just one daily crossing. This service proved successful and continued in 1923 with different boats. Soon the Puget Sound Navigation Company (Black Ball) took over the service. On San Juan Island, the boats continued to stop at Roche Harbor, not shifting to Friday Harbor until 1928. A Lopez Island stop, where today's ferries still call, came in 1926 and the Shaw Island stop in 1930. By the 1930s, today's routing was well-established, though the boats stopped at Shaw only upon a flag signal. Various additional operators ran ferries to the San Juans for relatively short periods. These included a route between Chuckanut, south of Bellingham, and a dock at Obstruction Pass on Orcas Island. In the late 1920s, a six-car ferry briefly operated between Lummi Island and Point Lawrence, on the east side of Orcas Island.

Service between Port Townsend and the west side of Whidbey Island became available in the mid-1920s via a tug-and-barge combination. Loading and unloading on Whidbey was problematic, however, because the approach was a bank of gravel. In 1927, Black Ball took over the route, using a newly built dock on the island about one-and-one-half miles from the site of the present dock, near the other end of Crockett Lake. As World War II began, though, Black Ball quit providing the service, which had run only during the summers. Despite citizen concern, not until several years after the end of the war did the ferry operate again. The federal government built the current harbor and three Port Townsend businessmen formed Olympic Ferries to reinstate the service. By 1973, constituents were pressing for year-round boats instead of six-month service. Olympic then found it could no longer sustain the route and Washington State legislators ordered Washington State Ferries to take over, so the state bought out Olympic Ferries.

Car-carrying boats to South Whidbey Island began operating in 1919, but sparked arguments between islanders who wanted a Langley-Everett service and those who preferred a Clinton-Mukilteo route. Willis Nearhoff's company, Central Ferry Lines, began a Clinton-Everett route, but in 1923 the Whidbey Island Transportation Company opened a Langley-Clinton-mainland service. Nearhoff bought the Langley dock in 1926, hoping to put the rival firm out of business, but finally sold out in 1928 and direct service including Langley ended in 1929. Since then, South Whidbey service has run between Clinton and Mukilteo.

King County began the first automobile ferry service to Vashon Island in 1916, using the first diesel vessel specifically built to carry cars, the *Vashon Island*. The route joined Des Moines, south of Seattle, to the Portage area. In 1919 the county also started running car ferries from Harper, on the South Kitsap mainland, via the north end of Vashon Island to downtown Seattle. Island berry farmers had a hand in getting the service to the King County mainland moved away from the Des Moines terminal location, for they wanted a route closer to Seattle and its public market.

The Kitsap County Transportation Company took over service to Vashon in 1925 and soon stopped docking in downtown Seattle, instead going to Fauntleroy. The company continued to run a foot passenger boat on the old route to downtown Seattle for a while. The shift to Fauntleroy created some controversy on Vashon Island, but in 1939, when Black Ball suggested including downtown Seattle in the route, a survey found that Vashon folks preferred the more frequent service the shorter Fauntleroy route could provide. Today this is seen as a decision that helped prevent rampant development on the island.

Ferry runs between Tahlequah, at the far south end of Vashon Island, and Point Defiance in Tacoma began in 1920. Pierce County arranged for a boat that could carry up to thirty-two cars on its two daily round trips. Zilfa Phillips opined in the *Tacoma News Tribune* that despite the island being in King County, "in interests and spirit [it] belongs so much to Pierce County."[3] During 1920 Vashon Island had three car ferry routes: north end to Harper and Seattle, Portage to Des Moines and south end to Tacoma, as well as a few remaining Mosquito Fleet passenger routes. Operations between Portage and Des Moines ended in 1922.

The Skansie brothers took over the Tacoma-Vashon Island route in 1927. One of their ferries on the route was the *Skansonia*, built, of course, by the Skansie firm in 1929. Her sister ferry, the *Defiance*, served the Keystone-Port Townsend run in the 1950s, and after her retirement traveled around the Sound processing dogfish. Later she moved on to Alaska. Meanwhile, the *Skansonia* sits today in Seattle's Lake Union as a venue for parties, weddings, and receptions.

Larger firms, most prominently Black Ball, eventually took over the runs serving the main islands, but today Whatcom, Skagit and Pierce Counties each run a small operation serving a Puget Sound island or two. The Whatcom County ferry travels to Lummi Island from a dock at Gooseberry Point on the Lummi Indian Reservation north of Bellingham. It takes eight minutes for the nine-tenths-of-a-mile route crossing of Hale Passage. A private company began operating boats here in 1921, but the service was undependable. In 1923, the *Central*, which burned wood by the cord, took over and in 1929 the county replaced it with the *Chief Kwina*, which could carry six cars per trip—if they were small. In 1962, the sixteen-to-twenty-car *Whatcom Chief*, built for the county, went into service. Given her half-century history on the run, she has been remarkably trouble-free. Unfortunately, the county has a passenger-only replacement vessel to use when the *Whatcom Chief* needs maintenance, which is scheduled each September for two or three weeks, depending on what must be done. Meanwhile, the boat too often fills to capacity, leaving cars sitting on the dock, and the vessel is nearing the end of its useful life. It probably will be replaced within the next decade, and planners suggest obtaining a hybrid diesel-electric boat that will carry about twice as many cars as does the *Chief*.

Lummi Island's ferry service has had its troubles. The Inlandboatmen's Union struck for twenty days in the summer of 1976, after members had worked without a contract for half a year. Islanders had only a six-hour notice that service would stop, and some vehicles stranded on the mainland were vandalized while gas was siphoned from others. During the strike, the county furnished a free passenger ferry, but boarding was treacherous, requiring one to climb a ladder, and a few passengers slipped into the water. After settlement of the strike, ferry rates soon rose. Later another problem surfaced. A new dock built on the island in 1977 proved unreliable, with its ramp collapsing into the water in March 1979. The old dock continued in service but had trouble with heavily loaded trucks, so the county had to rebuild it.

A problem with long-term implications faced the Lummi ferry recently. Until 1962, Whatcom County had no formal lease with the Lummi Nation to allow use of the mainland landing site. The lease expired in 2010 and only an interim agreement allowed use of the dock to continue. The tribe asked for greater compensation and threatened to shut down the ferry system. After extension of the deadline for agreement and negotiations that sometimes became tense, Lummi and county officials finally reached an accord in September 2011. The new lease, which costs ferry riders and county taxpayers well more than the old one, extends use of the dock on the Lummi Reservation for another thirty-five years.

Skagit County runs the *Guemes* between Anacortes and Guemes Island, just north of the city across Guemes Channel. The ferry makes the not-quite-two-mile trip in about seven minutes. The first *Guemes*, built in Anacortes in 1917, took foot passengers to the island, and horses sometimes pulled wagons on to the boat for the crossing. In 1927, remodeling allowed the boat to carry up to six motor vehicles. Skagit County long helped subsidize the privately-operated ferry service and in 1965 took over the operation. The *Guemes* served the island until 1960. The larger boat that then assumed the route, the *Almar*, had been ferrying people across the Columbia River at Maryhill until construction of a bridge there. The *Almar*, a "rinky-dink ferry," in the words of Guemes Island Community Club President Ralph Stockton,[4] could hold nine to twelve cars. In 1979, an even larger boat, again named the *Guemes*, took over. It can carry twenty-one cars. A Seattle firm designed this boat, but a Massachusetts yard built it. The vessel took just over a month to make the six-thousand-mile trip to Anacortes via the Panama Canal. Today the *Guemes* uses the dock in Anacortes near the city center that once served San Juan Island runs.

Disruptions large and small have occurred on the Guemes route.. When gasoline supplies in the United States were short in 1973, Skagit County cut the number of ferry runs to Guemes Island in order to conserve fuel. Three years later it was a labor problem, with Inlandboatmen's Union members striking for higher wages on June 25, 1976, when they also stopped service to Lummi Island. A mere twelve striking workers stranded residents of both islands. Interestingly, many on Guemes blamed Skagit County commissioners, not the ferry workers, for the stoppage. Some islanders claimed that the commissioners' lack of support was a reaction to Guemes Islanders' opposition a decade earlier to the plan to build an aluminum smelter on their island. The ferry strike lasted for almost three weeks, with private boats stepping in to provide some passenger service. Guemes Island had a 4th of July parade scheduled, but floats being prepared for it were stuck in Anacortes. As on Lummi Island, the strike came when island population was at its highest, perhaps two or three times its winter figure.

Court orders in both counties sent the men back to work. Despite disruptions such as these, the ferry rides to Lummi and Guemes Islands are pleasant and relaxing in good weather because the boats are small and unpretentious and the journeys are short, but in both boats, only very small cabins offer cover for foot passengers during wind and rain. These days, replacing the Guemes boat is being considered, and acquisition of an all-electric ferry is one of the possibilities.

Much farther south, Pierce County runs a ferry to Ketron and Anderson Islands from a dock in the mainland town of Steilacoom. Starting in 1922, the Skansie brothers operated the run to Anderson Island under contract with the county. They made the three-and-one-half-mile run first with the *Elk*, then the larger *City of Steilacoom*. For a time, these three or four daily trips to and from Steilacoom served Anderson and McNeil Islands plus Longbranch on the mainland just northwest of Anderson. In 1937, briefly, Anderson had no car service, but Pierce County established a route serving Steilacoom and Anderson and McNeil Islands via the *Tahoma*, which could carry only nine—perhaps ten—cars per trip. In 1961 the county added Ketron Island to the route. In 1967 the county bought the larger *Tourister*, which had been crossing the mouth of the Columbia River near Astoria, Oregon, until a bridge opened there. Pierce County officials renamed the boat, for *Tourister* seemed inappropriate for a boat that served an island dominated by a prison. The vessel therefore became the *Islander*.

For twenty-three years Anderson elementary pupils took the ferry to McNeil Island to go to a one-room school there with prison staff members' children. After a new Anderson Island school opened in 1981, Pierce County dropped McNeil from its Anderson Island service, because almost no one was using the boat between these islands. McNeil Island has a separate vessel, though, provided by Washington State. After the McNeil Island school closed, employees' children have used this vessel to attend a mainland school. The state's Department of Corrections now has responsibility to provide all transportation to McNeil Island.

In 1977, a larger boat, the *Steilacoom*, began operating the Steilacoom-Anderson-Ketron route. Since 1994, the *Christine Anderson*, built by Whidbey Island's Nichols Brothers, has served the two islands, taking over after continued complaints about inadequate space on the *Steilacoom*, which was only half its size. This newer boat, with a capacity of fifty-four cars and a large passenger cabin above, commemorates islander Christine Anderson's long and varied service to her Anderson Island community, especially its children.

A more recent and slightly larger boat, the *Steilacoom II*, also built by Nichols Bros., has more recently become the main boat, supplemented by the *Christine Anderson*. Today, ferries make fifteen trips a day to Anderson Island and more to serve weekend travelers, especially in July and August. Many fewer runs also stop at small, private Ketron Island. Pierce County's one-route ferry system is unusual in that it commissioned a spare boat to use when necessary. Having a spare boat does not solve every problem, though. On a late Sunday afternoon in August 2019, the Anderson Island loading ramp failed, stranding some two hundred people overnight. The island's fire boat made multiple runs to get people to the mainland and Anderson's fire station opened so people could spend the night there. Ferry officials, however, closed the restrooms at the dock, where some people were sleeping in their cars.

One small privately-owned island in Puget Sound has car ferry service. Herron Island's south Puget Sound community of about 150 people maintains a ferry, the *Charlie Wells*, named for the man who ran the island's first ferry, the *Annabelle*, for thirty years. Nichols Brothers built the *Charlie Wells* for the island in 1989. Fares plus homeowners' assessments support the boat, which is only available for Herron Islanders and their guests.

Herron Islanders had to go without their ferry for forty-seven days in the late summer of 1969 when the island's ferry slip broke down. While small boats carried passengers, owners of cars stranded on the island parked their vehicles—with keys in the ignition—at the dock, so others could use them to transport supplies home. A barge that was able to land did arrive to carry some cars stranded on the island to the mainland where they were needed, and ferry captain Charlie Wells and his friend Del Koski used their own boats twice a day to take local children to and from the mainland, so they could go to school.

While these small ferry systems continue to play an important role in Puget Sound waters, two strong competitors emerged to serve more populous islands, having bought up some smaller ferry systems by the 1930s and becoming responsible for most of the ferry service on the Sound. These firms were the Kitsap County Transportation Company and the Puget Sound Navigation Company, or Black Ball. Strikes began plaguing both companies during that decade, however, as the Depression helped spur labor union activity.

The first strike that had a strong impact on ferry service to the islands came on November 7, 1935. After unsuccessful arbitration, the Masters, Mates and Pilots Association and the Ferryboatmen's Union struck the Kitsap County Transportation Company and the Whidbey Island Transportation Company over wages and an eight-hour day, then soon walked off Black Ball boats, too. To compensate, the *Virginia V* offered rides to passengers between Seattle and Vashon Island since the ferries to Vashon's north end were not running, though the island's south end ferry, operated by Skansie Brothers, operated as usual. Fox Island service was also not affected. The Bainbridge Island situation was similar to Vashon's, with a passenger steamer to Seattle while the Bainbridge to Kitsap mainland run operated by the Kitsap company continued to serve the public. Union Business Manager Capt. John M. Fox stated, "It's such a small operation we don't care about it."[5]

The strike continued over the Thanksgiving Day holiday and led to all sorts of coping methods. On November 22 the King County Commissioners authorized county operation of service to Vashon Island's north end, striking workers agreed, and this service began on the county-owned *Washington* with a full schedule. The boat held only thirty-five cars and the need to serve Fauntleroy, Vashon Island and Kitsap County's terminal at Harper meant that service at each dock came only every two hours. Finally, after thirty-three days, arbitration led to the resumption of service. The settlement came January 28, 1936, but economic losses exacerbated by the strike precipitated the sale of Kitsap Transportation to Alexander Peabody and his Black Ball operation.

Again, workers walked out on May 28, 1937, tying up Black Ball boats from the San Juans south to Vashon, once more with wages and hours the issues. Again, holiday weekend traffic felt the impact, though the Inlandboatmen's Union had given a few days' warning. Some Island farmers worried. While strawberries ripened, how could the growers get them to market? Service between the south end of Vashon island and Tacoma meanwhile continued, and once again the *Virginia V* offered passenger service.

The Bainbridge Island Chamber of Commerce telegraphed Governor Clarence D. Martin, describing the island's predicament: "The Island is completely isolated without hospital service, wholesale food supplies cannot be obtained, and island stocks are dangerously low. Stop. Strawberry pickers cannot be brought in nor can berries be shipped." Walt Woodward, who lived on Bainbridge Island and then worked for the *Seattle Times*, complained because he got his pants wet while commuting to work in his sixteen-foot outboard.[6] Meanwhile, Port Blakely residents chartered a forty-five foot yacht and some islanders pleaded for at least one trip daily by a vessel that could load autos, since their cars were marooned on the island.

In time, the King County Commissioners agreed that a boat could be chartered to run on the route to Vashon Island's north end. The *Washington* began service June 16, 1937. The first few runs from Vashon on the two-hour schedule necessitated by single-boat service left cars stranded on the docks, just as in 1935. Bainbridge Island, meanwhile, remained totally cut off, except for temporary passenger service. The Deception Pass bridge provided a route to the mainland from Whidbey Island's far north, but that did not help South Whidbey commuters.

This time, the strike lasted twenty-seven days. Captain Peabody "reluctantly" accepted a proposal submitted by Governor Martin which included temporary wage increases and a nine-hour day consisting of consecutive working hours. When service resumed, riders found that fares had gone up, some of them by twenty-five percent or more. The State Public Service Commission held hearings on the rate question. It had the final say, and upheld only a partial raise.

Except for a brief wildcat strike in 1938 that disrupted service only to Vashon, relative peace lasted until 1939. In March, the State Senate defeated a bill that would have allowed a state-operated ferry system and the *Vashon Island News-Record* reported that "a King County senator (the one that lives at the Olympic Hotel) dismissed the matter by saying, 'Well, they're all millionaires over there on the islands, so high ferry fares don't make any difference to them.'"[7]

The agreement that ended the 1937 strike had lapsed. Negotiations between the company and the unions failed, and the unions announced an August 1939 strike date. Customers—especially islanders—became more irate and better organized. To dramatize their plight, at least two hundred Vashon Islanders appeared on the dock, some armed with ax handles, rocks, and clubs. Thirty Vashon men took the last boat scheduled to leave the island and attempted to seize her, rushing onto the vessel before her departure. When she reached the Kitsap County dock at Harper, where the schedule showed she would sit overnight, the islanders stayed on board, holding a sit-down strike. They used the boat's galley to cook for themselves. After a one-night stay, though, the insurance company that provided coverage to the ferries asked the islanders to leave, and they complied.

The August 1939 strike lasted twenty-three days. Walt Woodward, still commuting, wondered whether he should wear bathing trunks to the job. Again, King County soon began to help some islanders. Officials arranged that the *Washington* temporarily serve Vashon and Bainbridge, alternating trips between Vashon and Seattle with trips between Bainbridge and Seattle. Meanwhile, San Juan islanders felt despondent, worried both about their crops and the tourists who would not arrive. The union agreed to one trip daily between Anacortes and the San Juans normally served by Black Ball. A Ferry Users' Committee made up of people who relied on various ferries urged arbitration. Many frustrated islanders pleaded for Washington State to provide service, but legal barriers made this nearly impossible. The strike continued, and in response, the committee urged that any new agreement include a no-strike provision.

Could the government condemn ferry company-owned property—the docks? Could two counties work together—King and Kitsap, for example—to establish ferry service? After twenty-three days, the ferries were back in service, as the various parties had finally agreed to arbitration. Arbitration meant compromise, with some workers receiving a wage increase—much smaller than they had asked—along with an eight-hour day. Bitterness among all remained, but with World War II intervening, the next strike did not occur until 1947.

In the late 1930s, Captain Peabody expanded his Black Ball fleet considerably. Fortuitously, the Golden Gate Bridge and other spans opened in California, meaning that ferries were now available. As war approached, traffic on Puget Sound was growing, while the Black Ball boats were aging. Black Ball bought the *Quinault*, *Nisqually*, *Illahee* and *Klickitat*, which originally were the *Redwood Empire*, the *Mendocino*, *Lake Tahoe* and *Stockton*. Known as the steel-electrics, they remained in use on Puget Sound until 2007.

Difficulties with ferry service crop up unexpectedly, and this happened when The Narrows Bridge suddenly collapsed on November 7, 1940. Ferry service between Tacoma's Point Defiance and the south end of Vashon Island immediately took a back seat to getting people across The Narrows. Vashon Islanders found themselves waiting for ferries that were either late or nonexistent, their boat having been diverted to a run across The Narrows. It took more than a week for Vashon service to return to what islanders, thought was normal, but boats continued to be shifted from the

Vashon run unexpectedly. Service improved when Black Ball took over the Point Defiance-Tahlequah franchise in the spring of 1941.

The World War II years proved a bonanza for Black Ball due to the growth of defense jobs on both sides of Puget Sound. The ferry company deserves credit for aligning its policies with defense needs. The war brought increased service. Peabody replaced the Fletcher Bay-Brownsville run with a new route from Bainbridge Island's Point White closer to Bremerton, largely to help commuters. By 1943, the sixteen runs from Point White to the Kitsap mainland spanned eighteen hours each day. Captain Peabody decreased fares on his routes both for vehicles and passengers, and his ferries saw profit during the war years despite the lower fares. With men needed in the armed forces or defense industries, staffing the boats caused some difficulty, however.

It was after the war that ferry problems became acute. Captain Peabody wanted to restore fares to their higher prewar level while employees wanted higher wages to cope with increases in the cost of living. Meanwhile, customers were irate because Peabody cut service in 1946 because no longer were a great number of war workers riding the boats. He also reimposed the higher prewar rates, to take effect January 1, 1947. Then, on January 16, Peabody applied to state officials to raise rates an additional thirty percent. While studying all aspects of the situation, the state approved this rate temporarily. Ferry riders complained—and organized. Six hundred islanders appeared at a meeting held at Vashon High School to protest. A caravan including representatives of various islands dependent on the ferries went to Olympia to meet with State Transportation Director Paul Revelle and others to protest the rate increase.

When the state legislature met in early 1947, members introduced measures that would allow the state to take over the ferry system. The legislature did not support this, but members did authorize creation of special districts to run ferries. Meanwhile, labor troubles added a complication. On March 14 marine engineers walked off the job, feeling that Black Ball had not treated them equitably. Members of other ferry unions agreed not to cross picket lines, and all Black Ball service stopped. The *Vashon Island News-Record* titled an editorial about ferry rates and strikes "The Public be Damned," a common feeling among ferry users, and declared, "As much as we are against public ownership, we believe that the State should operate our ferries." The *Bainbridge Review* railed against "high fares and undependable service," asserting that this combination has "always . . . made a hazard out of living on this island." One estimate suggested that the strike affected some ten thousand Puget Sound commuters.[8]

The strike was devastating to many islanders, as by this time Black Ball was the company serving the San Juans, south and west Whidbey Island, Eagle Harbor and Point White on Bainbridge Island, and both north and south ends of Vashon Island. On Bainbridge Island even the buses did not run during the nearly week-long strike, because Black Ball subsidized them. Again, commuters tried to cope by using private boats. After a few days, the *Silver Swan*, a cruise boat complete with dance floor—a "Floating Night Club," wrote the *Seattle Times*—began three daily round trips to Vashon.[9] Governor Mon Wallgren soon intervened and the strikers voted to accept a contract drawn up by negotiators meeting in the governor's office.

A few months later, Revelle announced the department's decision on rate increases. Instead of thirty percent, the state would allow a ten percent rise over prewar fares. Black Ball would have to refund customers any payments over that amount. The company appealed the ruling and continued to collect the higher rate, even requesting an additional ten percent. Vashon Islanders responded by collecting signatures calling for an election to create a ferry district now that state law permitted it, and in a September vote, islanders supported a ferry district, 326-38.

As these events in 1947 showed, the stakeholders in the ferry transportation system—Black Ball, its employees, Washington State government, and ferry riders—had very different viewpoints, needs and concerns. Troubles spilled over into 1948.

In January 1948, a Superior Court judge upheld the Transportation Department decision that the ferry rate increases recently imposed should be cut to ten percent. Captain Peabody announced that he would be forced to shut down the company at the end of February. He did this, and communities again chartered boats while small aircraft increased service to the San Juans. Freight traveled via tug and barge.

The 1948 ferry disruption was different than earlier stoppages. First, it was not instigated by a strike. Second, now that Vashon Island voters had authorized creation of a ferry district, King County commissioners leased a county boat, the *Lincoln*, to the new ferry district—officially, King County Ferry District No. 1. A steamboat built in 1914, the *Lincoln* had ferried people across Lake Washington until a floating bridge put it out of work in 1940. Vashon became the only island normally served by Black Ball system to have car ferry service during the stoppage, as the Vashon Ferry District ran boats between the island and Fauntleroy. Service was usually available hourly from six in the morning until an hour after midnight.

On the second day that his ferries did not run, Captain Peabody asked the state for an additional thirty percent rise in fares to be imposed on top of the thirty percent increase he had instituted the previous year, which would make the fare sixty-nine percent higher than it had been before February 1947. State officials reacted by looking more seriously into operating the ferry system. A woman broke her wrist when trying to step on to a Bainbridge dock from a passenger steamer rushed into temporary service. Bainbridge Islanders began studying the possibility of operating their own ferry district just as Vashon was doing.

On March 8, Captain Peabody and King County officials agreed that the county could run all the boats operating between King and Kitsap Counties except the Vashon run, which the Vashon Ferry District continued to operate. Other counties also made agreements with Captain Peabody. For example, Pierce County operated the run between Tacoma and South Vashon Island, leasing it to Black Ball. Thus, everybody had ferry service once again—but the Vashon fares were lower than those on other runs, for Black Ball's new, higher-than-ever fares were in effect elsewhere.

Black Ball announced that it would resume the Vashon Island-Fauntleroy run on May 15, 1948, but islanders were so angry at the company that they were determined to prevent this. A posse, the "Vashon Vigilantes," gathered at the dock to keep Captain Peabody's ferry away. With brute strength, plus ax handles and even billiard cues as weapons, they repelled the boat, and it left Vashon Island. The Vashon Ferry District had its own troubles with ferry breakdowns and barely adequate service, but islanders insisted on controlling their ferry service, and so they did, for more than three years. However, this meant that there was no direct Vashon-Kitsap County service during that time.

By mid-1948, serious talk that Washington State would purchase Black Ball was underway. Vashon residents were not the only islanders fed up with Black Ball. In September Bainbridge Islanders voted 333 to 289 to authorize creation of a ferry district. Instead, the state took over. Peabody's company rejected an offer by the state in August 1948 to buy the system;

the state increased the offer, and by September Peabody and his stock-holders accepted. But the Washington State Supreme Court ruled against this. It took a year before necessary changes in state law took effect and Peabody's company and the state government could come to an agreement that would stick, but finally the state bought all the Black Ball ferries and terminals except for those of the Port Angeles-Victoria, British Columbia, route. Washington State Ferries would begin operations on June 1, 1951.

Thus, Puget Sound's main ferry system evolved from private to public ownership, but boats continued to age, operating costs continued to rise, population in the Puget Sound region continued to grow, and in 1951, the question was whether state operation of Puget Sound's dominant ferry system could provide this crucial service to the public and, everyone hoped, improve it.

16 | Ferries: The Washington State Ferries Era

WASHINGTON STATE FERRIES NOW OPERATES one of the largest ferry systems in the United States, and unlike almost all other large ferry fleets, it is publicly owned, which means its focus is to provide service to the public rather than to make a profit. Over its seventy years of operation times have changed, and population has grown on the islands and the nearby mainland. In 1994, U.S. Senator Maria Cantwell of Washington State noted that WSF served more passengers than Amtrak.[1] Washington State has needed more and sometimes larger boats, and vessels and terminals need maintenance and sometimes renovation. The ferry system has had to cope with weather problems and labor issues. The ferries continue to provide a lifeline to islanders—and the boats provide at least a few minutes of relaxation en route.

To set up the state-run ferry system, Washington State purchased and leased terminals and boats from cities, counties, and other companies as well as Black Ball. WSF bought the boats used by Vashon's ferry district, and with the state now the premier ferry operator the Vashon Ferry District came to an end. State officials looked upon their new ferry system as temporary, however. The plan was to replace many routes with a series of bridges, but the state has built only two. One crosses Hood Canal. The other, across Agate Pass to Bainbridge Island, is the only one that reaches an island.

When the state took over ferry operations in 1951 not much seemed to have changed for riders, but no longer did people see the familiar black ball on the boats' smokestacks. The new era began amicably. Riders found the routes familiar, and most Black Ball employees came to work for Washington State Ferries with pay and benefits unchanged.

Most of the time, Washington State's ferries can be depended upon to take passengers where they want to go, but the boats make the news when problems surface. Even in the twenty-first century WSF does not have enough replacement boats to maintain all scheduled service during regular maintenance periods should a sudden breakdown occur. Money always seems tight. The state legislature has a crucial role in creating WSF's budget, and the ferry system is but one of many state responsibilities. Members from eastern Washington have no particular interest in subsidizing ferries, though ferry supporters point out how much money the state spends to build and maintain roads in the lightly populated eastern part of the state. In the early days of state operation, WSF made a small profit, even though ferry employees kept their union membership and benefits. The financial picture changed, and costs soon outran revenue. Rising fares could not always meet the need for funds, because if charges grew too high, riders would change their habits and desert the ferries. The financial quandary continues today.

Boat purchases have been an important priority. In 1953, after the Chesapeake Bay Bridge opened, Washington State acquired a boat no longer needed there and gave her the name *Rhododendron*. Two tugboats sent to the east coast brought the *Rhody* and her sister vessel, the *Olympic*, to Puget Sound via the Panama Canal. The two served the Sound well, and the *Olympic* retired in 1997. Her new owner's plans did not work out, and she sits derelict today next to the Ketron Island ferry dock. Meanwhile, the *Rhody*, with a sixty-five-car capacity, served the San Juans and later the south end of Vashon Island until 2012, then becoming a support vessel at a Vancouver Island scallop farm. People often lament boat retirements, and they did when the *Rhody* left. A more significant retirement had occurred in 1969, when the *San Mateo*, the last working steam-powered ferry on the Pacific Coast, was put out to pasture.

In 1969, WSF bought the *Kulshan*, which had run at San Diego as the *Crown City* until a bridge displaced it. Since then, the state has acquired only new boats. The first, the *Evergreen State*, came in 1954, well before the

Kulshan. Two sister vessels, the *Klahowya* and the *Tillicum*, began service a few years later, redesigned after it turned out that the *Evergreen State* had inadequate clearance for the tallest trucks, which were newly legal in Washington State. Only the *Tillicum* remains in service today.

The series of six boats built for WSF called the Issaquah Class ferries and delivered from 1980 to 1982 caused financial and political problems and worse, accidents. To support local industry, the state legislature had passed legislation to give firms in Washington State a preference over other shipbuilders. Thus, the state awarded the contract to a Seattle firm, Marine Power and Equipment, which had never built boats of that size and complexity. First, the *Issaquah* came into service in 1980. Its computer-operated propulsion system failed several times, and the boat slammed into the Fauntleroy landing on December 29, 1980, closing the dock for a month. WSF rerouted Vashon-bound boats to downtown Seattle, inconveniencing many islanders who worked south of downtown, for example at Boeing. In addition, the run to downtown Seattle used more fuel and took at least twice as long as the trip to Fauntleroy. Many islanders instead took the boat from Vashon's south end to Tacoma and this caused serious overloads on the southern route's *Hiyu,* the smallest vessel in the fleet. The system had no boats that could relieve the congestion.

Twice, Issaquah-class ferries suddenly began backing away from a dock while cars were loading, and once, in April 1982, a Mercedes Benz coming from Whidbey Island and disembarking from the *Cathlamet* at the Mukilteo dock landed on the floor of the Sound when the boat drifted sideways while unloading. A gap had resulted, with one of the car's wheels suddenly left in the air between the dock and the boat, and alert crewmen evacuated the occupants.

A ferry slammed into the Orcas Island dock on June 28, 1990, collapsing the protective wooden structure there and causing special anguish because this happened just before the busy Fourth of July weekend. A passenger-only boat provided by WSF began ferrying people to and from nearby Shaw Island to catch the regular ferry, and barge operators whose vessels could land on a beach took stranded motorists off Orcas Island. This was expensive and slow. Four days later, operations returned to normal.

The ferry system had to resolve the Issaquah class vessels' problems and eventually replaced the computer control systems on all the boats. Because of the problems, the 1980s saw charges of government ineptitude or political corruption, investigations, lawsuits and eventual settlement between the state and the shipbuilding company. Marine Power later declared bankruptcy and the debacle cost the state a lot of money.[2]

Accidents not involving Issaquah-class boats have occurred, too. In December 1972, a sleepy driver returning from Anderson Island drove his car off the boat about fifty feet from the Steilacoom landing. The car floated just long enough for the two passengers to get out, unhurt—but the driver had two outstanding warrants for traffic offenses, so he ended up in jail. In the San Juans, the *Elwha* lost power and rammed the Orcas Island dock in early September 1999, stalling auto traffic to the island. For more than a month while the dock was being repaired, car ferries could only dock at Orcas about twice daily, when the tide was at its highest. On a foggy day in September 2013, the *Hyak* collided with a sailboat between Lopez and Orcas Islands. Ferry crewmen rescued the boat's single occupant, but the sailboat sank.

Several very serious accidents have taken place. On an August 19, 1974 ferry from Vashon, a car bolted from the *Quinault*, jumping over wheel blocks, skidding almost six hundred feet down the ramp at the Fauntleroy dock and running into four passengers walking off the boat. Three of the four had significant injuries. The car dragged a fifteen-year-old Vashon Island High School student for thirty or more feet. He received head injuries that left him in critical condition, though he did recover. WSF considered installing overhead loading systems for Vashon foot passengers but dropped the idea because of cost and the relatively few pedestrians on this run. Docks serving islands do have overhead loading at Bainbridge Island, downtown Seattle, and Anacortes as well as at Mukilteo's new 2020 terminal.

On November 5, 1999, as the small private ferry serving Herron Island approached its mainland dock, a car carrying two women rolled off the boat into water about thirty feet deep. Only one of the women, a caregiver for an older wheelchair-bound woman, was able to get out of the car, while her patient died. As a ferry trip is beginning, deckhands routinely set a chock against one of the wheels of each car at the front of a boat to keep these cars from rolling forward during the journey. In this case, the deckhand had removed the block before the ferry reached the dock, and the car, in neutral gear, rolled forward while the boat was still about ninety feet out. The caregiver and two others on the boat tried unsuccessfully to rescue the victim, and Herron Islanders still grieve over the tragedy.

Accidents that damage docks prove the utility of providing two separate loading ramps at ferry docks. These docks used by boats on island runs have more than one such slip: downtown Seattle and Bainbridge Island, Clinton, Anacortes and Vashon Island's north end—but not Fauntleroy, where many neighborhood residents have long opposed any expansion of ferry service. In fact, they have wanted the dock closed. With more and more people using the ferries, lines of cars waiting on Fauntleroy Avenue approaching the dock get longer and longer and the traffic problem at Fauntleroy gets worse—while for ferry riders, the wait in line gets longer. In 1960 WSF ended similar neighborhood unhappiness in Anacortes by moving its operation from a dock in the middle of the city's residential area to an undeveloped, more spacious location at Ship Harbor a few miles away. Another dock relocation came in 1958. The Kitsap County landing on the route to Vashon Island and Fauntleroy was relocated from Harper to a new purpose-built dock at Southworth just over a mile to the southeast, shortening the ferry run, thus saving both time and money. The new site also includes a large parking lot.

Running the ferry system is a continuing challenge. Storms continue to create unexpected problems. A January 1954 blizzard stopped ferry service to the north end of Vashon Island. Strong winds led to a boat crashing into the single ferry slip there, rendering it useless. For a while, the boats stayed out in mid-channel and when waves subsided, dropped off only their foot passengers via a gangplank. WSF built a second slip at the Vashon dock in 1957.

The short Tahlequah-Point Defiance run is one of the most difficult in the state ferry system, one captain told the *Tacoma News Tribune* in the early 1970s. On an autumn Thursday morning in 1952, the ferry left Tahlequah on its regular eight o'clock morning run to Point Defiance, but the fog was so heavy the captain could not find the mainland dock. He kept sounding his whistle, hoping that an echo from the nearby smelter smokestack—later demolished—would help him figure out his position. He heard no echo and finally headed back to Vashon Island. There he picked up his nine o'clock passengers—and this time landed safely at Point Defiance. In September 1963, again in fog, the ferry ran aground on the slag heap next to the dock location. A nearby tugboat soon pulled the vessel away safely and the ferry suffered almost no damage. Not only do erratic currents and the somewhat frequent fog cause problems on this route, so do vacationers' sailboats, which can be especially troublesome near the Tacoma dock, which is located next to the Tacoma Yacht Club.

Bainbridge Islanders were startled on April 23, 1961, as the *Walla Walla*, heading for Seattle, grounded on an Eagle Harbor sandbar during an outgoing tide and heavy fog. After more than two hours, a barge took the 648 passengers off, but it was at least ten hours before people could retrieve their cars. WSF's most recent serious storm-related service interruption occurred on Thanksgiving Day, 1983, when a major storm's winds stopped the boats on the Vashon and Keystone runs and cut off electricity just when people had turkeys in their ovens. The only system-wide shutdown occurred on September 11, 2001, when officials ordered all vessels back to port as a security measure. On both occasions, service resumed after a few hours.

Just as during the Black Ball years, strikes interrupted WSF service too often—in 1974, 1976, 1980 and 1981. On Saturday morning, December 7, 1974, Inlandboatmen's Union members struck, after having worked without a contract for five months. While on strike they kept one boat running to the ferry-dependent islands, Vashon and the San Juans. But for Bainbridge and South Whidbey islanders with mainland jobs, commuting by car meant ninety miles or more of extra driving. Soon, the Bainbridge Island Chamber of Commerce chartered Seattle Harbor Tours boats to take foot passengers to and from downtown Seattle. Some commuters stayed on the mainland temporarily while others took sick leave or vacation time. Some union members stayed home because they refused to cross picket lines. Meanwhile, negotiations resumed and agreement came after five days.

The deck officers of the Masters, Mates and Pilots Union struck Thursday night, September 2, 1976, imperiling many people's plans for the upcoming Labor Day weekend. Work and seniority rules, not wages, were at issue. The Bainbridge Chamber of Commerce again arranged for Harbor Tours to carry riders between Winslow and Seattle. A ferry went to Orcas Island to pick up three hundred or more children including a few with special needs who had been at Camp Orkila. Irate vacationers wanting to return to the mainland watched the boat leave without them. With ferry service suspended, the Coast Guard brought mail to Vashon and Bainbridge Islands. A day after the strike began, the union agreed that Vashon and the San Juans could have limited service, only four daily runs to Vashon and two to the San Juans. The next day, the union agreed to more Vashon trips, eighteen in all instead of the usual thirty. Vashon's newspaper, the *Beachcomber*, pointed out, "Like the shade of Captain Alexander Peabody rising to tell the Island once again, 'Pay my price or there won't be any boats to ride,' the mates cut off service instead."[3]

Though the officers who staffed these boats to Vashon and the San Juans did so without pay during the strike, public reaction to the work stoppage became more and more negative. First, there had been no warning. Second, because it was Labor Day weekend, resort and shop owners lost their customers on perhaps the busiest weekend of the year. Washington State Governor Daniel J. Evans happened to be vacationing with his family on San Juan Island when the ferry officers stopped work, and he became heavily involved in the negotiations. By Sunday afternoon, the officers were back at work with the rest of the ferry crews, and full service resumed.

Again in 1980, a strike stopped the ferries. This time, people had about three days' warning that service would end on Saturday, April 5, disrupting Easter weekend plans. The Inlandboatmen's contract with the state had ended and the workers sought a raise above the state's offer, which the union charged was less than the cost of living increase in the Puget Sound area. Enough WSF crewmen volunteered—again without pay—to keep two boats running to the San Juans and one between Vashon and Fauntleroy. Because there were no trips between Vashon and the Kitsap mainland, the K2 ski factory then operating on Vashon Island chartered a vessel to bring employees who lived in Kitsap County to the island. An excursion boat took south end commuters to Tacoma, though the vessel, the *Gallant Lady*, departed the Island from Dockton, not Tahlequah. Private passenger boats served both Bainbridge and South Whidbey, and Whidbey commuters enjoyed the organ music played on an afternoon trip of the *Silver Swan*. This walkout lasted for eleven days. One thing Bainbridge folks enjoyed during that time was the disappearance of rush hour traffic on the highway across the island. A compromise agreement ended the strike.

Labor peace among WSF employees did not last, for on Monday, April 6, 1981, eighty-eight members of various ferry workers' unions walked out for twelve hours, protesting bills making their way through the Washington State Legislature. The proposed changes would bring ferry workers under the state civil service system and outlaw bargaining for wages. Union members had warned a few days earlier that ferry service might be interrupted, but no contingency plans were in place.

Perhaps the union warning stimulated the Legislature to adopt the legislation. Governor John Spellman let it become law without his signature. On May 19, members of the Marine Engineers Beneficial Association shut down the boats' engines and walked off the job—a wildcat strike. WSF employed only 140 members of this union, but, as engineers, they could not easily be replaced. No arrangements had been made to provide minimal service to Vashon and the San Juans but a member of WSF management who had an engineer's license fired up the tiny *Hiyu* and put it on the Vashon-Fauntleroy run. It loaded emergency vehicles and trucks provisioning the island and, if there was room, private automobiles. The *Seattle Times* delivered papers to the island by float plane. Vashon Islanders had no mail delivery on May 20, and in case of trouble or emergency on the island, a police boat sat at the marina in Burton. Vashon was well-equipped with police and firefighters, because some who lived on the island but worked on the mainland could not easily get to work. The vision of State Senator Pete von Reichbauer strike-bound in his Vashon Island home gave islanders something to smile about, for he was a leading proponent of the legislation that led to the walkout. Representative Bob Eberle, another Vashon resident, also supported the bill that precipitated the strike.

The strike disrupted life on the San Juan Islands, though San Juan Airlines did very well. Many prospective visitors canceled their reservations for the May 23-25 Memorial Day weekend. An Orcas storekeeper complained that Vashon got "preferential treatment" while the San Juan Islands had no service.[4] Private passenger boats were making runs there, though. Meanwhile, the private boats that served South Whidbey commuters charged more than three times the WSF rate.

The engineers went back to work after Governor Spellman appointed a commission to consider the issues. San Juan businessmen and other prominent islanders then met with union officials to get assurance that ferries would run as usual through the Fourth of July weekend. Meanwhile, making their feelings about the strike clear in a serious but good-natured way, some thirty islanders paraded through Friday Harbor, announcing that "being of Puget Sound mind," San Juan Islanders would secede from the state and the nation. "We're tired of being the state's stepchildren," read one protester's sign.[5] By August, the governor's commission had a proposal ready. Ferry workers would regain their right to negotiate wages, and ferry officials and workers would be subject to binding arbitration. Also, penalties for striking would be severe. As a result, islanders have not had to cope with striking Washington State ferry workers since 1981.

Ferry systems continue to struggle with other challenges, however. A continuing problem for WSF is the overload question. Having enough capacity to prevent all overloads, including those on holiday weekends, is financially impossible. Every year on Mother's Day morning, the line of cars waiting for a boat extends on and on and on, meaning that travelers sometimes have to wait until after several boats filled to capacity have left. On a July Sunday in 1954, shortly before the bridge to Fox Island ended ferry service there, sixty-five cars sat in line at 4:30 p.m., waiting for a ferry that could only take eighteen cars on a trip. The crewmen abandoned the schedule, skipped their dinner, and operated the boat as a shuttle until the line cleared. In 1958 WSF saw use of the route through the San Juans to Victoria B.C. suddenly increase when workers on Canadian Pacific Railway ferries went on strike.

The WSF route with the most troublesome recent history is that between Port Townsend and the dock on the west side of Whidbey Island. (This ferry terminal at Keystone received a new name, Coupeville, in 2010 because Coupeville was the destination for most of the passengers.) In March 2007, Paula Hammond, Washington State Secretary of Transportation, suddenly removed the two steel-electric ferries serving that route after maintenance showed a crack five inches long in the *Klickitat's* hull. Subsequent study of the four eighty-year-old boats in this class led her to ground all of them in November. The Coast Guard would have acted if she had not.

This almost meant the end of the ferry run, for the steel-electrics were the only boats owned by WSF that could navigate the strong cross-currents and the shallow and narrow approach to the Whidbey Island dock. WSF briefly shut down the run completely and then, for a time, instituted passenger-only service, but it proved inadequate. A temporary solution came when Pierce County agreed to let WSF lease the brand-new car ferry *Steilacoom II*, built to complement its sister vessel *Christine Anderson* on Pierce County's Anderson Island run. For more than two-and-one-half years, the *Steilacoom II* provided service for Washington State Ferries on the route to Whidbey Island. Finally, WSF's new boat planned expressly for that passage, the *Chetzemoka,* with superstructure built by Nichols Brothers, began service.

WSF had ordered three boats in the Chetzemoka's class to be built quickly because of the need to replace the borrowed boat on the Port Townsend-Coupeville route and to have a second boat to provide the extra service scheduled on that run each summer. This run continues to have cancellations now and then due to low tide, however. WSF had earlier studied several nearby sites and determined that moving the Whidbey Island terminal to one of these would both end the low-tide cancellations and provide an easier spot to dock. Island environmentalists fought a relocation, however, and WSF continues to dock at the Coupeville terminal.

The Coupeville ferry dock is not the only one where low tides have caused schedule cancellations. Tides also interrupted service on the South Whidbey-Mukilteo route until 1982 when the Mukilteo dock was extended seventy-five feet further out into the Sound. The Herron Island ferry has occasional low tide cancellations, and these days, the Anderson Island service restricts especially large vehicles during exceptionally low tides. The problem also exists on the Vashon Island runs, for very low tides make the ramp angle too steep for large vehicles with low ground clearance.

When the Port Townsend-Coupeville route suddenly had drastically reduced capacity after the steel-electric ferries were pulled from service, WSF adopted a reservation system for that run. As of January 2015, motorists traveling between the San Juan Islands and Anacortes could also make reservations. WSF has estimated that such a program can save millions of dollars otherwise necessary for enlarging terminals and automobile holding areas. Islanders have had mixed feelings about reservations, though. Many now say the system generally works well, except that all reservations for high travel days get snapped up immediately once they become available. Related to reservations is priority loading, which the ferry system allows for medical needs. Priority loading for all island residents on various runs has been raised as a possibility, too, especially in the San Juans. Given the relatively small number of sailings to these islands and the great number of summer tourists who visit the islands by ferry, it is no surprise that the residents want some assurance that their needs can be met.

Residents of different islands sometimes resent each other, islanders feeling that another island gets better ferry service. This perception can arise after a boat goes out of service because of a mechanical problem, for breakdowns can ripple throughout the system. If one of the large boats serving a major route is out of service, WSF might bring a slightly smaller replacement from another route, where a yet smaller boat replaces it. This vessel may in turn come from a different run. For example, on June 1, 2007, the *Cathlamet*, en route from Whidbey Island, barreled into the Mukilteo dock and needed immediate repair. As a result, Vashon Island's north-end run temporarily got a smaller boat and the Keystone-Port Townsend route lost one of its two boats. When a boat on the Fauntleroy-Vashon-Southworth route has a sudden mechanical problem or is taken to a different route, now service simply changes for the duration from three boats to two boats.

Even when accidents have not occurred, regular vessel maintenance often means replacing a regular boat with a smaller one. Sometimes car ferry service has been suspended with foot-passenger-only service offered instead while docks undergo extensive repair or reconstruction, as on Orcas Island in February 1987 and on Lopez Island in November 2006. During work on Lopez, car ferry service continued but boats could only dock when winds were not strong. Islanders wondered why the construction occurred in winter when storms were common, but WSF announced that it was to protect young salmon during other seasons, as the Endangered Species Act requires.

Complicating ferry travel are the routes with multiple stops: the Fauntleroy-Vashon-Southworth run—these days called the Triangle Run—and the San Juan Islands route. Predetermined formulas determine how many vehicles heading for each destination should be loaded, and this can frustrate riders who do not understand the system. Deckhands follow a prescribed pattern in signaling drivers to board, and for some destinations, drivers must proceed all the way around the boat's deck to be headed in the proper direction or, if with a long vehicle, back onto the ferry. Sometimes, a car ends up in the wrong lane, but this happens because the driver in a hurry comes down the wrong lane on the dock.

Just as Vashon Island's "vigilantes" had kept Black Ball boats from docking on the island in 1948, irate residents of San Juan Island once blockaded the holding lanes in Anacortes for cars heading to Orcas Island. On a June Sunday in 1988, several incidents, including one boat's breakdown, had led to an exceptionally large number of cars on Orcas Island waiting for a boat to Anacortes. WSF officials in Anacortes sent a ferry to Orcas even though it was scheduled to go non-stop to Friday Harbor, and then announced that the next boat would also go to Orcas. This roused people in the Friday Harbor line to action. Ferry officials, fearing possible violence, capitulated and did not send the next boat to Orcas. What the incident really illustrated was the system's inability to deal with heavy crowds under exceptional circumstances.

Washington State Ferries continues to carry people and their vehicles but has as much trouble financing the ferry system as Black Ball did. When ferry fares rise, ridership drops. Some islanders move back to the mainland while mainlanders avoid trips to the islands. Ferry proponents argue that because the ferries are a vital part of the state highway system, they should be financed in the same way as roads, for WSF routes are officially designated as extensions of the state highways that approach them. In 2012, Mary Margaret Haugen of Camano Island, head of the Washington State Senate Transportation Committee, stated, "I'd cut back on road maintenance before I'd cut a ferry . . . people can drive on a bad road and still get where they're going."[8]

Proposals for new ferry routes on Puget Sound appear every so often. Few people travel to the very lightly populated islands because there is no ferry service, and there is no ferry service because few people travel there. Ferry patrons urge expansion of ferry service, whether by using larger vessels, adding more boats for more frequent service, or by extending hours of service. Occasionally, however, islanders question expansion of service, as on Anderson Island in 2004. For years, the last boat left the mainland dock most weekdays at six in the evening. When Pierce County hoped to cut traffic congestion on earlier trips by adding a 7:30 evening run, what happened was an increase in people moving to the island and in part-time residents living there full-time. Ferry overcrowding continued and even extended to morning runs, which had not had the problem before. The 7:30 trip stayed on the schedule, and by the summer of 2014 some Anderson Islanders were again pressing for increased ferry service, even a later boat than 7:30. Beginning in June 2016, an earlier morning boat left Anderson and a 10 p.m. departure on Friday and Saturday nights began. Controversy also surfaced when Guemes Islanders opposed a 2006 increase in ferry service, fearing that later weekday boats and increased weekend runs would bring unwanted development to the island. The schedule eventually adopted includes more service than the islanders wanted but less than the county had implemented.

Ferry frustrations continue. Recently, ferry runs have also been canceled due to lack of crew. Coast Guard regulations mean a boat cannot sail without its specified crew, and the cash-strapped ferry system does not assign extra workers to a shift. Since September 11, 2001, security has had an impact. Officers with sniffer dogs sometimes walk up and down the line of cars waiting to board a boat and, at times, small Coast Guard vessels accompany the ferries en route. Occasional bomb threats occur, but the worst they have done is delay sailings. One security precaution has upset some riders, though. Border patrol agents have been spot-checking passenger vehicles on ferry runs near the international border, even on boats not coming from Canada. The concern is that terrorists might sneak on to one of the islands and take a ferry from there.

Ferries are a way of life to the people who need them. Islanders learn to live by the ferry schedule and to carefully plan their trips to the mainland. As many islanders say, "You don't leave the island without a lot of things to do." Almost everyone living on a ferry-dependent island has the current ferry schedule posted in a prominent place at home. Islanders learn mainland bus schedules and periodically request that they be better coordinated with the ferries. When off-island guests visit, it is not impolite for an island host to say, "You need to either leave now or stay another hour and a half." Also, islanders are often happy to meet visitors at the ferry dock so these mainlanders can park their car and become foot passengers, saving money and ensuring a place on the boat.

People who live on islands learn to cope with missing a ferry or failing to get on one because it is full. They avoid having to drive aboard at such times, as on the last evening of a summer holiday weekend. Island residents usually know when they need to arrive early to guarantee a space in line. Outsiders do not always understand the need to anticipate the length of a ferry line, though. In March 2010, the FBI made an elaborate plan on Orcas Island to catch Colton Harris-Moore, the young man known as the Barefoot Bandit, but the law enforcement team scheduled to participate could not get on the ferry, and Harris-Moore successfully fled.

The ferries are a lifeline to people who live on islands not reached by bridges, and because the boats are so important, it is easy to overemphasize problems that have arisen. Islanders live on the islands because they want to, and they take advantage of island amenities, avoiding ferry trips when they can. Ferry riders have good ferry experiences, too. On a few of the tables in the passenger cabins of some boats are partially-completed jigsaw puzzles ready for anyone to add the next piece. The ferry can be an island social center. Riders often see casual friends or acquaintances on the boat, giving them a chance to catch up on family news. One makes friends on the boats. The commuter can arrive home relaxed after a boat ride and a few miles driving on pleasant island roads rather than on mainland streets jammed with impatient motorists. Occasionally, a passenger may be immersed in a book or a conversation only to hear an announcement from the bridge that a group of orcas has been spotted ahead on the port side.

When a car in line cannot start, ferry workers have been known to push it *on* board as well as off. They awaken drivers who fall asleep on the boat—background noise and gentle motion seem to induce sleep—and they are even pleasant to the occasional islander who walks off the boat while forgetting that he happened to drive on board that day. Crew members open car doors for embarrassed drivers who have left keys in locked vehicles. More important, ferry workers have saved nearby boaters in danger of hypothermia or even drowning, whether an unfortunate sailor fell off a boat or the vessel started to sink. At least once, a crew has rescued a dog that went overboard. More than five hundred babies have been born on the ferries, sometimes with crew members assisting at the birth.

Nothing can beat walking down the dock to catch an early morning boat as the sun rises. Even if the day features clouds and rain, the freshness of the air, the different stripes of grey swirling through the water and the dark green of the distant evergreens can invigorate the commuter. The ferry ride brings relaxation during the commuter's day. Whatever awaits one across the water, the minutes on the boat offer a time for repose.

For twenty-seven years, riders on any of the San Juan Island ferries that stopped at Shaw Island could look forward to docking there, where Franciscan nuns maneuvered the ramp while wearing fluorescent orange life vests atop their long brown habits. As the women aged and no one came to join their group, they retired to a Franciscan center in Oregon, saying farewell to the affection and good will they had found on Shaw Island.

As long as people live on these islands, the ferry follies, as some have called the various controversies over the years, will no doubt continue. Financing, labor issues, population growth, weather, mechanical issues,

WSF has had to deal with all of these. Despite the furor that can ensue over ferry policies—especially finances—one very positive aspect has been the unity exhibited among residents of the various islands whenever ferry service is threatened. Citizens come together and, significantly, people from different islands do join forces. No topic but ferry service seems to generate both such rivalry and cooperation between the people of the different islands.

17 | Bridges

B RIDGES ALTER AN ISLAND'S CHARACTER. Every aspect of an islander's life seems to change. Once a bridge is built, people can easily leave an island at any time of day or night. There is no waiting in line for a boat or arriving an hour early to make sure the boat has room for one's car. One no longer pays ferry fare. For the State of Washington, replacing ferries with bridges could bring great savings, for taxes would no longer have to cover the ferry deficit. Bridge tolls can cost more than ferry fare, and islanders would continue to pay as long as the tolls last. Once a bridge reaches an island, property values might rise and population increase, and if tolls are later removed, grow quickly. Yes, a bridge will change an island.

People who lived on the islands in the nineteenth century mostly had their own boats or lived near Mosquito Fleet stops. In the next century more and more automobiles and trucks appeared. Not surprisingly, that semi-island, Fidalgo, was the first Puget Sound island to gain road access to the mainland. A rail connection to Anacortes had opened more than a decade before the beginning of the twentieth century, but in 1907 came a road bridge over the Swinomish Channel which separates Fidalgo Island from the mainland.

Camano Island's bridge access came early, too. This crossing requires two bridges, one from the mainland across the Stillaguamish River to small, flat Leque Island and the other spanning Davis Slough between

Leque and Camano. A simple slough bridge probably came in the first decade of the twentieth century and in 1912 construction began on a steel bridge to replace it. To cross the wider channel between Leque Island and the mainland, a ferry attached to a cable across the water served travelers until a swing bridge opened in 1909. When a vessel in the river gave a signal, a bridge tender would open the bridge, which would swing from its center, turning ninety degrees to open a passage for boat traffic. One former student, Mary Margaret Haugen, remembered the bridge shuddering when her school bus traveled across it.[1] Replacement of this bridge to the mainland did not come until 1949, after years of lobbying. The road across the channel was now a state highway and the state legislature made funds available to build a high level, twenty-six-foot-wide bridge. This also eventually proved inadequate, congestion helping lead to accidents. The new Camano Gateway Bridge opened in 2010. It is fifty-six feet wide and can accommodate four lanes of traffic. As for the slough, it too had received a new bridge, about 1949. An even newer one came in 2014 because possible flood waters and the piles of driftwood that had collected could have made the postwar structure unusable.

Bridges have been built to connect Puget Sound islands with the mainland only where the channels to be crossed are narrow. After years of interest and citizen lobbying efforts, two large islands on the Sound gained bridges which spanned narrow, but deep, channels. These bridges cross Deception Pass, connecting Whidbey and Fidalgo Islands, and Agate Pass between Bainbridge Island and the Kitsap County mainland.

The most spectacular bridges to any of the islands cross the double channel usually called Deception Pass. Even before a ferry began operating here in 1913, promoters were active with a bridge proposal, and legislator George Morse secured an appropriation in 1907 to survey a planned bridge site. Because Fort Casey sat on Whidbey Island, bridge proponents during World War I and the 1920s urged construction of a Deception Pass bridge to improve access to the fort. Most Island County voters wanted a bridge but not Captain Berte Olson, who ran the Deception Pass ferry. Despite her opposition, legislation authorizing a bridge finally passed in 1933.

Federal funds, a state bond issue earmarked for relief, and county money paid for the construction, so tolls were unnecessary. Island County had responsibility for the approach road to the south, as did Skagit County for the access route north of the channels.

Bridging required two spans, one from Whidbey north across Deception Pass to tiny Pass Island. This bridge is a 976-foot-long steel cantilever structure. From Pass Island, a 350-foot span crosses to Fidalgo Island. All three islands, Whidbey, Pass and Fidalgo, rise precipitously from the water and the bridge decks sit about 180 feet above the channels. Piers rise from the three islands and support the two-lane bridges and their sidewalks. From the piers, construction of the two spans headed toward their midpoints, where they would meet. This required getting supplies to Pass Island, so workers installed a gasoline-driven cableway system from Fidalgo. Steel and cement aggregate traveled by cable to the small central island, while a pump delivered water for the concrete from lakes almost a mile distant.

The Puget Construction Company began work August 6, 1934. One especially tense moment during construction came during lowering of the central span of the longer bridge from a crane to its place between two cantilever sections. The span proved to be three inches too long. But the day was hot and construction firm founder Paul Jarvis quickly figured out that heat-caused expansion could be the problem. Another attempt to join the sections scheduled for just before dawn the next day worked perfectly. The official dedication and opening of the two bridges took place July 31, 1935 and these have remained the only bridges to Whidbey Island.

Bridging Agate Pass between Bainbridge Island and the Kitsap County mainland was another long-hoped-for project. Even before 1930, influential Bainbridge residents, including Chamber of Commerce members and the local newspaper editor, urged a bridge, and in 1929 Seattle's Manson Construction Company carried out test drilling at the proposed location. By the early 1930s, state officials were seriously exploring the possibility of construction. In the Depression year of 1934, issue after issue of the *Bainbridge Review* carried the same page one message above the masthead: "Agate Pass Bridge is The Most Important Need For The Development of Bainbridge Island and a Splendid Labor Project."[2] Ferry workers' strikes spurred interest in the project, and finally, in the late 1930s, the Washington State Legislature gave approval, though not an appropriation, for a bridge crossing Agate Pass.

World War II intervened, but when Washington State bought the Black Ball ferry system, part of the plan was to replace ferries with bridges wherever it was technically and financially feasible. In 1949, the Manson Company received a contract to build the Agate Pass bridge, and the

Bainbridge Review celebrated with the headline, "At Last; A Bridge!" in huge type, covering two-thirds of the newspaper's front page.[3] Work started that summer. The project included building temporary coffer dams to hold back the strong current that coursed through the passage. The cantilevered two-lane bridge put in place is 1,229 feet long and seventy-five feet above high tide level. Black Ball, still operating the ferries, anticipated more vehicle traffic across Bainbridge Island and built a new terminal at Winslow to coincide with the bridge opening.

On October 7, 1950, the bridge connecting Bainbridge Island to the mainland opened. Construction funds had come from the state motor vehicle fund. Meanwhile, drivers and passengers paid tolls, but these lasted for less than a year. The popular bridge stimulated the island's population growth and development. Even before the bridge opened, the *Bainbridge Review* urged that a second bridge to the Kitsap mainland soon follow, this one directly toward Bremerton. Similar bridge proposals have continued to surface, but no such bridge has been built.

Other bridges connecting smaller Puget Sound islands to the mainland have been constructed since World War II. One would replace the small ferry running from Fox's north coast to Tacoma's Sixth Avenue. Hoping to end the costly ferry service—which included paying overtime salaries to the ferry crew for their thirteen-hour workday—the Pierce County Commissioners put a bridge proposal to county voters in 1950, but it did not gain the sixty percent majority necessary for a bond issue to pass. Next, the county asked the state, which had recently acquired the Black Ball ferries, to take over the Fox Island ferry route, but the state declined. County commissioners used traffic projections to show that a bridge would soon pay for itself, and the Washington State Grange and other organizations convinced the state legislature in 1951 to pass a law arranging for bridge construction. The project was related to the nearby Narrows Bridge work, replacing the bridge that had collapsed during high winds in 1940. After this bridge opened in 1950, building one to Fox Island seemed to be the obvious next step for a modern transportation system.

The Fox Island Bridge, which opened to use in 1954, is 1,950 feet long and 26 feet wide, providing room for two lanes of traffic and a sidewalk on one side. Twelve piers rise from the seabed to support the structure, and the clearance under the roadbed is a little over thirty feet at high tide, adequate clearance, because large vessels were not expected to need to navigate Hale Passage. The bridge is near the northern tip of the Island, where tiny Towhead Island sat just offshore and could be used for a bridge approach; fill for the approach obliterated this island. Once construction erased the water channel between Fox and Towhead Islands, residents noted stronger currents through Hale Passage during tidal changes.

When drivers began using the bridge, they faced a toll plaza on Towhead Island, but people crossing both the Fox Island and the Narrows Bridges now necessary for getting to Tacoma received a discount. To the surprise of many, the Fox Island Bridge did not immediately prove an economic benefit to islanders. Residents who worked in Tacoma had been able to drive any vehicle, whether tractor or barely-running rattletrap, to the Fox Island ferry dock, step aboard the ferry as foot passengers, and in Tacoma catch a bus to work. Now it was necessary to have a reliable car, pay the discounted toll for both bridges, pay for gas and perhaps to park in the city. Due to hardship, about thirty-five of the island's one hundred fifty families left the island where they could no longer afford to live, and traffic over the bridge began to decrease. Sometimes the tolls collected were not even enough to pay the toll collectors' salaries. Worried, state legislators decided to use motor vehicle tax receipts to help pay off the bonds that financed the bridge, and soon bridge tolls became about forty percent less expensive. A 1956 study on the question of paying off the bridge cost suggested that one problem was the zoning change adopted for Fox Island after the bridge was built. The new rules precluded development of shops or "public pleasure or recreational facilities" which could have enticed Tacoma-area folks to visit the island—and pay to cross the bridge.[4]

Tolls ended in 1965, and because of the bridge, Fox Island became a very desirable suburban residential area no longer dominated by small farms. The Fox Island story thus indicates that a bridge can change an island in a fundamental way. Bridges do not last forever, though, and in 2013 a county study found the 1954 bridge, built with an estimated fifty-year life span, "structurally deficient." Neither Pierce County nor island residents want to bear the financial cost of either retrofitting or replacing the bridge, but the lack of commerce or industry on Fox Island means that funds from the state or federal government might not be available.[5]

Meanwhile, farther north, Marrowstone and Indian Islanders wanted a bridge, something verbally promised when the Navy created Portage Canal and cut off land access to their islands. In the mid-1930s, Port Townsend community leaders as well as islanders pressed the state legislature to work on the problem. Money remained an obstacle. In 1940, the Navy bought Indian Island and instituted a military ferry to serve the base built there. Once World War II ended, clamor resurfaced for a bridge, even though the small public ferry had been free since 1936. Marrowstone Islanders spoke of the problems they had with their inadequate and undependable ferry service. A 1950 Jefferson County bond issue to help finance a bridge carried easily, for the federal government had agreed to pay much of the cost because the Navy had created the canal. Moreover, the Fort Flagler military base on Marrowstone Island's north end contributed some of the traffic. In mid-1951 the Manson firm began construction.

The 670-foot-long bridge that opened in January 1952 between the mainland and Indian Island sits seventy feet above the water so that traffic through the channel is not impeded. Designer Homer M. Hadley took an innovative approach with this bridge, using hollow steel box girders rather than ones of solid steel in building the cantilever structure. Therefore, the main span—250 feet—could be longer than usual. Otherwise, two additional piers would have been needed to support the structure. The bridge has eased access for the Navy to its Indian Island facility, for Marrowstone Island residents, and for visitors to island parks, notably Fort Flagler, which became a park in 1955.

A few mostly very small islands in the southern reaches of the Sound have bridges. Day Island, snuggled close against the Tacoma shore, acquired a bridge in 1908 built by the company formed to develop the island. Early landowners on Raft Island wanted to build a bridge, and Archie l. Matthew, who bought most of the island in 1957, directed its construction. The bridge, not quite eight hundred feet long, opened in 1958 without a toll. The island drew many residents, and eventually the bridge needed either serious renovation or replacement. Islanders voted in 1996 for annual assessments to create a bridge replacement fund. With the addition of a loan, construction could finally begin, and a new bridge opened with much fanfare in June 2014. The private span is open only to islanders and invited guests.

When Pope & Talbot developed Reach island in the early 1950s, the firm built a timber bridge 789 feet long for access. In 1974 a concrete deck replaced the original wooden one. This one-lane bridge even had a traffic light. Islanders owned and maintained the bridge, but in recent years, it continued to need repairs. Islanders offered the bridge to the county, which would not accept it as a gift. Finally, the community funded a two-lane replacement in 2012.

Like Raft and Reach islands, nearby Stretch Island never had auto ferry service. A timber bridge opened in 1920 to serve the farms that had long existed there. Reconditioned in 1973, it is only 360 feet long and twenty-four feet wide. At extreme low tide, the channel it spans can be nearly dry.

Harstine Island is much larger than these nearby islands. As early as 1935, the State Grange urged a bridge be built. After World War II, the island's small ferry operated by Mason County often left cars at the docks. Vehicle use increased from 8,305 in 1956 to 33,047 in 1968, and, like Washington State Ferries, this operation ran a deficit. County officials expressed concern that the old boat was not safe, because when it was fully loaded, passengers could not get out of their cars easily. In 1961, Mason County began investigating the possibility of replacing the ferry with a bridge. A federal grant made planning and surveying possible, but in 1962, county voters rejected a bond issue for bridge construction. Again in 1964 and 1966 voters refused to adopt a similar plan. Most Mason County voters probably had neither need nor desire to travel to Harstine Island, so paying for its bridge seemed unreasonable. Financing with tolls would not work, for too few vehicles traversed the route. At the time of bridge construction, only about 160 people lived on Harstine Island, though the Island's seven hundred summer people annually swelled the population.

In late 1966, Mason County created a special road improvement district for the Island. With the district in place, Harstine property owners would support more of a bridge's cost. The Weyerhaeuser firm, originally a timber company, wanted a bridge to develop several hundred acres of land it held on the island's northern point. The company would pay about twenty-two percent of the funds provided by the new district. Finally, November 7, 1967, Mason County voters passed a proposition that would help finance the bridge through a bond issue. At the time, this was the biggest county-funded road project ever accomplished in Washington State.

Precast concrete piles and beams support the bridge. It is almost 1,500 feet long with a concrete deck. Bridge dedication came on June 22, 1969, beginning with a ceremonial cavalcade crossing the span. A horse and buggy carrying some of the island's pioneers led the procession of vehicles, but beyond the bridge, the road on Harstine climbs a bit of a hill, and the horse pulling the buggy slipped on wet pavement, overturning the buggy—though luckily not injuring anyone. Soon after the bridge began serving traffic, Weyerhaeuser opened its development, Hartstene Pointe, for prospective homeowners. It features beach, pool, marina, tennis courts and trails as well as homesites.

The idea of connecting Harstine and Squaxin Islands by bridge emerged about 1970, but Squaxin Island tribe members, who did not control all their island at the time, were dubious. Dewey Sigo of the band said, "The people on Harstine Island are ready to blow up the new bridge leading to it. Now vandals can come on the island any time they want to and break into the homes." This echoes what Harstine Islander Esther Goetsch said when her island still had a ferry, not a bridge: "[We] like to say we draw our bridge up behind us at night."[6] Whether or not the Harstine bridge brought crime to that island, there is no bridge to Squaxin Island.

One proposal much farther north emerged in the late 1950s but did not lead to action, though it suggested some interesting ideas. The plan envisioned a bridge from the Lummi Indian Reservation on the mainland across narrow Hale Passage to Lummi Island.[7] Some islanders strongly supported a bridge, noting the many summer ferry overloads and the too-frequent need to take the route's one small boat out of service for maintenance or repair. Whatcom County would finance a bridge with a bond issue. Making the proposal unusual, the state legislature authorized establishment of ferry service between Lummi Island and Orcas Island, but only if Whatcom County did build the mainland-Lummi bridge. A study showed that the ferry route to Orcas would be feasible, though protective measures would be needed at both terminals because weather could be severe. Perhaps other, less expensive bridges could then be built to link the main San Juan Islands to each other and the Orcas-Lummi ferry.

Various objections scuttled these plans. Concern grew in maritime circles about navigation through Hale Passage with bridge approaches impeding this narrow channel. Mariners also noted the challenges of rough weather to a Lummi-Orcas ferry. In addition, the unstable clay seabed at the mainland dock in the Lummi Reservation made building a bridge there unfeasible. Most important, the Lummi bridge project would cost more than anyone wanted to pay. A satisfactory route nearby might have worked, had the voters of Whatcom County passed a bond issue in November 1960. Instead, Lummi Island got a new ferry.

The suggestion for another possible ferry route in Puget Sound has been resuscitated occasionally. After the Boeing Company opened a factory in 1967 not far from the mainland ferry dock in Mukilteo that serves the ferry to South Whidbey Island, suggestions to replace the boats with a bridge appeared. The next year, Governor Dan Evans arranged for study of such a bridge. This "sent ripples of shock through the populace," Dorothy Neil has written,[8] for South Whidbey residents feared irrevocable change in their rural setting should this occur. Expense halted any project, and an updated study in 1985 concluded once again that such a bridge would be too expensive. A different bridge to Whidbey Island had been studied in the 1950s, this one from Camano Island. Expense also caused the death of this idea.

The greatest bridge project of all has not yet been accomplished—and may never be. This is bridging Puget Sound. As with the bridges that have been built and the plans that never came to fruition, the failure to bridge Puget Sound via one of the islands has played a decisive role in island history.

After World War II, future-minded people in Western Washington dreamed of bridging the Sound. Including an island in the project made sense for two reasons. It would preclude the need for ferry service to that island as well as across the Sound. Also, two shorter spans are more feasible than one longer one, both technically and economically. Because the most useful route would be the one that best served the two population centers of Seattle and Bremerton, Bainbridge and Vashon were the two islands under consideration for this project.

Charles E. Andrew, Washington Toll Bridge Authority's chief engineer, announced in 1951 that a floating bridge from Seattle to one of the islands would be feasible. A suspension bridge from the chosen island to the Kitsap mainland would complete the route. Andrew predicted that if bridges were built from West Seattle via either Bainbridge or Vashon Island and on to the Kitsap County mainland, then in twenty-five years a second bridge would have to be built farther north to cope with traffic.

Three routes received serious consideration: West Point, in Fort Lawton, north of downtown Seattle, to Bainbridge Island; Alki Point, south of downtown Seattle, to Bainbridge; and Brace Point, just south of the current Fauntleroy ferry dock, to the northern point of Vashon. The main bridge would be floating, like the 1940 floating bridge built across Lake Washington. Another suggested alternative was a tube submerged about fifty feet below the surface.

During the early 1950s, the Washington State Legislature adopted several bills to facilitate this bridge project. Meanwhile, an Army engineering report did not oppose cross-Sound bridging. With this a real possibility, the *Bainbridge Review* and Vashon's *Islander News-Record* carried article after article and almost as many editorials explaining why their island was preferable. Other, more dispassionate, voices spoke up, too. Commercial carriers did not want a floating bridge interfering with travel. Tacoma interests expressed concern, fearing both the loss of business and interference with marine traffic to the city. The Army Corps of Engineers needed to approve any bridge project, and some local seafarers backed a Vashon route because it would interfere less with naval traffic, leaving the passage to the Navy Yard at Bremerton unimpeded.

After state officials formally chose a Vashon route in May 1955, Bainbridge folks worried about losing their direct ferry to Seattle. Planners considered providing a foot-passenger boat between Eagle Harbor and Seattle, but to many people this seemed inadequate. A few Bainbridge and Vashon men held a contest to see which bridge route could be crossed faster by rowboat. The Bainbridge route taken was four tenths of a nautical mile shorter than the Vashon route, and Rev. Vincent Gowen of Port Blakely in his cedar boat, the *F.O.G.*, won by just under thirteen minutes. Gowen's rowboat is now on display at the Bainbridge Island Historical Museum.

By autumn 1955, the cross-Sound project was dead, at least temporarily. The reason: cost. State Senator and later Governor Albert J. Rosellini charged that the state could have financed the bridge project, but "our present state administration simply does not want to build it at this time." In 1957, State Highway Director William A. Bugge predicted that a cross-Sound bridge system would carry traffic by 1964.[9]

Bridge talk continued, by 1960 centering on "consolidation." For example, a bridge could be built from Bainbridge directly to Bremerton, with the Seattle-Bremerton ferry route closed and twenty-four-hour passenger service provided between Seattle and Bainbridge. Various versions of consolidation engendered consideration for years, but few of the passengers involved liked any of them. "Or how about helicopters instead of bridges for Bainbridge Island and other places," journalist Polly Lane joked in 1960. By this time, some islanders were expressing the desire to maintain their isolation. The *Bainbridge Review* editorialized in 1961 that bridges could cause unwanted island population and development.[10] Since then, whenever Puget Sound bridges are promoted, such concerns arise.

Another cross-Sound bridge proposal in 1965 supported bridges across the Sound via Vashon Island plus another from the Port Orchard vicinity to Bainbridge Island. The State Highway Department recommended this combination as the most economical to build. Bainbridge interests opposed this because they would then have such a roundabout route to Seattle. Cost again doomed the project—and opposition to a bridge kept growing. More people, especially residents of Vashon and Bainbridge Islands, had indicated that they would rather keep ferries. Throughout the late 1960s, bridge discussions continued but did not lead to action. More than once, Puget Sounders would hear that the bridge idea was dead, only for it to revive a few years later. In 1969, one more study looked at consolidation of Bremerton and Bainbridge runs.

For a while, the issue remained dormant, but a state report in 1984 suggested different ideas: consolidation of nearby ferry routes and, in addition, bridges between some of the San Juan Islands. The *Seattle Post-Intelligencer* editorialized that the "spans would be economic millstones and environmental abominations" and that bridge suggestions were "harmless enough. The danger is that people may begin to take them seriously."[11] Once again, nothing happened.

The idea of a cross-Sound bridge never quite died. In 1992, a study by the state about the future of transportation across the Sound included the possibility of a bridge. Again, the best bridge alternative seemed to be a Vashon route plus feeder bridges in Kitsap County. To sample opinion, consultants hired by the state traveled to the various communities that could be impacted by a bridge. Mainlanders living south of Seattle felt that approaches for a Vashon bridge would "destroy neighborhoods" and cause traffic jams in their area. Then, at the South Kitsap County meeting, one area resident pointed out that "Puget Sound is a friendly barrier" which the bridge would "break."[12]

The Vashon Island meeting came on the evening of March 9, 1992, and took place in the high school gymnasium, the largest venue on the island. People streamed in, even latecomers who had to park their cars far from the school, until about one-fifth of the island's population was in the building. Speakers went to the microphone and audience members held up signs while they clapped and booed, depending on the message. No islander defended the bridge proposal. The newspapers which described the scene, including the *New York Times*, mentioned the sign, "If you build it they will come." One speaker asked audience members which of them opposed the bridges. As Timothy Egan wrote, "The room thundered with applause, a five-minute standing ovation." When asked who favored the bridges, no one responded.[13] After this, the Bainbridge Island meeting the next night seemed tame. People there were just as adamant that there should be no bridge via Bainbridge Island. Throughout the Puget Sound region, county and city officials plus island residents opposed the bridge plans.

The 1992 study did not lead to cross-Sound bridges and no serious attempt to design, finance and build them has since arisen. The idea continues to surface, however. When considering ways to relieve congestion on the very busy Tacoma Narrows Bridge, one alternative under study was a cross-Sound bridge via Vashon Island. In 1996, officials of the State Department of Transportation again came to Vashon and other communities. Just as in 1992, islanders expressed strong opposition to a bridge across their island. Project manager Tim Horkan said, "A majority of Gig Harbor residents think building a bridge across Vashon to Burien . . . will resolve problems on the Tacoma Narrows Bridge." A Vashon Islander's response: "We want a Wal-Mart in Gig Harbor."[14] The eventual decision adopted the regional preference: a second span across The Narrows parallel to the existing one. This opened to traffic in 2007—and cross-Sound bridges have not been built. Islanders must remember, though, that island opinion may have little weight should bridge construction ever become imminent, because the purpose of such bridges is to *cross* Puget Sound rather than to provide convenient access to an island.

Have bridges changed the islands? They have brought more people and more development, but local conditions—island size, local geography, availability, and price of land for purchase, nearness of large mainland cities—all these influence patterns of settlement and change. If island characteristics encourage settlement, a bridge will bring it, especially if tolls are low or non-existent. Since Bainbridge and Vashon Islands both have many acres of land sitting vacant and both are near a large urban center or two, a bridge could alter their character significantly. Thus, residents of these two islands adamantly oppose a cross-Sound bridge.

It is hard today to envision new bridges—or tunnels, for that matter—to, or across, any of the Puget Sound islands. The area's population will probably continue to grow, however, and as additional land for housing around the cities, especially Seattle, becomes ever farther from the city core and more expensive, acreage on the islands and across the Sound in Kitsap County will look more and more attractive. More and more commuters come to Seattle today by ferry. If even more people join them, at a time when technological advances and economic conditions might make bridge construction a more attractive proposition, will the bridges come after all?

Sent from Anacortes in 1910, this postcard's message reads, "We girls are having a fine time. Going to climb a miniature mountain today." Perhaps the mountain was Mt. Erie. The old town section of the Anacortes city center does not look too different from this today, but the street is paved and rarely if ever includes vehicles such as the two shown here.

Schools were important assets to pioneer communities on the islands. Lopez Island once had four separate school districts. One was the Port Stanley District in the northern part of the island. This building opened in 1917 to replace an earlier Port Stanley school. When the island's districts were consolidated in 1941, students no longer came to school here. The building then saw various uses, finally falling into disrepair. The Lopez Island Historical Society has restored it and community events now take place in the historic schoolhouse.

The Anacortes Hotel at a corner of 8th Street and J Avenue was constructed to house both a hotel and a bank, but due to the Panic of 1893, both closed. For awhile, then, some people simply lived there without paying rent. Finally, 1907 remodeling made it suitable for a school, and it housed Whitney School until a new building became the elementary school about five years later.

Vashon Island's public schools attract a number of mainlanders, and during the school year four full-size school buses wait on the island's north end ferry dock to meet the arriving students. About 7:15 a.m., some two hundred students stream off the boat from Seattle. About two dozen from Kitsap County also arrive. Elementary school commuters arrive on a later ferry, accompanied by a Vashon Island School District aide. Since this picture was taken, the dock has been restriped and a lane now is designated solely for bus parking.

It looks as though Friday Harbor was a pleasant place to live in 1908 when this postcard was mailed. The city is the largest community both on San Juan Island and in the entire archipelago, and it remains a pleasant place, though affordable housing is now hard to find.

A narrow, winding road serves recently-built homes on Orcas Island's Buck Mountain and from one of them is this view of Eastsound, the island's largest community. To the left of the town is Madrona Point and beyond Eastsound on the left is Turtleback Mountain. Beyond Orcas Island is Waldron Island.

1188 Steamer Vashon One of Seattle's Numerous Ferries

In the first decade of the twentieth century, two vessels named *Vashon* served Puget Sounders. One was a sternwheeler built in Aberdeen on Washington State's Pacific coast in 1891 as the *City of Aberdeen*. It came to Puget Sound after the turn of the century, was rebuilt and renamed *Vashon*. Here it is on a postcard mailed in 1908. Maury Island's Martinolich Shipyard built the other *Vashon*, a propeller steamboat, in 1905.

Stuart Island is the westernmost of the San Juan Islands, only about a mile from the international border. Moreover, Turn Point, the site of this lighthouse, sits at the island's northwesternmost point, as close to Canada as one can be on one of the San Juans. The Turn Point Light dates from 1893; the lighthouse structure and a better light came in 1936, with automation in 1974. For many years lighthouse keepers were stationed at Turn Point and some lived with their families at this isolated location.

The Puget Sound Navigation Company, also known as Black Ball, operated steamboats during the Mosquito Fleet era, in 1914 serving some of the islands as well as mainland communities. As the top schedule shows, the *Rosalie* stopped at San Juan, Orcas and Lopez Islands.

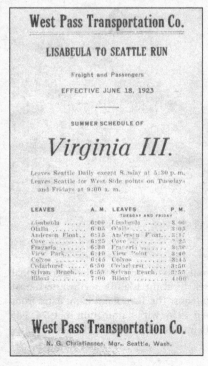

The West Pass Transportation Company offered passenger service along Colvos Passage, also known as West Passage, for about thirty years from 1909, using a series of boats each named *Virginia*. The *Virginia III* dates from 1914, when the West Pass company acquired the *Typhoon*, remodeled and renamed it. The firm ran the *Virginia III* until 1927, when it was sold. During summer 1923 the boat left Seattle for Colvos Passage in the late afternoon and started its route back northward along the passage in the early morning, stopping on both sides of the channel. For Vashon Islanders it stopped at Lisabeula, Cove, Colvos, Cedahurst, Sylvan Beach and Biloxi.

Railroad tracks once extended across Swinomish Slough all the way to downtown Anacortes. This causeway carried the tracks across Fidalgo Bay into the city. These days, with trains no longer going beyond March Point, the causeway has become a pedestrian walkway, a scenic sea-level trail. In the background is one of the refineries on March Point.

A dock once sat just southwest of Crockett Lake on Whidbey Island, and these pilings indicate the site of the causeway built across the lake in the late nineteenth century to reach the dock.

Driving on island roads is a pleasure. Most have only two lanes and traverse a rural or forested landscape, often with views of Puget Sound and perhaps other islands or distant mountains. This view looks north along North Whidbey Island's West Beach Road.

A rough wagon track to the top of Orcas Island's 2400-foot Mt. Constitution, the highest point in the Puget Sound islands, dates from 1894. In 1910, local citizens held money-raising events and donated their labor to improve the road. As shown in the photograph, tourists visited the mountaintop even before the days of the automobile. Nowadays a two-lane paved road makes the journey much easier. *Courtesy of Orcas Island Historical Society.*

Inns have welcomed visitors to the islands for well more than a century. Mt. Constitution Inn at Eastsound on Orcas Island began its life in the nineteenth century under another name and for awhile in the early twentieth century it was Mt. Constitution Inn, shown here with Buck Mountain in the distance. Today, as the Outlook Inn, this venerable inn still welcomes visitors to Eastsound. *Courtesy of Cherie Christensen. Les Irish enhanced this very dim postcard.*

Magnolia Beach on Vashon Island lies on the west side of Quartermaster Harbor beneath a steep hillside. Already by 1908 cabins lined the beach and the vacationer who sent the card mentioned swimming and canoeing in the harbor.

An unusual city park is Causland Park, which occupies a city block in Anacortes' residential area. The Seattle & Northern Railway donated the land for a park, and after World War I the city constructed this stone memorial and renamed the park for Guemes Islander Harry Causland who had died heroically in battle.

In the 1930s, the Leroy Stradley family built a resort on Camano Island. For fifty-five years visitors enjoyed waterside activities at Cama Beach. The two Stradley daughters inherited the property and instead of selling it to developers allowed Washington State to buy it at a lesser price. These days visitors stay in the original but refurbished cabins while enjoying an island stay at Cama Beach State Park.

One of the most scenic Washington State Ferry routes joins Orcas and San Juan Islands. Here in an August 2014 photograph the boat travels along Wasp Passage as it heads for Friday Harbor. To the left is Shaw Island; beyond the nearest forest is Shaw's Neck Point. In the far distance is San Juan Island. To the right are Cliff Island and, nearby, Crane Island.

This sign could warn visitors at many an island viewpoint, but it happens to be above the west shore of Whidbey Island at Fort Ebey State Park.

These buses lined up on the Orcas Island ferry dock await a ferry bringing a group of campers heading for camp. This is the most pleasant place in Puget Sound to wait for a WSF boat. Between the dock and the auto waiting area is a grassy hillside complete with picnic tables and a lovely view of the Sound with Shaw Island and its ferry dock in the distance. Next to the dock is a grocery store that provides sandwiches, salads and snacks for one's wait.

Many Western Washington school children have an opportunity to take a trip to Orcas Island and spend a little time at Camp Orkila. Mainland school buses drop off the students at Washington State Ferry's Anacortes dock and the youngsters have approximately an hour to enjoy the boat and the view before disembarking at Orcas Landing.

As the nineteenth century gave way to the twentieth, the United States built three coastal forts to guard Puget Sound. Fort Casey, on the western shore of Whidbey Island, was one of these harbor defenses. In 1912, when this photograph was taken, tensions were rising in Europe, though World War I did not begin there until 1914. Meanwhile, various types of training exercises took place at the fort. *Courtesy of Steven Kobylk.*

Fort Casey was armed with ten-inch guns before 1900. Earthworks built in front of the guns would prevent enemy ships in the Sound from seeing the weapons. This gun is shown in its lowered position, protected by the earthwork. These guns were obsolete by World War II and were salvaged then for scrap metal. After Fort Casey became a state park in 1955, several similar guns were discovered rusting away in a Philippines' forest and brought to Whidbey Island.

Here is a gun in raised position, ready to fire. In the background is the Admiralty Head Lighthouse. The guns in the "Triangle of Fire" were never fired as an act of war.

When World War II began, civil defense activities burgeoned in American communities. This March 1942 photograph published in the *Seattle Post-Intelligencer* pictures a civil defense drill on Vashon Island. Ironically, one of the women, Pauline Sakahara (shown in uniform wearing an armband), was soon forced to leave her home because the government ordered West Coast Japanese Americans interned. Her husband had donated a truck to the Red Cross to be used as an ambulance during the war, but they both had to leave Vashon Island--and for a time a relocation, or concentration, camp became the Sakahara family home. *Museum of History and Industry, Seattle.*

Bainbridge Island's ethnic Japanese were evacuated on the ferry Kehloken at the Eagledale ferry dock. A memorial, "Nidoto nai yoni," meaning "Let it not happen again," has been established at the approach to the dock site. Along this walkway curving towards the water are posted the names of all the people, from babies to grandparents, who had to leave.

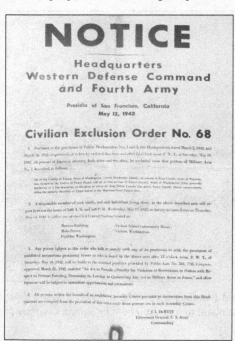

This sign, posted on Vashon Island in early May 1942, announced that ethnic Japanese would be transported away from the island on May 16. Bainbridge Islanders had received a similar announcement about six weeks earlier. Both groups were sent to temporary camps at first and then to more permanent camps, the Vashon Islanders to Tule Lake and the Bainbridge group to Minidoka.

First row: Kimi Takatsuka, Amy Woo Boo, Nora Hoshi. *Second row:* Bob Wight, Alfred Nordeng, Mr. Ostrom, Masa Kunugi.

Vashon High School's annual, the Vashonian, included a photograph of the 1940 tennis team. Three of the members were from Japanese families and one from a Chinese family. The two Japanese American girls, Kimi and Nora, graduated in 1941. Masa was a member of the class of 1942 and while his classmates attended their Vashon Island commencement ceremony, he was at the temporary relocation camp at Pinedale, California. He did, however, receive a diploma. *Courtesy of Vashon-Maury Island Heritage Museum.*

Harstine Island's first ferry, the Island Belle, served islanders from 1922 to 1929. It had a short run between the island and the Mason County mainland to its west. *Photo by author. Courtesy of Harstine Island Community Club.*

Until the Fox Island Bridge opened in 1954, ferries plied a route from Tacoma's Sixth Avenue to Fox Island. This 2009 photograph shows the island's old dock site and looks north across Hale Passage to the mainland west of The Narrows. The remains of the dock were removed in 2013 to prevent creosote that covered pilings from continuing to leach into Puget Sound and potentially harm sea life.

Skagit County has operated the ferries between Anacortes and Guemes Island for half a century. The *Guemes*, which has served the route since 1980, can carry up to 22 vehicles and is licensed to carry ninety-nine foot passengers. A small cabin provides protection from the elements on the seven-minute run. Annually, some 200,000 vehicles take this vessel across Guemes Channel. Guemes Island appears in the background.

The only regularly-scheduled private ferry upon which patrons can drive their cars from the mainland to a Puget Sound island serves Herron Island in Case Inlet in the South Sound. The *Charlie Wells* is docked at Herron Island; in the background to the left is Key Peninsula, part of the Pierce County mainland.

Here is the complete summer 1931 schedule for the Kitsap County Transportation Company. This was one of two companies that dominated ferry service on Puget Sound then. Notice that the firm ran boats from Bainbridge and Vashon Islands to both the eastern and western shores of Puget Sound.

VICTORIA, B. C.
SEATTLE-PORT ANGELES-VICTORIA
Ferry Iroquois

Read Down			Read Up
Lv. *11:45 pm	Seattle	Ar. 6:00 pm
Lv. 3:00 am	Port Townsend	Lv. 3:00 pm
Ar. 5:45 am	Port Angeles	Lv. 12:15 pm
Lv. 7:00 am	Port Angeles	Ar. 11:30 am
Ar. 8:45 am	Victoria	Lv. 9:45 am

Staterooms $2.01 to $5.75

*On night sailing, autos handled on advance arrangement only, due to limited space.

PORT ANGELES-VICTORIA
Ferry Iroquois

Lv. Port Angeles: 7:00 am Lv. Victoria: 9:45 am
Ar. Victoria: 8:45 am Ar. Port Angeles: 11:30 am

SAN JUAN ISLANDS
ANACORTES TO SAN JUAN ISLANDS
Daily Except Sundays and Holidays

Lv. Anacortes	10:00 am	6:00 pm
Lv. Lopez	11:05	7:05
Lv. Shaw	*11:15	*7:15
Lv. Orcas	11:35	7:35
Ar. Friday Harbor	12:15 pm	8:15

SAN JUAN ISLANDS TO ANACORTES

Lv. Friday Harbor	7:15 am	3:15 pm
Lv. Orcas	7:55	3:55
Lv. Shaw	*7:57	*3:57
Lv. Lopez	8:25	4:25
Ar. Anacortes	9:30	5:30

Sundays and Holidays
ANACORTES TO SAN JUAN ISLANDS

Lv. Anacortes	10:30 am	4:00 pm	8:45 pm
Lv. Lopez	11:35	*5:00	9:50
Lv. Shaw			*10:00
Lv. Orcas	12:00		10:15
Ar. Friday Harbor	12:40 pm	5:50	11:00

SAN JUAN ISLANDS TO ANACORTES

Lv. Friday Harbor	7:45 am	1:10 pm	6:00
Lv. Orcas	8:25	2:00	6:50
Lv. Shaw	*8:27	*2:02	*6:52
Lv. Lopez	8:50	2:25	7:15
Ar. Anacortes	9:55	3:30	8:20

*Stops on Flag Signal Only.

Sydney service discontinued during Winter

These fares include All U.S. Transportation Taxes

FARES
Children—6 to 12, half fare

	Passengers		Car & Driver	
	One Way	Rnd Trip	One Way	Rnd Trip
Anacortes to—				
Friday Harbor	5.81	$1.61	$1.89	$3.34
Lopez Island	.46	.92	.87	1.74
Orcas	.58	1.15	1.19	2.39
Shaw	.52	1.04	.88	1.76
Edmonds-Kingston	.30	.60	.82	1.63
Edmonds-Port Ludlow	.63	1.27	1.77	3.64
Fauntleroy-Harper	.30	.60	.82	1.63
Fauntleroy-Vashon	.20	.35	.51	1.02
Vashon-Harper	.20	.40	.51	1.02
Friday Harbor-Lopez	.46	.92	.87	1.74
Friday Harbor-Shaw	.35	.70	.81	1.63
Friday Harbor-Orcas	.35	.70	.81	1.63
Between other San Juan Points	.20	.40	.51	1.02
Mukilteo-Columbia Beach	.28	.40	.61	1.02
Point Defiance-Tahlequah	.20	.35	.51	1.02
Point White-Bremerton	.40	.40	.51	1.02
Port Gamble-Shine	.28	.45	1.02	1.83
Seattle to—				
Bremerton	.52	1.04	.88	1.76
Bainbridge Island	.75	.60	.91	1.63
Indianola	.38	.92	.87	1.74
Manchester	.36	.70	.93	1.68
Port Angeles	2.47	4.95	6.05	10.10
Port Townsend	1.50	2.99	3.14	6.29
Suquamish	.46	.92	.87	1.74

INTERNATIONAL ROUTES

CARS (Driver Extra) Wheelbase (Hub to Hub)		Passen-gers	Up to 115"	116" to 125"	Over 125"
Anacortes-Sidney	One Way	$1.44	$2.60	$3.10	$3.60
	Round Trip	2.59	4.70	5.60	6.50
Port Angeles-Victoria	One Way	1.21	2.18	2.60	3.10
	Round Trip	2.19	3.80	4.70	5.60
Seattle-Victoria	One Way	2.89	3.50	4.00	4.30
	Round Trip	5.19	6.30	7.20	9.10

CIRCUIT RATES

Port Angeles-Victoria and Sidney-Anacortes		2.84	4.35	6.15	6.06
Seattle-Victoria and Victoria-Port Angeles		3.68	6.05	6.95	4.85
Seattle-Victoria and Sidney-Anacortes		3.91	5.60	6.40	7.30

Take a Trip on the Sound

Ships of the Black Ball Fleet leave the Colman Ferry Terminal several times each hour. An interesting short water trip can take a couple of hours or half a day, and the cost is very nominal.

Ask for descriptive folder or call MAin 2222.

PUGET SOUND FERRIES
WINTER SCHEDULE
177
Effective November 1, 1946

Subject to Change Without Notice

Holidays referred to in connection with schedules shown herein are New Year's Day, Washington's Birthday, Memorial Day, Independence Day, Labor Day, Thanksgiving Day, and Christmas Day.

BLACK BALL LINE
PUGET SOUND NAVIGATION COMPANY
COLMAN FERRY TERMINAL — MAin 2222
FOOT OF MARION STREET — SEATTLE

PRINTED IN U.S.A.

OLYMPIC PENINSULA AND HOOD CANAL

SEATTLE-BREMERTON
Ferries Chippewa, Willapa, Enetai, and Kalakala
Daily Except Sunday

Lv. Seattle	Lv. Bremerton
1:10 AM	12:15 AM
5:00	*12:55
*5:45	*5:45
6:15	6:15
*7:00	*7:00
7:30	7:30
8:10	8:15
8:45	8:45
9:30	9:25
10:00	10:00
10:45	10:45
11:15	11:15
12:00	11:50
12:30 PM	12:30 PM
1:00	1:15
1:45	1:45
2:30	2:15
3:00	3:00
3:30	3:45
4:15	4:15
5:00	4:55
5:30	5:30
6:15	6:15
*6:45	6:45
*7:00	7:30
*7:30	*8:00
8:00	*8:30
*8:45	*8:45
*9:00	*9:15
*9:15	*9:30
10:00	*10:00
*10:30	10:30
*11:00	11:15
*11:45	*11:45
*12:00	

* Daily Except Sunday
● 12:45 on Monday morning
‡ 1:10 on Monday morning

EDMONDS-PORT LUDLOW
Ferries Klickitat and Nisqually

Lv. Edmonds	Lv. Port Ludlow
6:00 AM	6:00 AM
7:30	7:30
9:00	9:00
10:45	10:45
12:15 PM	12:15 PM
1:55	1:55
3:30	3:30
5:15	5:15
6:50	6:50
8:20	8:20
10:00	10:00

EDMONDS-KINGSTON
Ferry Quillayute
EFFECTIVE OCT. 1, 1946

Lv. Edmonds	Lv. Kingston
7:45 AM	6:50 AM
9:30	8:40
11:15	10:32
1:00 PM	12:15 PM
2:40	2:00
4:40	3:45
6:15	5:30
8:00	7:15
9:30	8:50

SEATTLE-SUQUAMISH-INDIANOLA
Daily except Sundays & Holidays

Lv. Seattle	Lv. Suquamish	Lv. Indianola
7:45 AM	6:20 AM	6:30 AM
10:25	9:00	9:10
12:00 PM	11:45	11:30
5:20	2:35 PM	2:10 PM
8:15	6:25	6:35

SUNDAYS & HOLIDAYS

Lv. Seattle	Lv. Suquamish	Lv. Indianola
7:45 AM	6:30 AM	6:30 AM
10:25	9:00	9:10
1:10 PM	11:45	11:50
3:50	2:35 PM	2:10 PM
9:00	7:35	7:40

HOOD CANAL AND VASHON ISLAND

FAUNTLEROY-VASHON-HARPER
Ferries Illahee and Quinault
Daily Except Sundays and Holidays

Lv. Fauntleroy	Lv. Vashon	Lv. Harper
12:45 AM	12:30 AM	
6:35	6:10	5:45
*7:40	7:10	6:45
8:10	7:40	7:15
9:00	8:05	8:50
10:00	9:15	9:40
10:30	10:00	10:40
11:30	11:00	11:15
12:00	11:30	12:10 PM
1:00 PM	12:30 PM	12:40
1:30	1:00	1:40
2:30	2:00	2:15
3:00	2:30	3:10
4:00	3:30	3:40
4:35	4:00	4:45
*5:00	4:25	6:30
5:50	5:25	7:15
6:20	5:45	8:15
7:30	6:45	9:40
*8:15	7:30	11:05
9:00	8:30	
10:25	9:55	
11:50	11:20	

*To Vashon only

Sundays and Holidays

Lv. Fauntleroy	Lv. Vashon	Lv. Harper
1:10 AM	12:45 AM	12:30 AM
7:00	6:30	6:10
8:10	7:20	7:45
9:00	8:10	8:50
10:00	9:15	9:40
11:30	11:00	11:15
12:00	11:30	12:10 PM
1:30	1:00	1:40
2:30	2:00	2:15
3:00	2:30	3:10
4:00	3:30	3:40
4:35	4:00	4:45
*5:40	5:00	6:20
6:15	5:45	*7:10
*6:45	6:15	*8:45
*7:45	7:15	10:20
8:00	8:15	
*8:45	9:15	
9:30	10:45	
*9:45		
11:50		

To Fauntleroy Direct

SEATTLE-MANCHESTER
Ferry Kehanla

Lv. Seattle	Lv. Manchester
7:50 AM	6:00 AM
10:05	9:00
12:20 PM	11:10
3:15	1:25 PM
5:30	4:25
7:35	6:40
9:15	9:15

POINT DEFIANCE-TAHLEQUAH
Ferry Vashonia

Lv. Point Defiance	Lv. Tahlequah
6:30 AM	6:00 AM
7:30	7:00

AND HOURLY UNTIL

| 11:30 PM | 11:00 PM |

BAINBRIDGE IS.

SEATTLE-EAGLE HARBOR
Ferries Shasta and Kehloken

Lv. Seattle	Lv. Winslow	Lv. Eagledale
12:45 AM		
6:30	5:30	5:35 AM
7:35	6:45	6:35
8:40	7:45	7:30
9:30	8:30	8:35
*10:30	9:30	9:35
11:30	10:25	10:15
1:00 PM	11:20	12:15 PM
2:10	12:25 PM	2:00
*3:15	1:50	3:10
4:05	3:00	4:50
*5:30	4:15	*6:25
*6:05	5:05	*6:50
*7:20	6:15	
*8:15	7:15	
*9:20	8:30	
*11:10	10:20	
	11:55	

*To Winslow only.
A-All vehicles discharged at Winslow on Sundays and Holidays
C-Passengers only on Sundays and Holidays

POINT WHITE-BREMERTON

Lv. Point White	Lv. Bremerton
*6:45 AM	7:15 AM
8:00	8:30
9:10	9:40
10:30	10:00
12:05 PM	12:40 PM
1:25	1:55
3:00	3:30
4:30	5:00
6:45	7:35
8:40	9:10
10:45	11:00

*Stops at Waterman except Sat., Sun. & Holidays (Passgrs. only)

WHIDBY ISLAND

MUKILTEO-COLUMBIA BEACH
Ferries Bainbridge and Kitsap

Lv. Mukilteo	Lv. Col. Beach
6:10 AM	5:45 AM
7:15	6:45
8:10	7:40
9:00	8:30

and every
HALF HOUR including

| 9:00 PM | 8:30 PM |

THEN

10:00	9:30
11:00	10:30
12:00 MIDNITE	11:30

Extra trips Monday mornings:

6:40 AM	6:10 AM
7:45	7:15
8:35	8:10

PORT GAMBLE-SHINE

Lv. Port Gamble: Hourly, 7:00 a.m. to 7:00 p.m. Lv. Shine: Hourly, 7:15 a.m. to 7:15 p.m.
Extra trips Saturdays, Sundays and Holidays one hour later.

By being at the terminal, ready to board the ferry, a few minutes before the scheduled time of departure you can help maintain prompt, dependable service.

This complete Black Ball schedule for summer 1945, during World War II, bears some resemblance to today's Washington State Ferries schedules. Three of the cross-Sound routes no longer operate and two others--the Hood Canal crossing and Point White (on Bainbridge Island) to Bremerton have been replaced by bridges. The Seattle-Bremerton route featured frequent service because of the many wartime defense workers who needed to cross the Sound to get to work.

To cope with the severe shortage of low-income housing on San Juan Island, the San Juan Community Home Trust has been bringing older houses to the island by barge. These came from Victoria, British Columbia. New construction was replacing older homes on that city's outskirts and some of the older ones are finding new life near Friday Harbor. *Courtesy of Nancy DeVaux.*

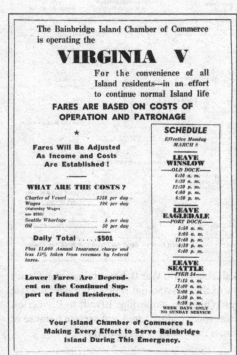

The Bainbridge Island Chamber of Commerce is operating the

VIRGINIA V

For the convenience of all Island residents---in an effort to continue normal Island life

FARES ARE BASED ON COSTS OF OPERATION AND PATRONAGE

★

Fares Will Be Adjusted As Income and Costs Are Established !

WHAT ARE THE COSTS ?

Charter of Vessel	$250 per day
Wages (Saturday Wages are $295)	196 per day
Seattle Wharfage	5 per day
Oil	50 per day

Daily Total $501

Plus $1,000 Annual Insurance charge and less 15% taken from revenues by federal taxes.

Lower Fares Are Dependent on the Continued Support of Island Residents.

SCHEDULE

Effective Monday MARCH 8

LEAVE WINSLOW
----OLD DOCK----
6:10 a. m.
8:30 a. m.
12:30 p. m.
4:00 p. m.
6:30 p. m.

LEAVE EAGLEDALE
----PORT DOCK----
6:50 a. m.
8:05 a. m.
12:40 p. m.
4:10 p. m.
6:40 p. m.

LEAVE SEATTLE
----PIER 54----
7:15 a. m.
11:00 a. m.
3:00 p. m.
5:30 p. m.
8:30 p. m.
WEEK DAYS ONLY
NO SUNDAY SERVICE

Your Island Chamber of Commerce is Making Every Effort to Serve Bainbridge Island During This Emergency.

Strikes disrupted ferry service on Puget Sound during the 1930s, 1940s, 1970s and 1980s, and islanders had to find alternate ways to travel between their homes and the mainland. Community organizations stepped in and chartered passenger boats, as did the Bainbridge Island Chamber of Commerce during a March 1948 strike. Advertisement in *Bainbridge Review*, March 4, 1948.

Once the houses reach San Juan Island, much work remains. *Courtesy of Nancy DeVaux.*

This sign appeared at the entrance to the development called Lummi Island Scenic Estates when the photograph was taken in March 2011. Limited water resources are a concern on many islands; new housing construction can be prevented if the builder cannot identify an adequate water source.

Very near the summit of Fidalgo Island's 1273-foot Mt. Erie is this opening in the forest showing the view to the south. Jane Irish sat here on a family trip some years ago. Nearby is Fidalgo Island's Lake Campbell. In the distance to the right sits Whidbey Island. To the left beyond Fidalgo Island are Skagit and Hope Islands and farthest away, Goat Island.

Small planes provide a useful service to island residents and visitors, and float planes do not need an airstrip. This plane is landing at Deer Harbor on the south shore of Orcas Island.

In emergencies the San Juan County sheriff's boat can transport people from islands which do not have needed medical services. Deputies also respond to boaters in difficulties whether because of stormy seas, sudden illness or problems with the vessel--anything from running out of gas to engine failure. With its gurney-accommodating ramp lowered, this boat sits at Orcas Landing.

Many a visit to an island begins this way. What will a visitor see on this island? It is Ketron Island in the south Sound. The ferry to Anderson Island includes a stop at Ketron on a few of its trips.

III
THE PRESENT
AND THE FUTURE

18 | Island Life

ISLAND LIFE HAS CHANGED GREATLY SINCE THE EARLY DAYS of white settlement, both for the Native people and for the settlers' descendants. The people who came to the islands during the second half of the nineteenth century used the natural resources of the region to support themselves. Forestry, fishing and extraction of clay and limestone provided a livelihood, but over the years, exploitation of these resources led to their depletion. Islanders developed agriculture; growing tree fruit and berries proved successful until development of irrigation elsewhere and decreasing costs of long-distance transportation meant that island fruit could no longer compete. Meanwhile, resorts and summer camps brought part-time residents and tourists to the islands. Communities provided the amenities for pleasant small-town and rural life, and at the same time more and more people who came to the islands near cities commuted to mainland jobs. Today, living on the islands has become expensive, and challenges like a rising sea level lead islanders to wonder what the future will bring.

In the first few decades after World War II, island life seemed to reflect mainland life in many ways. In the 1950s and 60s, housing developments appeared throughout the United States, including, on the islands, Neck Point Coves on Shaw, Riviera on Anderson, and others. More recently, islanders have opposed such developments, but the demand for homes increases as more people come to the Puget Sound region. In 1979, at a time when Winslow was growing rapidly, with new apartment buildings and condominiums built or planned, Bainbridge resident Jerome Hellmuth declared that islanders did not want the island to become a "dormitory."[1]

While more and more breadwinners on some islands commuted to mainland jobs, local work provided income for others. Shopkeepers, doctors and dentists, construction workers and real estate agents, school employees from teachers to bus drivers and more—all could live and work on an island. In 1950, Bainbridge High School students in shop class were doing some of the construction work on modest homes meant to attract schoolteachers who had found a housing shortage on this island. The opening of the Agate Pass Bridge soon afterward helped solve the Bainbridge teachers' problem, but today, the larger islands still ferry-dependent—Vashon and the San Juans—have similar problems regarding affordable housing for teachers.

In mid-century one could find small industries on the islands. Some have existed since well before World War II, and more opened in postwar years. Most industries that have emerged on the islands in recent years employ few people and are relatively non-polluting. In the computer age, more and more people can work from their island homes. Meanwhile, for industries that produce physical products, island locations, even Fidalgo, have become more difficult to sustain because rising transportation costs or changing zoning requirements or both restrict industrial activity.

Islanders continued to create local entertainment in the mid-twentieth century era. Some of the larger islands featured a movie theater as well as a bowling alley and lots of clubhouses. Organizations like the Elks, Eagles, Veterans of Foreign Wars, and various women's guilds carried out useful projects as they provided social gatherings and entertainment, just as non-profit organizations do these days. Local high school sports, especially football, have been important on the islands, though it has often been difficult for islanders to attend sporting events where their boys—in the 1950s and 60s, very few girls could participate—were the visiting team.

Special accommodations have been necessary to make some modern necessities available to islanders. An example is electricity, which people on various islands had to provide for themselves until the mid-twentieth century. On Lummi Island, electricity became available to all the residents in 1945. Guemes Island only received island-wide power in 1949, and until

1960, Anderson Islanders, too, relied on private generators. A two-mile-long underwater cable began providing electricity then. On January 31, 2009, however, the cable ruptured. Tanner Electric Cooperative, the provider, brought in two massive generators. Finding the break in the submarine cable took time as did the repair, but finally, in early April, Anderson Island's regular power supply became available again.

In the San Juan Islands, OPALCO—Orcas Power and Light Cooperative—originally served only Orcas Island but expanded coverage to all the major islands in the 1940s. Generators supplied power until OPALCO laid its first submarine cable, seven-and-one-half miles long, in 1951. At the time this was the longest high-voltage cable ever made for underwater use. During subsequent years, a few major storms have caused power interruptions on the San Juans, as in October 1962 and January 1972. Also, in November 1964, an underwater cable broke. Emergency generators, including one on a Washington National Guard maintenance ship, provided power for twenty days during repairs. Newer cables have been installed over the years, and to prevent storm damage as well as visual pollution, as of 2011, 87% of OPALCO's power lines were underground.[2] Today OPALCO is known for the annual meetings a cooperative must legally hold, for they take place on a regular Washington State Ferries run. Like electricity, telephone service for the islands cannot be taken for granted. Provider CenturyLink had an underwater cable break in November 2013, and San Juan County lost almost all telephone service, both by land line and cell phone. Quick work restored 911 service two days later, but cable repairs took ten days.

Aviation has decreased island isolation and emergency services by air are on hand in case of medical need. On Vashon Island, Masa Mukai built an airstrip on his land after World War II and voters purchased it around 1950. The field became King County's Airport District #1 and Mukai became one of the first airport commissioners. Voters on both Orcas and Lopez Islands created island-wide port districts mainly to support air transportation, Orcas in 1958 and Lopez in 1968. Until airstrips were built, aviators landed on the beach or on farm fields or arrived in float planes. San Juan, Orcas and Lopez all have scheduled air service these days. Tiny Hat Island has no airstrip, but if a speedy medical evacuation is warranted, a helicopter lands on the golf course's third fairway.

The increased accessibility of aviation is crucial in emergencies, but aviation along with telecommuting attract wealthy folk who can commute directly to Puget Sound island homes by air. On San Juan Island, Friday Harbor residents have noticed the number of planes that fly in on summer Friday afternoons and sit at the airport over the weekend. Also, some part-timers with homes on islands not served by ferries fly their own planes. Not all island airfields are available to the public—except for emergency use.

The islands that become less rural and more suburban are generally the ones close to mainland cities with relatively convenient transportation links. As early as 1962, the *Seattle Times* wrote that Bainbridge and Vashon "share the same principal industry—Seattle commuters." When the Boeing Company cut its workforce in Puget Sound country by two-thirds in the early 1970s, nearby island areas saw their population drop. In 1984, though, more than forty percent of Vashon Islanders holding down jobs were commuters, including many Boeing workers. Some thirty years later, the Vashon-Maury Island Heritage Association noted, "We are a rural community geographically but a suburban community in terms of employment."[3] The ferry system played its part, for when auto capacity of boats serving Vashon Island increased by forty percent in the final two decades of the twentieth century and passenger service to downtown Seattle began in 1990, Vashon population rose faster than before. The passenger service encouraged urban professionals to move to the island, something that had happened earlier on Bainbridge Island, whose car ferry connects the island's commercial center directly with downtown Seattle.

Vashon Island has remained more affordable than Bainbridge because it is harder to reach. Vashon does not have a bridge to Kitsap County. Its car ferries do not run to the Seattle city center. Also, on Vashon, unlike Bainbridge, there is nothing for the casual visitor near a ferry dock. And when King County planned improvements at Maury Island's Dockton Park in the mid-1970s, islanders resisted, fearing that improvements would bring more people. Vashon Islanders have expressed concern about beginning to resemble Bainbridge, while in 1972, one-time Winslow city councilman Jim Taniguchi worried that Bainbridge was becoming too much like Mercer Island, the wealthy bedroom community in Lake Washington just east of Seattle. Other islands, not just Vashon and Bainbridge, have changed, too, but "except for the ferries, Orcas is uncrowded," visiting journalist Jerry Hulse wrote in 1987, and this is still more or less true—but perhaps only for about nine out of twelve months each year, from Labor Day until Memorial Day.[4]

Just after World War II, the islands were scenic but relatively undeveloped. However, even during the depression years of the 1930s, island waterfront prices had risen substantially, partly due to improved ferry service. Several decades later, the islands were becoming communities of commuters and retirees. The islands evolved from places where the residents made their livings locally—working at a boatyard, fishing, growing strawberries, teaching school—to locations featuring many vacation retreats or homes for commuters to the mainland. In the late 1960s, "tourism, retirement, real estate construction, the arts and a variety of cottage industries began to take hold" on San Juan Island, according to a sign in Friday Harbor. By the 1970s, Whidbey Island, once mainly rural, had become "Residential, Recreational and Retirement," Ken Brydges wrote. Waterfront properties and, to a lesser extent, view properties in the Puget Sound area have become more and more desirable. Through the years land values and property taxes have inevitably risen. Real estate prices skyrocketed in the late 1970s and this has continued. By the early 1990s one could read that many people who grew up on Bainbridge Island could not afford to live on the island,[5] and one hears this on other islands, too.

The San Juan Islands saw little if any population growth from the time the orchard business faded in the early twentieth century until after World War II. In the next decade, the traveling public discovered them. Purchasers mostly from California drove real estate prices up twelve to fifteen percent in just one year, the *Seattle Times* reported in 1989. *Post-Intelligencer* journalist Thomas Shapley wrote bitterly about the archipelago in 1990, "The battle and the islands are lost to the super rich. Within a few years, no more than a decade, no one will live on the islands but the very rich—and the people they hire to serve them." An editorial in the *Journal of the San Juan Islands* worried in 1994 that "we have an economy that cannot take care of people who need to work for a living."[6]

Most service jobs on the San Juans do not pay enough to enable people to live there, and affordable rental property is more and more difficult to find. Organizations on various islands have created initiatives to develop more low-cost housing, sometimes through sweat-equity programs. The San Juan Community Home Trust has acquired small, older houses that were about to be torn down on Vancouver Island to be replaced by larger up-to-date houses. The organization brings them by barge to San Juan Island, then refurbishes them and sells them to low-income residents. Meanwhile, long-timers continue to live on the islands and strive to keep them pleasant—and open not only to the wealthy. Perhaps some long-time residents want to keep their island the way it was when they first saw it.

As people keep coming to the islands, water may be the ultimate factor that limits development. Studies on various islands have identified them as dependent on sole source aquifers. This Environmental Protection Agency designation means that a specified area contains an aquifer—underground water source—that supplies more than half of the area's drinking water, and that additional or alternative sources are not available. The islands do not tend to have rivers or lakes free of pollution that could also be used as water sources. Therefore, the aquifers warrant protection, and the islands face two main threats to drinking water supplies. If people use too much water, rainfall will not be able to fully replenish the aquifers. Second, salt water intrusion from the sea can contaminate water sources, as has already begun to occur on some islands, such as Guemes.

The EPA has defined Guemes, Marrowstone, Vashon-Maury, Whidbey, Camano and Bainbridge Islands as dependent on sole source aquifers. For some of these islands, water piped from the mainland would appear to be an obvious possibility but is mostly too expensive to consider. Island population growth is thus limited by the amount of fresh water available— but no one can tell how many people are too many. In 1994, due to scant rainfall, Friday Harbor instituted a temporary "water emergency,"[7] and in 2013, because of limited availability of groundwater supplies not compromised by sea water intrusion, some home-owners in San Juan County received permits to use rainwater when necessary. Sometimes needed water has been delivered by truck.

Desalination supplies fresh water in some Puget Sound island communities, but this is an expensive alternative. Five systems are in San Juan County and others serve Eliza, Hat, and part of Guemes Islands. A few of them supply only two or three properties, but several have fifty or more customers. Among the islands where desalination provides water is 178-acre Center Island in the San Juans. This tiny island has an airstrip and a community building serving all the residents, who get around the island in golf carts. Fewer than two dozen people are full-time residents, but the population increases dramatically in the summer. For a populous Puget Sound island, though, desalination is not a solution.

Marrowstone Island has seen the angriest battle over water. During the first decade of the twenty-first century, island residents found themselves strongly divided on the question of whether to create a public water district for the island. People depended on wells, but some had run dry, and saltwater had seeped into some others, making perhaps twenty percent of the island's wells unusable. Some residents began collecting rainwater, and people without good well water began hauling water from the mainland. The residents whose wells worked just fine were not anxious to pay the cost of water supplied by a public utility district (PUD), and some residents feared that an island-wide water system would bring unwanted development to the island. It took six years of controversy, but the island finally began to receive PUD water piped from the mainland by the beginning of 2009.

While water sources can be a limiting factor, waste disposal is also a problem. Some island landfills have reached capacity, and their solid waste must go to the mainland, which is often expensive. Moreover, the necessary vehicles fill a lot of space on the ferries. Also harming the Puget Sound environment is the discharge of sewage from waterfront homes and businesses directly into the Sound, which was general practice in earlier years. It is no longer condoned, but dwellings here and there on the islands still pollute the Sound. Official efforts to curb this are continuing.

In 1971 Washington State adopted the Shoreline Management Act, which regulates use of land close to the shore. The first criminal conviction for violation of the Act involved a road being built on Maury Island's southernmost shore. The developer had continued work on his project even after being ordered to stop construction. Despite examples of environmental degradation such as this, most islanders are sensitive to environmental concerns. They work tirelessly to protect cherished land, like Guemes Mountain, Orcas Island's Turtleback Mountain or Bainbridge Island's Grand Forest. In a very different kind of environmental action, San Juan County voters passed an initiative in 2012 that forbade the planting of genetically modified seeds. Winning environmental battles takes hard work. Though many people move to the islands for privacy and tranquility, they may find they have to become active in battles to protect these values because other people want to develop the land and make money or attract more residents, visitors and businesses. An island life can offer serenity and peace of mind, but islanders may have to strive to keep such contentment possible.

Many islanders are working on preparation for the future. Residents on various islands have developed community plans to try to cope with major catastrophes, such as beachfront inundations brought on by climate change. Islanders realize that should a regionwide crisis occur, they could be on their own for a long time. Their self-reliance will help. People come to the islands to live despite the challenges of such possible emergency situations. In 2016 Vashon Islanders faced a serious problem when their major health provider announced that its island clinic would close. For almost two months, many Vashon Islanders found that they had to find all medical care off-island. An interim provider came, but with long-term needs in mind islanders voted to create a hospital district, which helps support a clinic and provides stronger emergency services. San Juan, Orcas, Lopez, and Whidbey Islanders have also set up local hospital districts, which appear to be the best answer these days to providing medical services in isolated communities.

Vaccination has been a medical issue. A relatively high rate of Vashon Island parents did not have their children vaccinated against communicable diseases in early 2015, when measles cases led to nationwide concern. 17.8% of the students in Vashon Island's public schools were exempt from vaccination requirements due to medical conditions or personal beliefs. A year later, however, Vashon's exemptions were much fewer. Some other islands, too, have faced a similar problem. In 2019, Washington State made it mandatory for children attending school to be vaccinated, with exceptions permitted only for medical or religious reasons.

San Juan County has had the healthiest residents of any Washington State county, studies have shown. Positive factors include relatively low rates of smoking and obesity and an active lifestyle, along with a low crime rate and lots of opportunities for recreation. It is also true that as islanders age and need more medical care, many of them move to the mainland. On the other hand, study also indicates that San Juan County residents are above the state average in consuming too much alcohol.

Facing the ferry-dependent islands is the future of the ferry system. What will ever-increasing fares and possible decreases in frequency of sailings do to impact island life, and how will the price of fuel for the boats affect the system? Ferry service has been a concern since well before World War II and will always remain so unless or until bridges or tunnels replace the boats. Islanders who are dependent on ferries have a different concept of time and distance, even space, because of the ferries. One is either "on the island" or "off island." An islander with a problem will ask, "Can I get it taken care of on the island?" Residents understand that island life can be inconvenient at times but are willing to put up with this because they feel the advantages of island living so far outweigh the disadvantages. Islanders are resilient and can depend on themselves, even when the boats stop running or the power is off.

During difficult economic times in the twenty-first century, island communities have struggled as have towns throughout the nation and beyond. Restaurants go out of business and empty storefronts on main streets face the tourist. Even businesses that remain open find profits declining. On the San Juan Islands, some residents take two, even three jobs, to be able to afford to live there. Some islanders on the San Juans live in a rental house for nine months of a year but make do with a tent or a friend's sofa during the summers when the owner reclaims his home. The Puget Sound islands also have year-round homeless people. In 2019, 166 people on Whidbey and Camano Islands were identified as homeless and Vashon Island's January 2019 count found 97 homeless people.[8] The islands have plenty of forested land where people sometimes camp with little fear of detection or removal. For low-income people, various volunteer organizations on the islands provide hot meals while food banks also help meet needs. With such programs, islands continue to be a refuge to all, not only the wealthy.

Islands respect privacy, for example in secluded spots where a person can live mostly undisturbed. In the twenty-first century, the story of Camano Island teenager Colton Harris-Moore, called the "Barefoot Bandit," spread across the nation. This young man lived with his sometimes-violent mother in a trailer in the wooded, less populated southern part of the island. Students taunted him at school for wearing dirty and torn clothes, he often was belligerent, and he dropped out of school in ninth grade. At an Island County hearing in December 2011, Judge Vickie Churchill described his childhood as "little better than a dog's."[9] Many places in Western Washington, especially Camano Island and the San Juans, saw break-ins and thefts attributed to Harris-Moore. He taught himself to fly, stealing airplanes. Eventually caught in the Bahamas in 2010, he received a seven-and-one-fourth year prison sentence from Washington State with a federal sentence to run concurrently. One wonders whether greater community involvement during Colton-Moore's early years could have helped him.

The islands have attracted some rebellious and potentially dangerous groups since World War II. A serious confrontation occurred on Whidbey Island on December 8, 1984, when the FBI targeted several neo-Nazis, including Robert Mathews, who were living in three beach houses in the Greenbank area. Agents sought Mathews for having shot an FBI agent in Portland, Oregon, several weeks earlier. When he resisted capture on Whidbey, the FBI kept boat traffic away from the vicinity while surrounding Mathews' refuge. A shootout ensued and later a fire, after which Mathews was discovered dead.

In 1991, a small racist group with ties to the Aryan Nation rented a Bainbridge Island house and apparently distributed hate literature on Bainbridge Island. Later, leaders of a committee founded to combat this racial harassment on the island found themselves harassed by telephone. However, the hate group decamped one November night, perhaps in response to community opposition.

McNeil island has long been a home to miscreants—for many years, prisoners, and now, detainees. The federal prison built on the island in the nineteenth century held inmates for just over one hundred years, but by the 1970s, the U.S. government wanted to close the aging facility. No longer was an island location an asset, for transporting people and provisions cost too much. McNeil Island remains a detention center, though, as it now houses Washington State sex offenders who have finished their sentences but are deemed still to be sexually dangerous. However, descendants of McNeil Island settlers would like to reclaim the island where their families put down roots. Others would like to see the island named a nature preserve.

Are islands safer than other areas? Islanders know that when they set foot on their islands, they leave the stress of city streets behind. They feel safe from crime. On some islands, people still leave their doors unlocked and their car keys in the ignition. Many homes are used only during summer and on some weekends. These houses tempt squatters or thieves, as Harris-Moore demonstrated. Somewhere on the islands you will find most of the problems Americans face in communities elsewhere, for the islands are part of the modern world.

Some people have safety in mind when they decide to move to an island, but these days many island parents wait at school bus stops with their young children just as do mainlanders. Islanders have found that burglars sometime arrive and depart—with stolen items—by boat. The islands have attracted some habitual drug users who often steal to support their drug habits. On the larger islands, petty crimes often occur. Vashon and Bainbridge have at times been described as places rampant with illicit drugs. On Whidbey, some students have become homeless because their military families were relocated from the Naval Air Station and arrangements for the youngsters to live with friends while finishing high school on the island did not work out. These islands and others feature programs to counsel and help people deal with issues of various kinds, including drug and alcohol use and homelessness.

Island teenagers often complain, "There's nothing to do," but many mainland teens feel the same. Concerned adults have responded by opening teen centers and organizing activities while the local schools offer many different sports and other extra-curricular activities. After high school graduation, disenchanted young people often leave their islands to make their futures on the mainland. Other island youth leave because they cannot find local jobs and, moreover, cannot find places to live which they can afford. Some do return years later, sometimes moving into the homes where they grew up, now that the older generation needs family care or has left the house.

On some islands, islanders can make decisions regarding official policies. In the San Juans and on Whidbey and Camano Islands, islanders run the county government, as Island County—Whidbey, Camano and a few tiny islands—and San Juan County consist of nothing but islands. These counties provide services keyed specifically to island residents (and visitors) and county officials are easily accessible. County government offers employment as well as decision-making. Yet islands with local government do not find themselves free of political controversy, for factions develop among residents. These are often characterized as newcomers versus old-timers, groups who have widely divergent ideas of what the future should be. Long-time islanders sometimes resent newcomers because they represent population growth and change, while in other cases, they are blamed for stifling desired development.

And though Camano Island's county government administers only islands, Camano Islanders face the problem of distance from their county seat on Whidbey Island. Modern communications and a branch office on Camano meet some of the difficulties, but Camano people summoned for jury duty still have to travel to Coupeville, about sixty miles and perhaps an hour and a half away. Other inhabited islands are part of much larger counties. People living on these islands can find themselves with little say when county officials make decisions. Vashon-Maury Island, for example, contains only about one-half of one percent of King County's population. Residents may feel that officials in county government do not always recognize that islanders' needs and desires can be different from those of mainland folks, or islanders may feel that they are not adequately consulted when the county officials create policies. Consider the county's role in the negotiations between Whatcom County commissioners and Lummi Indian Nation officials over the future of ferry service to Lummi Island. Islanders had no official say on the issue, though it was their future which was at stake. For such reasons, Bainbridge islanders incorporated, shifting much authority to islanders. The ultimate example of what the lack of local control might bring could be a bridge across one's island to ease mainlanders' trips across Puget Sound. Most ferry-dependent islanders do not want such a bridge, but sometimes the mainland comes to an island anyway.

Summer people continue to swell island populations from June through August, even a bit longer. In 1968, only two-thirds of the residences on Whidbey Island were occupied all year and the 2000 census found the same on Orcas, while about 2015 Camano Island's population went from about 15,000 to 20,000 in the summer. People with summer homes on the islands can feel that year-round islanders resent them. What the locals see are crowded ferries and restaurants. More strangers appear. Tourists predominate along Winslow Way on Bainbridge Island during the summer, and residents of Bainbridge and other islands will complain that it is hard to find a parking place in their island's commercial center because of tourists or summer people.

When people open new businesses on the islands, some are for tourists but quite a few primarily serve residents. One can no longer shop on an island for many items connected with everyday life, however, but these can be ordered online and delivered to islanders' homes. Meanwhile, "Buy local" campaigns take place on the islands to keep small businesses profitable. The larger islands all still have at least one bookstore. Chain stores and fast-food operations are rare. San Juan County has none but Vashon Island has a Subway. The larger islands have a number of restaurants, and you can find at least one on a few of the lightly-populated ones.

Islands offer a strong sense of community. Consider three South Sound islands: Reach (Treasure), Harstine and Anderson. Reach is a tiny private island with a short bridge, Harstine a larger island, also bridged, and Anderson, fairly large, and accessible by a twenty-minute ferry ride. Harstine and Anderson Islands each have about one thousand residents and Reach many fewer. These islands differ in important ways, but they all have tightly-knit communities. Everyone knows each other and offers help when needed. On these islands, people see their neighbors at potluck dinners and other community functions. They step into each other's homes by the back door, which for many houses on all the islands is the obvious way to enter. These islands feature social gatherings, arts presentations and lots of volunteer organizations and projects.

On the islands with much larger populations, community feeling is still strong, but different. Fewer causes bring an entire island together—though a ferry or bridge issue can do this. School and development questions also bring out the crowds. When someone is severely ill, needing off-island treatment, islanders respond, offering transportation, child care, food, and more, even ferry tickets. Perhaps the clear boundary of an island enhances community feeling. On the other hand, it is important to remember that some islanders do not become involved in community affairs. Island residents are ordinary but independent folks, and many may want to live their own lives without participating in island causes or activities.

Little interaction among residents of different islands seems to occur. These people can feel like rivals, but they sometimes work together to influence decisions or events that impact the islands. For example, in 1997, residents of Anderson, Vashon and Whidbey Islands joined forces to urge Washington State officials to better regulate logging. Cooperation sometimes occurs when ferry service is the issue, but in the days soon after World War II when most islanders supported construction of a cross-Sound bridge, Bainbridge and Vashon Islanders vied with each other for the bridge route.

The islands are similar, but also in many ways different from each other. Visitors can peruse island historical museums and libraries to get an idea of an island's particular features, especially its history. San Juan and Anderson Islands have museums located on pioneer farms, while museums on other islands are mostly in historic town buildings. On Bainbridge, Lopez and Orcas, schoolhouses form part of the local historical museum complexes. On Orcas Island, six cabins, all built on the island between 1870 and 1900, now sit together on a site in Eastsound, where they make up the main Orcas Island museum.

On Vashon Island, the museum is the one-time Lutheran Church. Built in 1907, the sanctuary served the congregation until a new, larger church building opened in 1959 and in 2003, the Vashon-Maury Island Heritage Museum opened there. On Fidalgo Island, the Anacortes Museum is in a charming building in a pleasant residential neighborhood. The structure originated as the city's Carnegie Library, which opened in 1911. Shaw and Fox Islands both have historical museums, and Whidbey Island has several—one in Coupeville and another in Langley as well as the PBY-Naval Air Museum in Oak Harbor. Friday Harbor and Langley both have whale museums.

Island museums are an afterthought, begun in more recent years to preserve what came before. For earlier settlers, libraries were important, just as they are now, and some began very long ago. On Bainbridge Island, Port Madison had a library by 1863 and Winslow opened one in 1913. Almost all island libraries have now been incorporated into countywide systems or the two-county Sno-Isle Libraries serving Snohomish and Island Counties. However, through volunteer efforts, Shaw Islanders fund and operate their own independent library.

Community support can enhance community life. A wonderful example is the Bainbridge Island Library's new building, opened on July 6, 1997. Islanders sorely needed better library facilities, and islanders raised funds for extensive remodeling, creating what amounts to a new structure. Supporters collected enough money to avoid calling for a special tax levy to finance the library upgrades.

In the museums and libraries one can learn about interesting incidents that have occurred on the islands. One event that reaped publicity in 1947 was a reputed Maury Island flying saucer sighting. Unidentified Flying Objects were just beginning to make the news in those days, and a boater reported six UFOs flying over the island on June 21. These objects, shaped rather like doughnuts, ejected some debris and something that fell killed the boater's dog. The story spread widely, but who knows what, if anything, truly happened.

An internationally significant gathering took place on Blake Island in 1993 when President Bill Clinton hosted a meeting of the Asia Pacific Economic Cooperation, or APEC, leaders there. The visitors included the prime ministers of Japan, New Zealand, Australia, Singapore and Thailand, presidents of the People's Republic of China, Indonesia, South Korea, the Philippines, the United States, and others, including the Sultan of Brunei. They arrived at the island in the WSF passenger boat *Tyee* and sat down to a meal highlighted by salmon and wild blackberry cobbler, but the political leaders did not have a chance to see the Native American dances shown to tourists.

We can hear lots of stories about the islands. Bellingham area entrepreneur James F. Wardner announced about 1890 that his company, Consolidated Black Cats Co. Ltd., would be raising black cats on Eliza Island to sell their pelts. After this story appeared in the *Fairhaven Herald*, various newspapers throughout the country reported the enterprise which, of course, never existed except as Wardner's prank. Also perhaps meant as a hoax are the fake San Juan Islands recorded on a Wilkes Expedition map. Perhaps true is this tale from the beginning of the twentieth century: A North Whidbey farmer found hidden cans of what he thought was paint. Therefore, he painted his house, but after rain dislodged the "paint," he found that he had covered his house, temporarily, with some $1,500 worth of opium.[10]

Genuine in every way are other stories. Friday Harbor men once held a tea party modeled on the famous Boston protest. In August 1974, a Sunday *Seattle Post-Intelligencer* article had vilified the town, calling Friday Harbor "the armpit of the San Juans." So, a few weeks later, some wrathful residents done up as Indians boarded an arriving ferry, seized the Sunday *Post-Intelligencers* it was bringing to the island and threw them overboard.[11] Well known is Vashon Island's bicycle enveloped high in the trunk of a tree, while Orcas Islanders know about the rocks placed in the shape of an anchor on top of Turtleback Mountain long ago.

For residents and visitors alike, the islands are special places. One needs make an effort to get to an island. A traveler does not just happen to discover one while on a road trip somewhere. People have enjoyed island life but also have faced challenges over the years, and this will continue.

Today's challenges are different from those the Native Americans and European-American pioneers faced during their nineteenth century lives on the islands. The twentieth century brought challenges of wartime and development, while the twenty-first century sees climate change and COVID-19 and may face future unknown trials. Like the Native peoples' way of treasuring culture since time immemorial, so do we cherish the islands. The islands are the jewels of Puget Sound, havens of tranquility, and islanders struggle to find the balance between honoring the past and navigating the days to come.

Acknowledgments

INFORMATION ABOUT ISLAND HISTORY CAN BE FOUND far and wide and I owe thanks to many people and institutions which helped me find it. The smallest islands do not boast museums, but nearby county museums and research facilities offer lots of resources. Both the Shelton Timberland Library and the Mason County Historical Society Museum furnished information to me regarding Harstine, Squaxin, and neighboring small islands, as did the beautiful museum of the Squaxin Island Tribe. Representing the tribe, Kathy Block and Charlene Krise read the two chapters regarding Native Americans and made valuable comments about them. The helpful people at the Jefferson County Historical Society Research Center outside Port Townsend, especially Cathy Beatty-O'Shea, assisted me in delving for information about Marrowstone and Indian Islands. In addition, Ron Hirschi, Josh Wisniewski and Toni Whalen offered suggestions regarding the S'Klallam people and Indian and Marrowstone Islands. In Bellingham, both the public library and the Center for Pacific Northwest Studies at Western Washington University made research a pleasure. Thanks to Eric Mastor and Roz Koester for assisting me at the Center.

Other mainland institutions have been invaluable. These include the downtown branch of the Tacoma Public Library, whose Northwest Room has an extensive clipping file and a comprehensive book collection. The Washington State Historical Society Research Center is also in Tacoma.

This institution holds manuscripts and ephemera not available elsewhere. Joy Werlink makes it possible for researchers there to use their time efficiently, and I thank her for the time and energy she expended in searching out many items for me. I also used the Everett Public Library's clipping file. In Seattle, I sought material in the Seattle Room of the Seattle Public Library downtown, ably assisted by Ann Ferguson and others. At the University of Washington, the microform collections of weekly island newspapers and other items were invaluable. Glenda Pearson and her staff were very helpful as I worked with the materials. At the University's Special Collections, staff members have made useful suggestions and have retrieved many items for me to peruse. Carolyn Marr at Seattle's Museum of History and Industry Archives took time to fulfill my requests. I received helpful attention at the Washington State Library in Tumwater, which maintains an extensive and useful collection of books, microfilmed newspapers from all over the state, and manuscripts. In Olympia, Kathy Szolomayer of the Washington State Department of Transportation Library was especially helpful, and librarians at the Washington State Archives found important information for me.

The island museums are great! I heartily recommend them. Not only are their displays and collections useful, their staff members are eager to help. I should add that the museums differ from each other, so people should visit all of them. The Anacortes Museum in its beautiful historic building—once the city's Carnegie Library—includes historic information on Guemes and Sinclair Islands as well as Fidalgo Island. On Fidalgo, I appreciate the insights I received from Theresa Trebon, Archivist and Historian for the Swinomish Indian Tribal Community. I visited island museums on San Juan, Orcas, Lopez and Shaw Islands in the San Juans, in Oak Harbor, Coupeville and Langley on Whidbey Island, and on Bainbridge, Vashon, Fox and Anderson Islands. Island historians and museum personnel are generous with their time. Terry Slotemaker and Bret Lunsford kindly answered my many questions at the Anacortes Museum, as Kevin Loftis and Mary Jean Cahail did at the San Juan Island Museum. Liz Illg and Nancy DeVaux made interesting San Juan Island photographs available to me. I learned about Orcas Island thanks to Jim and Kay Clark, Eirena Birkenfeld, Clark McAbee, Tom Welch and the late Jane Barfoot-Hodde. Mark Thompson-Klein helped me on Lopez Island and Cherie Christensen and the late Geb Nichols showed me around Shaw Island while imparting much about island life and history. Two one-time teachers at the Shaw Island School, Dick Cvitanich and Diane Tuttle, shared memories of life on Shaw. At the libraries on San Juan, Orcas and Lopez Islands, too, I found both useful information and helpful people. Others who have helped me include Karen Jones-Lamb concerning Decatur Island and Paul Davis on Lummi Island. Deb Martyn and the late Margaret Philbrick have lived on both Vashon and Orcas and thus offered important insight. Thanks to Pastor Beth Purdum of the San Juan Islands.

Whidbey Island boasts the Island County Historical Museum in Coupeville and the South Whidbey Historical Museum in Langley as well as the PBY military museum, which presents military history in Oak Harbor. Rick Castellano, Joan Peters and Gordon Grant at the Coupeville museum and Sue Hoelscher in Langley helped me. The late Roger Sherman enhanced my knowledge of the island's maritime history and Steven Kobylk was a military history mentor, giving me more of his time than I deserved. The Sno-Isle Library branches on Whidbey Island also have useful historical data as well as helpful librarians. Barbara Gordon made my time on Whidbey Island even more rewarding by urging my sister and me to take the loop trail from Ebey Landing. And thanks to Eleanor Brugeman, who knows everything there is to know about Hat Island. Karen Prasse shared her extensive knowledge of Camano Island history. At the Bainbridge Island Historical Museum I appreciate help from many people, especially Rick Chandler, the late Hank Helm, Reid Hansen, Katy Curtis and Dick Berg. The Kitsap Regional Library's Bainbridge Island branch also contains useful historical information about the island.

On Anderson Island, Mikey Sleight opened the museum for me, while Liz Galentine and Pete Cammon shared their insights. At the Fox Island Museum, Marie Weis spent several hours responding to my many queries. In the South Sound, Judy Prior made it possible for me to visit privately-owned Reach (Treasure) Island and shared island information. Claudia Ellsworth, Judy Greinke, Mary Turpin, Charles Smith and Steve Kramer made Herron Island come to life. Thanks also to Kae Paterson and long-time resident Jean Springer for details about Raft Island history and to Shirley Erhart of the Mason County Historical Society for Stretch Island particulars. Deborah and Ken Hoy shared their knowledge and photographs of South Sound Islands. Finally, I treasure the chance I had to learn from the late Robin Paterson, Mosquito Fleet expert.

My friends and colleagues at the Vashon-Maury Island Heritage Museum of course offered information, memories, and ideas. I will include names of only a few of my many friends there who shared evidence and encouragement. Lifelong islander Barbara Steen seemingly knows everything there is to know about the island, as did the late Mary Jo Barrentine. Laurie Tucker, Rayna and Jay Holtz and Peter Rinearson have given me assistance. David Perley was especially helpful in sharing information regarding Vashon Island's Japanese American community. The Vashon Island branch of the King County Library System is also a useful source of information and I especially appreciate its Interlibrary Loan service.

Friends and family are always important to anyone doing research and writing. George Foster's analytical mind and knowledge of Puget Sound history was very helpful. On island trips, friends offered lodging. While I studied Indian and Marrowstone Islands, Penny Ridderbusch and Kathleen Croston hosted me in the beautiful and historic Port Townsend house they are restoring. On Orcas Island, Anne Thomas and her family welcomed me at their beach cabin, while my hosts Judy and Mike Callaghan on Harstine shared island events and information in addition to hospitality.

My travel companions, too, made my trips more enjoyable and often contributed knowledge and insight. Thank you, Mary Mullen, Mary Grayson, Rosemary Shattuck, Yvonne Kuperberg and Bea Jackson.

Thanks to paper ephemera dealer Michael Maslan for his help and to Kate Blackmer, who not only created wonderful maps, but expanded my understanding of the islands. My Vashon Island friend Alice Larson provided necessary assistance in computer use.

Those who read a manuscript critically are irreplaceable and I owe immense thanks to them. Mike Vouri, Laurie Tucker, Dick Blumenthal, Tom DeVries, Steven Kobylk, Roger Sherman and Robin Paterson each read the chapter or chapters dealing with their area of expertise. They not only offered important suggestions, they prevented mistakes and misinterpretations. Family members Les Irish, Mary Mullen, Ellen Irish, Rosemary Shattuck and Jane Irish Nelson read the entire manuscript for me. Les also prepared the photographs for publication. Finally, extra thanks are due to fellow Vashon Island historians Jean Cammon Findlay and Bruce Haulman for critically reading the entire manuscript as well as sharing information, insight, encouragement, and research trips. Long conversations with them also improved this work immeasurably. Jean deserves additional recognition, for she suggested the book's title.

I am indebted to Epicenter Press for making publication of this book possible. Megan Stills' editing expertise guided me in improving the text, while Phil Garrett and Jennifer McCord kept me on track throughout the process of publication. All of them answered many queries and offered encouragement and suggestions

Finally, islanders throughout Puget Sound, from Lummi Island in the far north to Anderson in the far south have inspired me. Thanks to all of you.

This work is one person's look at the islands. As well as being responsible for any factual errors that appear, I am the person who decided what to say and what not to say about the islands. I hope you agree that I have included most of the important things, fairly and accurately.

Notes

Preface

1. "Deadman Island Purchased from Seattle Contest Winner," *Seattle Times*, November 16, 1948.
2. Radio program, "The Vinyl Cafe," November 29, 2010, KUOW, Seattle.
3. Alexandra Harmon, *The Power of Promise* (Seattle: University of Washington Press, 2008), 14-15.

1 | On the Map

1. Richard W. Blumenthal, ed., *Charles Wilkes and the Exploration of Inland Washington Waters* (Jefferson, NC: McFarland, 2009), 96, 211.
2. Blumenthal, ed., *Charles Wilkes*, 83-4.
3. "Oliver Scott Van Olinda: Island Chronicler—Newspaperman, Photographer, Author," Vashon-Maury Island Heritage Association Bulletin 25: 3, Summer 2010.
4. William A. Peck, Jr., *The Pig War and Other Experiences of William Peck—Soldier 1858-1862—U.S. Army Corps of Engineers: The Journal of William A. Peck, Jr.*, eds. C. Brewster Coulter and Bert Webber (Medford, OR: Webb Research Group, 1993), 131.
5. Richard W. Blumenthal, ed., *With Vancouver in Inland Washington Waters: Journals of 12 Crewmen, April—June 1792* (Jefferson, NC: McFarland, 2007), 19, 20, 80; Hardin Craig, Jr., ed., "A Letter from the Vancouver Expedition," *Pacific Northwest Quarterly* 41 (October 1950), 354.

6. Ann Nugent, ed., *Lummi Elders Speak* (Lynden, WA: *Lynden Tribune*, 1982), 31, 32.

7. Arthur R. Kruckeberg, *The Natural History of Puget Sound Country* (Seattle: University of Washington Press, 1991), 413; Blumenthal, ed., *With Vancouver*, 85.

8. Blumenthal, ed., *With Vancouver*, 195; *Told by the Pioneers III*, (Olympia, WA?, 1938), 51.

9. Blumenthal, ed., *With Vancouver*, 20.

10. Dorothy Neil in *Spirit of the Island . . . A Photo History of Oak Harbor*, comp. Peggy Christine Darst (Peggy C. Darst, 2005), 4.

11. George A. Kellogg, *A History of Whidbey's Island* (Coupeville, WA: Island County Historical Society, 2001), 88.

2 | The Early Inhabitants

1. Julie K. Stein, "Stratigraphy and Dating," in Julie K. Stein and Laura S. Phillips, eds., *Vashon Island Archaeology: A View from Burton Acres* (Seattle: Burke Museum, 2002), 59; Julie K. Stein, *Exploring Coast Salish Prehistory: The Archaeology of San Juan Island* (Seattle: University of Washington Press, 2000), 104, 48.

2. Stein, *Exploring Coast Salish* Prehistory, 105; Court of Claims of the United States. No. F-275. Duwamish et al. v. U.S.A. 1927. The Indian Claims Commission considered claims made by Native American groups against the government regarding compensation promised in nineteenth century treaties.

3. Court of Claims, 833.

4. George Gibbs, *Indian Tribes of Washington Territory* (Fairfield, WA: Ye Galleon Press, 1967), 35, 37. This is a reprint from Exec. Doc. no. 91, House of Representatives, 33rd Congress, 2nd session.

5. Though Puyallup Tribe officials have indicated that S'Homamish is less accurate than other spellings such as Sxwobabc, S'Homamish has appeared in federal government documents; Natalie Martin, "New exhibit delves into Vashon's Native American past," *Vashon-Maury Island Beachcomber*, June 4, 2014; LLyn De Danaan, "Ethnographic Background," in Stein and Phillips, ed., *Vashon Island Archaeology*, 19.

6. Court of Claims (Lucy Gurand), 648.

7. Daniel L. Boxberger, *To Fish in Common: The Ethnohistory of Lummi Indian Salmon Fishing* (Seattle: University of Washington Press, 2000), 15; Court of Claims (Caroline Ewing), 439.

8. T. T. Waterman, *Notes on the Ethnology of the Indians of Puget Sound* (New York: Museum of the American Indian, Heye Foundation, 1973), 54; Nugent, ed., *Lummi Elders*, 56.

9. Richard W. Blumenthal, ed., *The Early Explorers of Inland Washington Waters: Journals and Logs from Six Expeditions, 1786-1792* (Jefferson, NC: McFarland, 2004), 159.

10. Court of Claims (Caroline Ewing), 439.

11. Gibbs, *Indian Tribes*, 39.

12. Deur, Douglas. *An Ethnohistory of Traditionally Associated Contemporary Populations.* United States Department of the Interior, Pacific West Series in Social Science, Publication Number 2009-02, 54.

13. Blumenthal, ed., *With Vancouver*, 19.

14. Robert H. Ruby and John A. Brown, *Indian Slavery in the Pacific Northwest* (Spokane: Arthur H. Clark, 1993), 292.

15. Nugent, ed., *Lummi Elders*, 88-89.

16. Bernhard J. Stern, *The Lummi Indians of Northwest Washington* (New York: Columbia University Press, 1969), 112.

17. George L. Miller, ed., *Fox Island: A History* (1982), 4. Variations on this tale appear in other publications.

18. Judy Wright, "The Project: A Tribal Perspective," in Stein and Phillips, ed., 2. We know Mt. Takoma as Mt. Rainier.

3 | The Explorers

1. Blumenthal, ed., *Early Exploration*, 58. Blumenthal uses a translation from Spanish by Henry R. Wagner. Note that Blumenthal's editions of explorers' journals and diaries are especially helpful because footnotes indicate, as much as is possible, where events occurred.

2. Blumenthal, ed., *With Vancouver*, 209.

3. Blumenthal, ed., *Early Exploration*, 152, 125.

4. Blumenthal, ed., *Early Exploration*, 153.

5. Blumenthal, ed., *With Vancouver*, 30.

6. Peter Puget, in Blumenthal, ed., *With Vancouver*, 32.

7. Blumenthal, ed., *With Vancouver*, 36.

8. Blumenthal, ed., *With Vancouver*, 78 and 78 n.53.

9. Blumenthal, ed., *Early Exploration*, 167.

10. Blumenthal, ed., *Early Exploration*, 173, 174 and 174 n.123.

11. Sam McKinney, *Sailing with Vancouver* (Victoria, B.C.: Touch Wood editions, 2004), 87.

12. Blumenthal, ed., *Early Exploration*, 178.

13. Blumenthal, ed., *With Vancouver*, 49, 50.

14. Blumenthal, ed., *Early Exploration*, 184, 187, 186.

15. Craig, ed., "A Letter from the Vancouver Expedition," 354.

16. *Journal of John Work: January to October 1835* (Victoria, BC: Charles F. Banfield, 1945), 91, 92.

17. Blumenthal, ed., *Charles Wilkes*, 170, 16.

18. Blumenthal, ed., *Charles Wilkes*, 17, 31.

19. Blumenthal, ed., *Charles Wilkes*, 175, 203, 135.

20. Blumenthal, ed., *Charles Wilkes*, 136, 143.

21. Blumenthal, ed., *Charles Wilkes*, 221, 153, 83.

22. 22. John Frazier Henry, "The Midshipman's Revenge: Or, The Case of the Missing Islands," *Pacific Northwest Quarterly* 73 (October 1982), 159, 161, 162.

4 | The Pig War

1. Michael Vouri, *The Pig War: Standoff at Griffin Bay*, 2nd ed. (Seattle: Discover Your Northwest, 2013), 25.

2. Vouri, *The Pig War*, 59.

3. Peck, *The Pig War and Other Experiences*, 100, 101, 105, 226 n. 24.

4. Jo Bailey-Cummings and Al Cummings, *San Juan: The Power-Keg Island* (Friday Harbor, WA: Beach Combers, Inc., 1987), 66; A Settler of Ten Years, "San Juan Island," *Washington Standard*, September 30, 1865.

5. James O. McCabe, *The San Juan Water Boundary Question* (Toronto: University of Toronto Press, 1964), 123; Hunter Miller, ed. and trans., *Northwest Water Boundary: Report of the Experts Summoned by the German Emperor as Arbitrator under Articles 34-42 of the Treaty of Washington of May 8, 1871, Preliminary to His Award dated October 21, 1872* (Seattle: University of Washington Press, 1942).

6. "U.S.-Canadian Friendship Symbolized by New Park," *U.S. Department of State Bulletin*, October 3, 1966, 499.

5 | The Forests

1. *Jerry Silverman's Folk Song Encyclopedia*, V. I (New York: Chappell Music, 1975), 21.

2. Art Kimball and John Dean, *Camano Island: Life and Times in Island Paradise* (Stanwood, WA: Stanwood/Camano News, 1994), 12.

3. Oliver S. Van Olinda, *Van Olinda's History of Vashon-Maury Island*, ed. Roland Carey (Seattle: Alderbrook, 1985), 5; "Vashon Island," *Weekly Intelligencer* (Seattle), April 20, 1878.

4. Henry Hoffman, *Henry's Stories: Tales of a Larger than Life Figure on a Smaller than Normal Island* (Shaw Island: Kitchen Garden Press, 2008), 106.

5. Tom Schroeder, "The Lime Industry and Timber Cutting: A Quantitative Analysis," in Forest Info for the San Juan Islands, www.rockisland.com/~tom/Limeindustry.html, accessed April 7, 2014.

6. "Trip to Mt. Erie," *Anacortes American*, August 7, 1890; *Congressional Record*, December 16, 1901, cited in Nancy L. McDaniel, *A Sound Defense: Military Sites, Lighthouses, and Memorials of Puget Sound* (Chimacum, WA: Nancy McDaniel, 2013), 16.

7. Elizabeth Moore, "Development Coming to Orcas," *Seattle Times*, August 24, 1988.

8. Todd C. Tucker, Land Use Planner, Lummi Tribe, to Skyanne Housser, U.S. Forest Service, August 10, 1998. Seen in Orcas Island Historical Museum Archives.

6 | The Settlers

1. Ezra Meeker, *Pioneer Reminiscences of Puget Sound: The Tragedy of Leschi* (Seattle: Lowman and Hanford, 1905), 85-86.

2. Betty Crookes, "Potlatch days on Guemes Island remembered," *Anacortes American*, May 18, 1977.

3. Reminiscences of Olive Blanche (Benson) Munks, in *Told by the Pioneers* II (1938), 177.

4. Karen Jones-Lamb, *Native American Wives of San Juan Settlers* (Bryn Tirion Publishing, 1994).

5. Peyton Kane, "The Whatcom County Nine: Legal and Political Ramifications of Metis Family Life in Washington Territory," *Columbia* 14 (Summer 2000), 42.

6. Jones-Lamb, *Native American* Wives, 5-7; Snyder, "San Juan County Items," *Anacortes Progress*, September 14, 1889; Washington State Office of Financial Management Small Area Estimate Program, saep.island10p_ xlsx. 2015 populations indicated for various islands come from this report.

7. Christopher L. White, "The Rise and Fall of Civilization on Cypress Island: A Historical Report" (Olympia, WA: Department of Natural Resources, Division of Land and Water Conservation, 1991), 5; "Cypress Island NRCA," Washington State Department of Natural Resources, www.dnr.wa.gov/CypressIsland.

8. June Burn, *100 Days in the San Juans* (Friday Harbor: Long House Printcrafters and Publishers, 1946), 118.

9. Gail Lee Dubrow, "Traces of the Chinese in Ebey's Landing National Historical Reserve, Whidbey Island, Washington."

10. Van Olinda, *Van Olinda's History*, 26.

11. "Filipinos ordered off of Vashon Island," *Vashon Island News-Record*, June 14, 1934.

12. Joe Symons, *Potholes in Paradise* (Olga, WA: Centripetus, 2009), 8; Virginia Jensen, interview by author, Eastsound, Orcas Island, April 26, 2011.

13. Dan Coughlin, "Vashon Urged to Plan for Expansion," *Seattle Post-Intelligencer*, February 16, 1954.

7 | Meeting of Cultures

1. Blumenthal, *With Vancouver*, 144.

2. *Notices and Voyages of the Famed Quebec Mission to the Pacific Northwest* (Portland, OR: Champoeg Press for the Oregon Historical Society, 1956), 65; George Gibbs, Dr. William F. Tolmie and Father G. Mengarini, "Tribes of Western Washington and Northwestern Oregon," Extract from Vol. 1 of *Contributions of American Ethnology* (Washington, D.C., 1977), 196.

3. Wayne Suttles, "The Early Diffusion of the Potato among the Coast Salish," *Southwestern Journal of Anthropology* VII (1951), 280.

4. Richard White, "The Treaty of Medicine Creek: Indian-White Relations on Upper Puget Sound 1830-1880," M.A. Thesis, University of Washington, 1972, 44.

5. Olympic Peninsula Inter-tribal Cultural Advisory Committee, *Native Peoples of the Olympic Peninsula: Who We Are*, ed. Jacilee Wray (Norman: University of Oklahoma Press, 2002), 85.

6. Court of Claims, 853-54.

7. Cecelia Svinth Carpenter, *Tears of Internment: The Indian History of Fox Island and the Puget Sound Indian War* (Tacoma: Tahoma Research Service, 1996), 39.

8. Kellogg, *Whidbey's Island*, 86.

9. Court of Claims (Johnnie Scalopine), 219.

10. J. Ross Browne, "Indian Affairs in the Territories of Oregon and Washington," Secretary of the Interior's Report to the House of Representatives, 35th Cong., 1st sess.; Exec. Doc. 39, reprint: Fairfield, WA: Ye Galleon Press, 1977), 15.

11. Browne, "Indian Affairs," 16.

12. Court of Claims (Julian Sam Simmonds), 212, 213.

13. Court of Claims (Charley Sneatlium), 311. Note that this family name has been spelled in different ways, including Snatelum.

14. O. C. Upchurch, "The Swinomish People and Their State," *Pacific Northwest Quarterly* 27 (October 1936), 292.

15. Reported by Wayne Suttles, in Robert Boyd, *The Coming of the Spirit of Pestilence: Introduced Infectious Diseases and Population Decline among Northwest Coast Indians* (Vancouver: University of British Columbia Press and Seattle: University of Washington Press, 1999), 31.

16. Theresa L. Trebon, "Beyond Isaac Ebey: Tracing the Remnants of Native American Culture on Whidbey Island," *Columbia*, Fall 2000, 7, 9.

8 | Farming

1. Betsey Johnson Cammon, *Island Memoir: A Personal History of Anderson and McNeil Islands* (Puyallup, WA: Valley Press, n.d.), 165.

2. Court of Claims, 766.

3. Vouri, *The Pig War*, 37.

4. *The James Francis Tulloch Diary 1875-1910*, Gordon Keith comp. and ed. (Portland, OR: Binford & Mort, 1978), 17, 20.

5. *Bellingham Herald*, November 10, 1918, Peggy Alston Collection, I/1/23, Center for Pacific Northwest Studies, Bellingham.

6. Esther Goetsch, *Conversations with Esther: A Personal History of Harstine Island as told to John Erickson* (Hansville, WA: Acme Pack Distributing and Publishing Co., 1998), 17.

7. Patricia Klindienst, *The Earth Knows My Name: Food, Culture, and Sustainability in the Gardens of Ethnic Americans* (Boston: Beacon Press, 2006), 87, 95.

8. Mary Matsuda Gruenewald, *Looking Like the Enemy: My Story of Imprisonment in Japanese-American Internment Camps* (Troutdale, OR: NewSage Press, 2005), 17.

9. Gordon Keith, *Voices from the Islands: True Stories about Washington State's Fabulous San Juan Islands and Those Who Inhabit Them* (Portland, OR: Binford & Mort, 1982), 79.

10. "Springtide 2010-11" (*Journal of the San Juan Islands* and *The Islands' Sounder*), 12.

9 | Industries of Sea and Land

1. Bret Lunsford, *Anacortes* (Charleston, SC: Arcadia, 2009), 8; *Anacortes American*, August 16, 1923.

2. "Week is Active on Waterfront," *Anacortes American*, August 16, 1923; Craig Smith, "Anacortes," *Seattle Post-Intelligencer*, Northwest Today section, April 15, 1973.

3. Editorial, "Best solution: leave it alone," *Bainbridge Review*, January 15, 1992.

4. Dolly Connelly, "Is Guemes Island Doomed to Become Paradise Lost," *Seattle Magazine*, October 1966, 49; Bob Lane, "Suit Threatened If Guemes Island Is Rezoned," *Seattle Times*, November 7, 1966.

5. Shaw Island Subarea Plan as amended through Ordinance 21-2002, December 3, 2002.

10 | Communities

1. *The San Juan Islands: Illustrated Supplement to the San Juan Islander—Historical, Commercial, Industrial 1901* (Facsimile reproduction Seattle: Shorey Book Store, 1966), 37.

2. P. H. Knott, "Island County," *Seattle Daily News*, July 15, 1906.

3. Constantine Angelos, "Traveling teacher bridges educational strait," *Seattle Times*, February 26, 1978.

4. Mae Mark Nalder, "The Academy Era in the State of Washington," MA Thesis, State College of Washington, 1934, 216-17.

5. John Hessburg, "Vashon pastor denies sex accusations," *Seattle Post-Intelligencer*, May 15, 1983.

6. Carey Quan Gelernter, "Wandering Whidbey," *Seattle Times*, October 11, 1988.

7. "Anacortes, Skagit Co., Washington: The Great Railway Terminal of Puget Sound" (McNaught Land and Investment Co., 1891); Advertisement, *New York Tribune*, May 9, 1891.

8. "Hat Island Community Survey 2012," hatisland.org/library/surveys/2012Surveyresults.pdf. Accessed October 9, 2014.

11 | Mosquito Fleet Days

1. Current maps show Johnson Landing, but Anderson Islanders call the place Johnson's Landing.

2. Ida Lee, *Children of the Lighthouse* (published by author, 2003), 13, 17, 50, 55; Anneli Fogt, "Point Robinson lighthouse keeper's granddaughter returns to remember," *Vashon-Maury Island Beachcomber*, September 23, 2015.

3. Albert E. Parker, "Eagle Harbor, Washington," *The Coast*, February 1909, 130.

4. Nugent, *Lummi Elders*, 130.

5. Roland Carey, *The Steamboat Landing on Elliott Bay* (Seattle: Alderbrook, 1962), 66; History Link, "Puget Sound's Mosquito Fleet," www.historylink.org/_content/printer_friendly/pf_outpout.cfm?file_id=869.

6. "Public Ferries," *Seattle Mail and Herald*, June 16, 1906.

12 | Rails and Roads

1. George Foster, "4:10 to Glacier Creek," unpublished manuscript, 17; "A Solid Growth," *Anacortes Progress*, April 26, 1890.

2. "Award Franchise for Vashon Line," *Seattle Post-Intelligencer*, February 19, 1908; "All Aboard," *Vashon Island News*, January 3, 1908.

3. Court of Claims (Susie Kittle), 325; Jacob Anthes to George Kellogg, n.d., in *A Centennial Look at the Boy Who became the Father of Langley* (Langley: South Whidbey Historical Society, 1999), 21.

4. E. M. Hawes and Lou Clark, *Island County: A World Beater* (1911, reprinted by Elizabeth H. Dodge, 1979), 5; Black Ball Ferry Lines, "Romantic Whidby [sic] Island," n.d.

5. Phoebe Smith, ed., *Glimpses of Bainbridge: A Collection of Life Stories* (Bainbridge island: Bainbridge Island Senior Community Center, 1992), 36.

6. Editorial, "The Ferry Problem Remains," and "Chamber Asks United Island Support For Limited Access Bridge—Ferry Road," *Bainbridge Review*, October 12, 1950 and March 31, 1949.

7. Lucile S. McDonald, *Making History: The People Who Shaped the San Juan Islands* (Friday Harbor: Friday Harbor Press, 1990), 59.

8. "Lopez Island," *Washington Standard*, January 13, 1877.

9. Van Olinda, *Van Olinda's History*, 60.

10. "Many Island Road Projects Progressing," *Vashon Island News-Record*, April 10, 1930.

11. Fred John Splitstone, *Orcas: Gem of the San Juans* (East Sound: Fred T. Darvill 1954), 96.

13 | Leisure

1. William Ristow, "Island Living," *Seattle Times*, August 3, 1986.

2. Anacortes Mariners' Pageant Official Program, July 25-26-27-28 [1957], 5, 10.

3. Helen Starr, "A Motor Tour of the Puget Archipelago," *Travel*, October 1919, 27-8, 47

4. www.campfireseattle.org/council-history. Accessed April 12, 2014.

5. Washington State has two Hope Island State Parks. One is in Mason County, just west of Squaxin Island. The other is in Skagit County, between the north end of Whidbey Island and the Swinomish Reservation. Both parks are accessible only by boat.

6. "Spencer Tracy Ends Vacation In San Juans," *Seattle Times*, August 21, 1937.

7. Kate Archibald, "Gulf Islands Fit for a Queen," *Christian Science Monitor*, September 19, 1939; Brian J. Cantwell, "State's tourism bell-wether rings loudly in the San Juans," *Seattle Times*, May 19, 2012.

14 | Defense and War

1. Hoffman, *Henry's Stories*, 116, 117.

2. Gruenewald, *Looking Like the Enemy*, 27-9.

3. "New Rules Confine All Coast Japanese," *New York Times*, March 30, 1942; "Army Issues First Japanese Eviction Order," *New York Herald Tribune*, March 23, 1942.

4. Untitled editorial, March 10, 1938; Editorial, "Dual Responsibility," December 11, 1941; "Japanese Leave for Pinedale, Calif.," May 21, 1942; Editorial, "Leave the Japs Where They Are," June 24, 1943; all in *Vashon Island News-Record*; "Youth Faces Arson Trial," *Seattle Post-Intelligencer*, March 2, 1945.

5. Editorial: "The Anti-Japanese Speak," *Bainbridge Review*, November 10, 1944; Mary Woodward, *In Defense of Our Neighbors: The Walt and Mary Woodward Story* (Bainbridge Island: Fenwick, 2008), 115; Lisa Konick, "Japanese relive WW II days in internment camps," *Seattle Times*, November 10, 1986.

6. Stuart Whitehouse, "Navy Reveals Secrets of Whidby [sic]," *Seattle Star*, August 30, 1945.

7. David Brewster, "The Anti-Missiles Are Coming . . . or Are They?" *Seattle Magazine*, March 1969, 31.

15 | Ferries: Black Ball and More

1. Gretchen Huizinga, "Families Wanted: Stuart Island—Unspoiled, Uncomplicated, Uncrowded—A Little Too Uncrowded," *Seattle Times*, October 8, 1995.

2. "Fox Island Ferry Limps," *Tacoma News Tribune*, September 17, 1953.

3. Marie Rowe Dunbar, "Ferry Opens New Suburb," *Tacoma Ledger*, June 15, 1920; Zilfa Phillips, "Ferry Service to Vashon Makes Dream Real," *Tacoma News Tribune*, May 17, 1920.

4. Marshall Wilson, "Guemes Islanders See Way of Life Ending," *Seattle Times*, July 27, 1966.

5. "New Moves Under Way to Settle Walk-Out," *Seattle Times*, November 8, 1935.

6. "Island Civic Clubs Appeal To Governor Martin To End Strike," *Bainbridge Review*, June 4, 1937; Walter Woodward, "Nautical Scribe Complains; Ferry Strike Hard on Pants," *Seattle Times*, June 5, 1937.

7. "Ferry Bill Lost in Senate Vote," *Vashon Island News-Record*, March 9, 1939.

8. Editorial, *Vashon Island News-Record*, March 20, 1947; Walt and Mildred Woodward, Editorial: "Ferries: What to Do About Them," and "Chamber of Commerce Provides Boat Service during Ferry Strike," *Bainbridge Review*, March 21, 1947.

9. Lenny Anderson, "Floating Night Club Becomes 'Good Fairy' In Ferry-Strike Tale," *Seattle Times*, March 18, 1947.

16 | Ferries: The Washington State Ferries Era

1. Jack Swanson, "Four ferry routes could become U.S. highways," *The Bremerton Sun*, April 9, 1994.
2. The *Seattle Post-Intelligencer* published a sixteen-page special report on the ferry system, including details about the Marine Power contract, in the January 8, 1986 issue.
3. "Islanders cope with strike," *Vashon-Maury Island Beachcomber*, September 9, 1976.
4. "Orcas Island grocer gripes," *Seattle Post-Intelligencer*, May 22, 1981.
5. Peter Lewis, "Islanders are jest fed up with ferry strikes," *Seattle Times*, June 5, 1981; Photograph, *Friday Harbor Journal*, June 10, 1981.
6. C. B. Hall, "Gale force ferry service warnings," *Crosscut*, February 8, 2012.

17 | Bridges

1. Gale Fiege, "Drivers, your bridge to Camano Island awaits; New span between Stanwood and Camano Island opens Friday," *The Herald* [Everett], August 12, 2010.
2. See, for example, March 29, 1934.
3. Walt Woodward, in *Bainbridge Review*, March 31, 1949.
4. W. C. Gilman & Company, "Report on Fox Island and Tacoma Narrows Toll Bridges," June 8, 1956, 6.
5. Brynn Grimley, "Aging Fox Island Bridge: Replace it or repair it?" and "Fox Island residents to Pierce County: 'We don't want to be Mercer Island,'" *The News Tribune*, July 30 and August 3, 2016.
6. Archie Satterfield, "Almost Everyone Wants Some of Squaxin Island," *Seattle Times*, March 22, 1970; "County Ferry Links Island With Outside," *Shelton-Mason County Journal*, July 11, 1957.
7. Both this passage and the channel between Fox Island and the mainland called Hale Passage honor Horatio Hale of the Wilkes Expedition.
8. Dorothy Neil, *A Bridge over Troubled Water: The Legend of Deception Pass* (Bellingham, WA: Joel Douglas, 1999), 44.

9. "Cross-Sound Bridge Temporarily Shelved" and "Langlie Says Cross-Sound Bridge Not Dead," *Islander News-Record* [Vashon], October 13 and 20, 1955; "State Approves Vashon Bridges—Across Puget Sound," *Daily Journal of Commerce* [Seattle], July 20, 1957.

10. Polly Lane, "Passenger Interest Will Be Key to Helicopter Commuting, Survey Shows," *Bainbridge Review*, March 10, 1955; "When a Bridge Connects With an Island," *Bainbridge Review*, September 1, 1961.

11. Editorial, "Bridge humor," *Seattle Post-Intelligencer*, May 4, 1984.

12. Angelo Bruscas, "Bridge proposal soundly opposed by Seahurst folks," *Seattle Post-Intelligencer*, March 6, 1992; Travis Baker, " South Kitsapers say no to Bridge," *The Sun* [Bremerton], March 3, 1992.

13. Timothy Egan, "Islanders Envision a Bridge Too Near," *New York Times*, March 11, 1992.

14. Allison Arthur, "Islanders BOO bridge idea," *Vashon-Maury Island Beachcomber*, September 11, 1996.

18 | Conclusion

1. Charles Dunsire, "Islands in the Stream of Progress," *Seattle Post-Intelligencer*, February 11, 1979.

2. "About OPALCO," https://www.opalco.com/about-us/. Accessed August 30, 2014.

3. "Rush to Suburbs Felt By Island Communities, *Seattle Times,* April 8, 1962; Vashon-Maury Island Heritage Association Newsletter, Winter 2013.

4. Tim Menees, "Island Life: Bainbridge And Vashon," *Seattle Post-Intelligencer*, October 8, 1972; Jerry Hulse, "Washington's San Juan Islands," *Los Angeles Times*, July 26, 1987.

5. Informative sign in Friday Harbor, seen August 21, 2014; Ken Brydges, Introduction to reprint of Elizabeth H. Dodge, *Island County A World Beater* (E. M. Hawes and Lou Clark, 1911, reprint by Port Townsend Printery Communications, 1979); Brenda Bell, "Welcome To Fantasy Island—Bainbridge Is Having A Middle-Aged Identity Crisis, *Seattle Times*, May 19, 1991.

6. Theresa Morrow, "Golden Ghetto," *Seattle Times*, March 5, 1989; Thomas Shapley, "San Juans: Fated to be Martha's Vineyard West?," *Seattle Post-Intelligencer*, March 4, 1990; Editorial: "Islanders need to pull together," *Journal of the San Juan Islands*, June 15, 1994.

7. M. L. Lyke, "Drought Island," *Seattle Post-Intelligencer*, September 26, 1994.

8. Laura Guido, "Chronic homeless population hardest to help," *South Whidbey Record*, March 29, 2019; Susan Riemer, "Annual homeless count finds nearly 100 people on Vashon," *Vashon-Maury Island Beachcomber*, January 31, 2019.

9. Erik Lacitis, "Barefoot Bandit's letter moves judge to sympathy," *Seattle Times*, December 17, 2011.

10. "Jim Wardner's Biggest Whopper," www.shoshonenewspress.com/news/2020/apr/16/jim-wardners-biggest-whopper-8/. Accessed February 2, 2016; "Strange Story of Smugglers," *Seattle Post-Intelligencer*, May 29, 1902.

11. Stephen Green, "Friday Harbor: Outside Money Is Moving In," *Seattle Post-Intelligencer Northwest Magazine*, August 18, 1974; Lee Moriwaki, "'Boston Tea Party Against The P-I,'" *Seattle Post-Intelligencer*, September 23, 1974.

Suggested Reading

General

Blumenthal, Richard W. *Maritime Place Names: Inland Washington Waters.* Bellevue, WA: Inland Waters Publishing, 2012.

Friel, Bob. *The Barefoot Bandit: The True Tale of Colton Harris-Moore, New American Outlaw.* New York: Hyperion, 2012.

Gibbs, Jim and Joe Williamson. *Maritime Memories of Puget Sound: In Photographs and Text.* Atglen, PA: Schiffer, 1987.

Gregory, V. J. *Keepers at the Gate.* Port Townsend, WA: Port Townsend Publishing, 1976.

Hansen, David M. *Battle Ready: The National Coast Defense System and the Fortification of Puget Sound, 1894-1925.* Pullman, WA: Washington State University Press, 2014.

Hitchman, Robert. *Place Names of Washington.* Tacoma: Washington State Historical Society, 1985.

McDaniel, Nancy L. *A Sound Defense: Military Sites, Lighthouses, and Memorials of Puget Sound.* Chimacum, WA: Nancy L. McDaniel, 2013.

Told by the Pioneers: Tales of Frontier Life as Told by Those Who Remember The Days of the Territory and Early Statehood of Washington. Vols. 1-3. U.S. Works Progress Administration (Wash.), Olympia, 1937-38.

Native Americans

Batdorf, Carol. *The Feast is Rich: A Guide to Traditional Coast Salish Indian Food Gathering and Preparation*. Bellingham: Whatcom Museum of History and Art, 1980.

Carpenter, Cecelia Svinth. *Tears of Internment: The Indian History of Fox Island and the Puget Sound Indian War*. Tacoma: Tahoma Research Service, 1996.

Deur, Douglas. "Ebey's Landing National Historical Reserve: An Ethnohistory of Traditionally Associated Contemporary Populations." U.S. Department of the Interior, National Park Service, Pacific Region Series in Social Science, Publication Number 2009-02.

Kluger, Richard. *The Bitter Waters of Medicine Creek: A Tragic Clash between White and Native America*. New York: Knopf, 2011.

McDaniel, Nancy L. *The Snohomish Tribe of Indians: Our Heritage . . . Our People*. Nancy L. McDaniel, 2004.

Nugent, Ann, ed. *Lummi Elders Speak*. Lynden, WA: Lynden Tribune, 1982.

Ruby, Robert H. and John A. Brown. *A Guide to the Indian Tribes of the Pacific Northwest*. Norman: University of Oklahoma Press, 1992.

———. *Indians of the Pacific Northwest*. Norman: University of Oklahoma Press, 1981.

Stein, Julie K. *Exploring Coast Salish Prehistory: The Archaeology of San Juan Island*. Seattle: University of Washington, 2000.

Stein, Julie K. and Laura S. Phillips. *Vashon Island Archaeology: A View from Burton Acres Shell Midden*. Seattle: Burke Museum, 2002.

Wray, Jacilee. *Native Peoples of the Olympic Peninsula: Who We Are*. Norman: University of Oklahoma Press, 2002.

Exploration

Blumenthal, Richard W., ed. *Charles Wilkes and the Exploration of Inland Washington Waters: Journals from the Expedition of 1841*. Jefferson, NC: McFarland, 2009.

———. *The Early Exploration of Inland Washington Waters: Journals and Logs from Six Expeditions, 1786-1792*. Jefferson, NC: McFarland, 2004.

———. *With Vancouver in Inland Washington Waters: Journals of 12 Crewmen, April- June 1792*. Jefferson, NC: McFarland, 2007.

Mosquito Fleet

Carey, Roland. *The Sound and the Mountain*. Seattle: Alderbrook, 1970.

———. *The Steamboat Landing on Elliott Bay*. Seattle: Alderbrook, 1972.

Faber, Jim. *Steamer's Wake: Voyaging Down the Old Marine Highways of Puget Sound, British Columbia, and the Columbia River*. Seattle: Enetai Press, 1985.

Findlay, Jean Cammon and Robin Paterson. *Mosquito Fleet of South Puget Sound*. Charleston, SC: Arcadia, 2008.

Sherman, Roger M. *The Sinking of the Calista*. Coupeville: Roger M. Sherman, 1998.

Ferries

Kline, M.S. and G.A. Bayless. *Ferry Boats: A Legend on Puget Sound*. Seattle: Bayless, 1983.

Lander, Patricia. *Guide to Ferryboats of Puget Sound Past and Present*. Annapolis, MD: Lighthouse Press, 2002.

Neal, Carolyn and Thomas Kilday Janus. *Puget Sound Ferries: From Canoe to Catamaran*. Sun Valley, CA: American Historical Press, 2001.

Anderson Island

Cammon, Betsey Johnson. *Island Memoir*. Puyallup, WA: Valley Press, [1969].

Galentine, Elizabeth and the Anderson Island Historical Society. *Anderson Island*. Charleston, SC: Arcadia, 2006.

Heckman, Hazel. *Island in the Sound*. New York: Ballentine, 1969.

Bainbridge Island

Alcala, Kathleen. *The Deepest Roots: Finding Food and Community on a Pacific Northwest Island*. Seattle: University of Washington Press, 2016.

Perry, Fredi. *Port Madison Washington Territory 1854-1889*. Bremerton, WA: Perry Publishing, 1989.

Price, Andrew, Jr. *Port Blakely: The Community Captain Renton Built*. Bainbridge Island: Bainbridge Island Historical Society, 2005.

Swanson, Jack. *Picture Bainbridge: A Pictorial History of Bainbridge Island*. Bainbridge Island: Bainbridge Island Historical Society, 2002.

Woodward, Mary. *In Defense of Our Neighbors: The Walt and Milly Woodward Story*. Bainbridge Island: Fenwick, 2008.

Blakely Island

Roe, JoAnn. *Blakely: Island in Time.* Bellingham, WA: Montevista Press, 2005.

Camano Island

Kimball, Art and John Dean. *Camano Island: Life and Times in Island Paradise.* Stanwood, WA: Stanwood/Camano NEWS, 1994.

Prasse, Karen and the Stanwood Area Historical Society. *Camano Island.* Charleston, SC: Arcadia, 2006.

Schroeder, Val. *Exploring Camano Island: A History and Guide.* Charleston, SC: The History Press, 2014.

White, Richard. See entry under Whidbey Island.

Worthington, Gary. *Cama Beach.* Olympia, WA: TimeBridges, 2008.

Day Island

Tucker, Marcia Willoughby. *Day Island: a Glimpse of the Past.* Rhododendron Press, 1997.

Fidalgo Island

At Home on Fidalgo. Bellingham, WA: Premier Graphics, 1999.

Hartt, Jack and Sam Wotipka, eds., *Two Hands and a Shovel: An Illustrated Exploration of the Work of the Civilian Conservation Corps at Deception Pass State Park.* Anacortes: Deception Pass Park Foundation, 2013.

Lunsford, Bret. *Anacortes.* Charleston, SC: Arcadia, 2009.

Neal, Dorothy. *A Bridge over Troubled Water: The Legend of Deception Pass.* Bellingham: Joel Douglas, 1999.

Slotemaker, Terry. *Fidalgo Fishing: A History of a Commercial Fishing Industry.* Anacortes: Anacortes Museum, 2009.

———. *From Logs to Lumber: On Fidalgo, Guemes, Cypress, Burrows, and Sinclair Islands.* Anacortes: Anacortes Museum, 2007.

Trebon, Theresa. *The Skagit Collection: First Views: An Early History of Skagit County: 1850-1899, V. 2.* Skagit Valley Herald, 2002.

Fox Island

Edgers, Don. *Fox Island.* Charleston, SC: Arcadia, 2008.

Miller, George L., ed. *Fox Island: A History. 1982.*

Harstine Island

Goetsch, Esther as told to John Erickson. *Conversations with Esther: A Personal History of Harstine Island.* Hansville, WA: Acme Pack, 1998.

Hitchcock, Beulah and Helen Wingert. *The Island Remembers: A History of Harstine Island and Its People.* Shelton, WA: Harstine Women's Club, 1979.

Lopez Island

Ferguson, Susan Lehne and the Lopez Island Historical Society and Museum. *Lopez Island.* Charleston, SC: Arcadia, 2010.

Lummi Island

Finding Lummi Island: Stories of the Settlers. Lummi Island: Lummi Island Congregational Church, [2013].
Hutchings, Bobbie, Thurid Clark and Beth Hudson. *Shared Heritage: A History of Lummi Island.* Lummi Island: Lummi Island Heritage Trust, 2004.

Marrowstone Island

Grover, Lyman P. *Fort Flagler: Over 100 Years of History.* 2nd ed. Nordland, WA: Friends of Fort Flagler, 2006.
Russell, Karen and Jeanne Bean. *Marrowstone.* Port Townsend, WA: Port Townsend Publishing, 1978.

McNeil Island

Burkly, Ann Kane and Steve W. Dunkelberger, eds. *McNeil Island.* Charleston, SC: Arcadia, 2019.
Keve, Paul W. *The McNeil Century: The Life and Times of an Island Prison.* Chicago: Nelson-Hall, 1984.
See also Anderson Island entries.

Orcas Island

Orcas Island Historical Society and Museum. *Orcas Island.* Charleston, SC: Arcadia, 2006.
Peacock, Christopher M. *Rosario Yesterdays: A Pictorial History.* Eastsound, WA: Rosario Productions, 1985.

Philbrick, Margaret. *A Bit Off Center*. Eastsound: Paperjam Publishing, 2000.

Tulloch, James Francis. *The James Francis Tulloch Diary 1875-1910*. Gordon Keith, comp. and ed. Portland, OR: Binford & Mort, 1978.

San Juan Island

Peck, William A., Jr. *The Pig War: The Journal of William A. Peck, Jr.* C. Brewster Coulter and Bert Webber, eds. Medford, OR: Webb Research Group, 1993.

Vouri, Mike. *Outpost of Empire: The Royal Marines and the Joint Occupation of San Juan Island*. Seattle: Northwest Interpretive Association, 2004.

———. *The Pig War*. Charleston, SC: Arcadia, 2008.

———. *The Pig War: Standoff at Griffin Bay*. 2nd ed. Seattle: Discover Your Northwest, 2013.

Vouri, Mike and Julia and the San Juan Historical Society. *San Juan Island*. Charleston, SC: Arcadia, 2010.

Vouri, Mike and Julia and the San Juan Historical Society and Museum. *Friday Harbor*. Charleston, SC: Arcadia, 2009.

Walker, Richard. *Roche Harbor*. Charleston, SC: Arcadia, 2009.

San Juan Islands (general)

Jones-Lamb, Karen. *Native American Wives of San Juan Settlers*. Decatur Island: Bryn Tirion, 1994.

McCabe, James O. *The San Juan Water Boundary Question*. Toronto: University of Toronto Press, 1964.

McDonald, Lucile S. *Making History: The People Who Shaped the San Juan Islands*. Friday Harbor: Harbor Press, 1990.

Miller, Hunter, ed. *Northwest Water Boundary: Report of the Experts Summoned by the German Emperor as Arbitrator under Articles 34-42 of the Treaty of Washington of May 8, 1871, Preliminary to His Award Dated October 21, 1872*. Seattle: University of Washington Press, 1942.

Richardson, David. *Pig War Islands: The San Juans of Northwest Washington*. Eastsound: Orcas Publishing, 1990.

Roe, JoAnn. *The San Juan Islands: Into the 21st Century*. Caldwell, ID: Caxton Press, 2011.

Shaw Island

Hoffman, Henry. *Henry's Stories: Tales of a Larger than Life Figure on a Smaller than Normal Island*. Shaw Island: Kitchen Garden Press, 2008.

Sinclair Island

Leach, Mary March. *Cottonwood Collection: History of Sinclair Island*. Snohomish, WA: Snohomish Publishing, 1988.

Stuart Island

Bergquist, James. *The History of Stuart Island*. Privately published, 2012.

Vashon and Maury Islands

Caffiere, Blanche Hamilton and others. *The Past Remembered II*. Ed. Garland Baker Norin. Vashon: Vashon-Maury Island Heritage Association, 1991.

Gruenewald, Mary Matsuda. *Looking Like the Enemy: My Story of Imprisonment in Japanese-American Internment Camps*. Troutdale, OR: New Sage Press, 2005.

Haulman, Bruce. *A Brief History of Vashon Island*. Charleston, SC: The History Press, 2016.

Haulman, Bruce and Jean Cammon Findlay. *Vashon-Maury Island*. Charleston, SC: Arcadia, 2011.

Norin, Garland Baker, Blanche Hamilton Caffiere and others. *The Past Remembered III*. Eds. Mary Jo McCormick Barrentine and Barbara Crocker Steen. Vashon: Vashon-Maury Island Heritage Association, 2008.

Van Olinda, Oliver O. *Van Olinda's History of Vashon-Maury Island*. Ed. Roland Carey. Seattle: Alderbrook: 1985.

Watkins, Marj and Garland Norin, eds. *The Past Remembered*. Vashon: Vashon Island Public Schools, 1978.

Woodroffe, Pamela J. *Vashon Island's Agricultural Roots: Tales of the Tilth as Told by Island Farmers*. San Jose, CA: Writers Club Press, 2002.

Waldron Island

Lovering, Frances K. *Island Ebb and Flow: A Pioneer's Journal of Life on Waldron Island*. 2nd ed. Friday Harbor: Illumina, 2008.

Whidbey Island

Buchanan, Terry. *Fort Casey: The History of Fort Casey and the Defense of the Pacific Northwest*. Serenity Ridge Press, 2010.

Cherry, Lorna. *Langley, the Village by the Sea; South Whidbey and Its People*, V. 3. Langley: South Whidbey Historical Society, 1986.

———. *South Whidbey and Its People*. V. 2. Langley, South Whidbey Historical Society, 1985.

Darst, Peggy Christine. *Oak Harbor*. Charleston, SC: Arcadia, 2014.

Guss, Elizabeth, Janice O'Mahony and Mary Richardson. *Whidbey Island: Reflections on People and the Land*. Charleston, SC: History Press, 2014.

Haroldson, William and the South Whidbey Historical Society. *Resorts of South Whidbey Island*. Langley: South Whidbey Historical Society, 2013.

Hartt, Jack and Sam Wotipka, eds. See entry under Fidalgo Island.

Island County Historical Society. *Settlement, Trade and Transportation in Island County between 1850 and 1900*. Coupeville: Island County Historical Society, 1993.

Kellogg, George A. *A History of Whidbey's Island*. Coupeville: Island County Historical Society, 2002.

Lynn, Judy, Kay Foss, and the Island County Historical Society and Museum. *Coupeville*. Charleston, SC: Arcadia, 2012.

Neal, Dorothy. *A Bridge over Troubled Water*. See under Fidalgo.

Neal, Dorothy and Lee Brainard. *By Canoe and Sailing Ship They Came: A History of Whidbey's Island*. Oak Harbor, WA: Spindrift, 1989.

South Whidbey Historical Society. *South Whidbey and Its People*. V. 1. Greenbank, WA: 5 Center Publishing, 1983.

Waterman, Robert E. and Frances L. Wood. *Langley*. Charleston, SC: Arcadia, 2012.

White, Richard. *Land Use, Environment, and Social Change: The Shaping of Island County, Washington*. Seattle: University of Washington Press, 1992.

Wood, Frances L. *Community at the Crossroads: The History of Bayview on Whidbey Island*. Langley: The Goosefoot Community Fund, 2002.

———. *Down to Camp: A History of Summer Folk on Whidbey Island*. Mercer Island, WA: Blue Heron Press, 1997.

Index

Page numbers in *italics* refer to illustrations.

Born in Ohio, Ann B. Irish lived on Vashon Island for almost all of her adult life. She holds a doctorate in history from the University of Washington, and she retired from Vashon Island High School after having taught there for twenty-seven years. Her two previous books are a biography of distant relative and important national politician Joseph W. Byrns and a history of Japan's northern island, Hokkaido. Ms. Irish is a long-time volunteer at the Vashon-Maury Island Heritage Museum, where she has imparted details of island history to many school groups and other visitors. She has also been an active volunteer and docent for Friends of Mukai, an organization which celebrates Vashon-Maury Island's Japanese heritage. In addition, she has traveled widely in the United States and abroad and has taught in Japan and Laos.